The White Savage

Racial Fantasies
in the Postbellum South

LAWRENCE J. FRIEDMAN

I missed one thing in the South—African slavery.
That horror is gone, and permanently. Therefore,
half the South is at last emancipated, half the South is free.
But the white half is apparently as far from emancipated as ever.
—MARK TWAIN, 1883

Prentice-Hall, Inc. Englewood Cliffs, N. J.
A SPECTRUM BOOK

For my Mother and Father

LAWRENCE J. FRIEDMAN is Assistant Professor of History at Arizona State University. A member of the Association for the study of Negro Life and History, he has written articles and delivered papers on racism in America.

Current printing (last number):
10 9 8 7 6 5 4 3 2 1

PRENTICE-HALL INTERNATIONAL, INC. (*London*)
PRENTICE-HALL OF AUSTRALIA, PTY. LTD. (*Sydney*)
PRENTICE-HALL OF CANADA, LTD. (*Toronto*)
PRENTICE-HALL OF INDIA PRIVATE LIMITED (*New Delhi*)
PRENTICE-HALL OF JAPAN, INC. (*Tokyo*)

Contents

CONTENTS

Preface

Preface

A few years ago James Baldwin addressed a preponderantly white college audience. "I am not a nigger," he proclaimed. "I am a man. And the question is why do you need a nigger?" Why, Baldwin was asking, have white Americans spent so much time and energy searching for docile Negro behavior? Why have they been so fearful of bold, assertive blacks? Why has Nat Turner been the villain and Uncle Tom the hero in the white American melodrama? Why have whites reared their children on Stepin Fetchit and taught them to hate H. Rap Brown?

Baldwin's question was national in scope. The definitive studies of white racism in America—Gunnar Myrdal's *An American Dilemma: The Negro Problem and Modern Democracy* (1944) and Winthrop D. Jordan's *White Over Black: American Attitudes Toward the Negro 1550–1812* (1968)—make this evident. From the earliest settlements in British North America, whites everywhere craved servile Negro behavior. Nonetheless, the quest for docility has been particularly anxious and intense below the Mason-Dixon line. Sensitive analysts of the Southern scene from Frederick Douglass and Mark Twain to Robert Penn Warren and Lillian Smith have stressed how important servile Negro behavior has been to Southern whites. In 1928 historian Ulrich Bonnell Phillips maintained that a compulsion to perpetuate white supremacy by controlling Negro behavior was "the cardinal test of a Southerner and the central theme of Southern history." The heavily paternalistic Southern proslavery argument, the Southerner's traditional account of Reconstruction as an "unnatural" period of "vicious Negro rule," and the long-standing Southern habit of assigning "uppity niggers" to the court of Judge Lynch all validate Phillips' "central theme."

Baldwin's question is therefore particularly applicable to life below the Mason-Dixon line. Yet most historians of the post-Civil War South have been so preoccupied with the issues of segregation and integration that they have slighted the Southern search for Negro servility. Professor C. Vann Woodward is a case in point. Early in the fall of 1954, soon after the United States Supreme Court issued its landmark school desegregation decision (*Brown v. Board of Education of Topeka*), he delivered the James W. Richard Lectures at the University of Virginia. Published as *The Strange Career of Jim Crow*, these lectures reflected contemporary anxiety over the future of interracial relations. Woodward argued that segregation had not always been the way of the postbellum South. Between the demise of Reconstruction and the collapse of Southern Populism in the middle 1890s, race relations had remained fluid and relatively unstructured. "Conservative" Democrats ran Southern affairs. Viewing Negroes as children who required white guidance and care, they disapproved of rigid color lines. Hence, blacks generally received equality of treatment aboard trains and streetcars. They were admitted almost without restriction to restaurants, theaters, and bars that whites patronized. Many continued to vote. By the late 1890s, however, this fluid white-black relationship was on the wane. By then, Woodward argued, growing Northern indifference toward Southern Negroes, the declining political influence of Southern "conservatives" (Bourbons), and the rise of "radical" Southern politicians who appealed to poor white racism all combined to produce widespread Negro disfranchisement and rigid color lines below the Mason-Dixon line.

In the decade that followed the publication of *The Strange Career of Jim Crow*, students of the postbellum South were so preoccupied with Woodward's narrative of the chronological development of segregation that most of them ignored the crucial issue raised by Baldwin. For example, Charles E. Wynes' *Race Relations in Virginia, 1870–1902* (1961) and Frenise A. Logan's *The Negro in North Carolina, 1876–1894* (1964) did little more than test and validate the Woodward thesis on the state level. Others took issue with Woodward's chronology. In *Slavery in the Cities: The South, 1820–1860* (1964), Richard C. Wade tried to prove that segregation patterns had permeated the urban South even before the Civil War. In *After Slavery: The Negro in South Carolina during Reconstruction, 1861–1877* (1965), Joel Williamson demonstrated that relatively rigid color lines had been drawn in the Palmetto State soon after emancipation and persisted through and beyond Reconstruction. But despite criticisms of Woodward's chronology by such historians as Wade and Williamson, and despite the fact that their analyses of other qualities in Southern racial life were remarkably sensitive, the Woodward thesis continues to be widely accepted. Though certain historians are beginning to consider the thesis with increasing skepticism, they still represent little more than a "loyal opposition." Most of them accept Woodward's premise that the color line is the primary issue in the Southern racial experience. Questioning Woodward only as to *when* color lines first took meaningful hold in Southern life, too many of them have let Baldwin's question go unanswered.

It is easy to see why most historians of the postbellum South followed Woodward's lead and became almost totally immersed in the issues of segregation and integration during the decade that followed the *Brown* decision. The United States Supreme Court had overturned a fifty-eight-year-old "separate but equal" doctrine. Inspired by this decision and equating integration with "freedom," Martin Luther King, Jr., Fred T. Shuttlesworth, Ralph D. Abernathy, James Farmer, and countless other black leaders took to the streets of Montgomery, Albany, Birmingham, Selma, and other bastions of segregation demanding "freedom now." As articulate blacks in the decade after *Brown v. Board of Education* claimed that integration was the major racial issue below Mason-Dixon, sympathetic historians were inclined to think along these same lines.

In the last several years, the "freedom now" crusade sparked by the *Brown* decision has obviously passed. Many blacks and some whites now speak about the shallowness of their approach between 1954 and the mid-1960s. Though some color lines were broken below Mason-Dixon, many parts of the South have remained determined to deny blacks racial dignity. Lester G. Maddox can still be elected Governor of Georgia by threatening to strike out at "uppity niggers," and until quite recently George C. Wallace was perhaps the most popular Southerner since Robert E. Lee.

As *The Strange Career of Jim Crow* reflected the hope and optimism of the mid-1950s for a "new day" in Southern race relations, *The White Savage* reflects the cynicism of the late 1960s. Like Baldwin, I argue that segregation and integration are not the vital issues—that white Southern efforts at segregation have been no more than manifestations of a deeper Southern abhorrence of "uppity niggers." Because this abhorrence has never been eradicated, crusades for racial equality have had limited effectiveness. For this reason, I feel compelled to join Baldwin and ask why whites, particularly Southern whites, have sought "niggers."

By focusing on the South in the years between the Civil War and the first World War, I therefore hope to demonstrate the centrality of Baldwin's question and to answer it. The book is not a narrative of the central racial occurrences of these years. "Black Reconstruction," the "biracial" Populist crusade, the Atlanta Compromise, and "lilly white" Progressivism are not my focal points. Woodward's own *Origins of the New South 1877–1913* (1951) and other histories have covered these topics quite thoroughly. Instead, I seek to uncover the subjective racial world of white Southerners and to explain why the pursuit of "niggers" was so essential to that world.

Several good friends must be thanked for assisting me in this task. Professor Donald B. Meyer of Wesleyan University provided constant and brilliant suggestions while *The White Savage* was in its dissertation stage. Professor Keith B. Berwick of U.C.L.A. also offered creative criticism of the dissertation. The Indiana University and Arizona State University Grants Committees provided financial assistance during the process of revision. In addition, I received constant and useful advice and criticism from Professor Graham J. Barker-Benfield of the American University; Professor S. P. Fullinwider of Arizona State University; Professor Arthur H. Schaffer of the University of Missouri, St. Louis; Professor Martin J. Sherwin of the University of California, Berkeley; and Professor and Mrs. Sheldon A. Silverman of the University of Calgary. Two friends deserve special mention—Professor Ronald T. Takaki of U.C.L.A. and my wife, Sharon. For years they have perceptively criticized chapter after chapter and draft after draft of *The White Savage*. Without them, this would have been a very different volume.

Tempe, Arizona, 1970

PART ONE

Prologue

Use all the negroes you can get, for all the purposes for which you need them, but don't arm them. The day you make soldiers of them is the beginning of the end of the revolution. If slaves will make good soldiers our whole theory of slavery is wrong—but they won't make soldiers.

—Howell Cobb, 1864

Chapter One

"Gone Are the Days"

The Civil War represented a genuine watershed in white Southern racial thought. From proslavery advocates like James Henry Hammond to antislavery Negrophobes like Hinton Rowan Helper, antebellum racial theorists spoke and wrote with assurance and authority. They envisioned workable solutions to basic racial difficulties, and they believed that they knew how to transform their visions into realities. While Hammond considered the "peculiar institution" the key to racial utopia, Helper was certain that racial peace required expelling blacks from white society. These antebellum theorists had only two basic concerns: they feared that Southerners with racial solutions different from their own would predominate, and they were anxious that a Northern-controlled Federal Government might overturn their particular solution.

After Appomattox, white Southern theorists displayed far less intellectual clarity and certainty regarding racial goals. Old answers gave way to new questions. To Louisiana historian Charles Gayarré, Negro freedom burdened white Southerners with "a question far more difficult to solve satisfactorily, than one which formerly proceeded from his presence as a slave." [1] The "great question," wrote the Macon *Telegraph*, was the Negro; "what is to become of him is undecided." [2] A former Confederate officer charged that a "bloody war wiped out slavery" and that black bondage had ceased to be a viable concept.[3] Increasingly, Southern whites came to realize that they would have to uncover new racial solutions. They spoke and wrote with few exclamation points but with many question marks.

Clearly wartime events had a marked effect on white Southern thought. Promulgation of the Emancipation Proclamation was the most striking, but other occurrences also conditioned white racial attitudes. Negroes stole, deceived, and aided the enemy. On several

1. Thomas M'Caleb, ed., *The Louisiana Book: Selections from the Literature of the State* (New Orleans: R. F. Straughan, 1894), p. 199.
2. Macon *Daily Telegraph*, June 22, 1865. See also Macon *Daily Telegraph*, August 27, 1865.
3. Jackson *Daily Clarion*, July 4, 1867.

occasions they even plotted general insurrections.[4] The fact that
many blacks were "disloyal" to their white overlords and that the
Emancipation Proclamation encouraged "disloyal" conduct would
seem to explain the decisive change in white racial thought during
the war. But an analysis of this sort is grossly inadequate, for it
equates actual Negro wartime conduct with the modes of behavior
that whites believed were occurring. What men see is invariably
colored by dreams, fantasies, and irrational anxieties so that their
observations may only remotely correspond with actualities. Our concern must be with what white Southerners *thought was happening*
to the traditional white-black relationship between Sumter and
Appomattox.

II

During the Civil War, white Southerners persisted in characterizing blacks as a loyal and obedient race. Despite many social and
institutional dislocations, such rhetoric cascaded everywhere. Most
often, whites made warmhearted references to domestic servants—
physically perhaps the least exploited segment of the slave population. The editor of the Charleston *Courier* boasted about a domestic bondsman who left Union troops and freedom behind in
Knoxville and traveled one hundred and fifty miles to rejoin his
master.[5] The Mississippi legislature praised another house servant who
had "remained on the field [at Gettysburg], faithfully attached to the
person of his master," and who refused "to receive his liberty from
the hands of the murderers of his master. . . ." [6] Another domestic
bondsman was heralded for risking his own life to recover his master's
body from a battlefield.[7] Sometimes free Negroes were praised for
loyal, obedient behavior.[8] Occasionally the entire slave population
received commendation. Confederate newspapers never ceased to report cases of Yankee stragglers captured by the South's loyal, de-
pendable bondsmen. The "general fidelity and affectionate loyalty of

4. See, e.g., Harvey Wish, "Slavery Disloyalty under the Confederacy," *Journal
of Negro History*, XXIII, No. 4 (October, 1938), 435–50; Bell Irvin Wiley, *Southern Negroes 1861–1865* (New Haven: Yale University Press, 1938), pp. 63–84;
Herbert Aptheker, *American Negro Slave Revolts* (New York: International Publishers Co., Inc., 1952), pp. 359–67; Joe Gray Taylor, "Slavery in Louisiana During the Civil War," *Louisiana History*, VIII, No. 1 (Winter, 1967), 27–33.

5. Charleston *Daily Courier*, January 23, 1864.

6. John K. Bettersworth, ed., *Mississippi in the Confederacy* (Baton Rouge:
Louisiana State University Press, 1961), p. 244.

7. Bettersworth, ed., *Mississippi in the Confederacy*, p. 245.

8. See, e.g., the New Orleans *Picayune*, February 9, 1862, and the Richmond
Enquirer, September 13, 1861.

servants," a Charleston editor exclaimed, "is one of the most gratify-
ing results and indications elicited by the war. . . ." [9] Despite the
Emancipation Proclamation, an Alabamian observed, "our servants
all still loyal and never rendered more cheerful obedience; indeed
their interest in our soldiers and anxiety for the return of peace seems
as great as our own." [10] A clerk in the Confederate War Department
was so confident of slave loyalty that he saw little danger in federal
efforts to recruit black bondsmen. Armed and assigned duties within
the federal service, Negro bondsmen "would cut their way back to
their masters." War had wrought no substantial changes in the slave's
behavior.[11]

Though widespread, many such claims of black loyalty and docility
were misleading. Before the war, Southern defenders of the "peculiar
institution" had tailored their remarks to refute abolitionist charges.
But many had also attempted to assuage doubts about slavery among
fellow Southerners. In *Cannibals All!,* George Fitzhugh was gravely
concerned with a Southern sense of moral guilt over slavery. He
feared that Southerners could not effectively counter Northern criticism if they themselves were uneasy about the South's leading social
institution. Thus, Fitzhugh called for a campaign to vindicate the
"peculiar institution" in Southern eyes. William J. Grayson's *The
Hireling and the Slave* and Henry Hughes' *A Treatise on Sociology*
were designed, in part, for this same end. To allay pangs of guilt
among white Southerners, these propagandists tried to depict the
most depressing aspects of slavery as vital components of a near
utopian social order.[12] One must not assume that efforts to purge
Southerners of their guilt instantly ceased with the guns of Sumter,
for much of the Southern wartime rhetoric praising blacks as loyal,
happy, and obedient bondsmen bears a striking resemblance to the
antebellum rhetoric of a Fitzhugh, a Grayson, or a Hughes. By the
same token, wartime praise of Negro loyalty obviously persisted as a
way of telling Northerners that the Negro did not want Northern
aid. Finally, some who continued to speak of black docility may have
been trying to define acceptable norms for Negro behavior amidst
chaotic wartime conditions. Thus, though Southerners frequently
characterized their slaves as servile and loving, their characterizations
must not always be accepted at face value. Sometimes their rhetoric
was no more than propaganda. Often it merely underlined the

9. Charleston *Daily Courier,* March 5, 1864.
10. Robert D. Reid, "The Negro in Alabama During the Civil War," *Journal
of Negro History,* XXXV, No. 3 (July, 1950), 273–74.
11. Howard Swiggett, ed., *A Rebel War Clerk's Diary at the Confederate States'
Capital by J. B. Jones* (New York: Old Hickory Bookshop, 1935), I, 224.
12. For an excellent analysis of these efforts to eradicate Southern guilt, see
Ralph E. Morrow, "The Proslavery Argument Revisited," *Mississippi Valley Historical Review,* XLVIII, No. 1 (June, 1961), 70–94.

Southerner's desire for Negro docility. Nonetheless, there was some degree of candor in certain claims of exemplary black wartime behavior. Outwardly at least, some blacks had conducted themselves obediently in the presence of whites. White Southerners who desperately hoped to uncover servile Negro conduct for propagandistic advantages and for peace of mind probably cherished these moments to the exclusion of others, dwelling upon manifestations of black servility and dismissing contrary examples.

White Southern praise of a servile and obedient Negro population thus represented a strange blend of candor and propaganda. But though many whites had actually believed that they were encountering Negro docility, they nevertheless perceived contrary patterns of Negro behavior as well. Slave disloyalty in general and theft in particular seemed almost commonplace. Writing from federally occupied New Orleans early in 1863, a white woman noted the rise of a class of insolent and thievish Negroes.[13] A Richmond woman fretted over slaves who took vital provisions from their masters.[14] A South Carolina rice planter complained that the blacks had raided and pillaged his home.[15] A Mississippian reported how his haughty slaves had assumed "that the plantation and every thing on it belongs to them." [16]

Southern whites also claimed that slaves were taking advantage of wartime conditions through massive desertions. In 1862 a Confederate General estimated that desertion was costing North Carolina a million dollars every week.[17] The following year a woman from Snyder's Bluff, Mississippi, claimed that every Negro on her plantation had deserted.[18] From Fort Gibson, a planter wrote that "two men, three women, and eight children were all that remained with us, and they were much demoralized." [19] By November of 1863, a distressed white resident of Warrentown, Alabama, predicted that in view of the high rate of desertion, the day was near when there "will not be a negro left in the country. . . ." [20]

Whites frequently tried to explain black defections. Usually they concluded that the proximity of federal troops caused desertion. A

13. Kate Mason Rowland and Mrs. Morris L. Croxall, eds., *Journal of Julia Le Grand: New Orleans 1862–1863* (Richmond: Everett Waddey Co., 1911), p. 112.

14. Ben Ames Williams, ed., *A Diary from Dixie by Mary Boykin Chesnut* (Boston: Houghton Mifflin Company, 1949), p. 348.

15. Joel Williamson, *After Slavery: The Negro in South Carolina During Reconstruction, 1861–1877* (Chapel Hill: University of North Carolina Press, 1965), p. 5.

16. Theodore Bratner Wilson, *The Black Codes of the South* (University, Alabama: Univerity of Alabama Press, 1965), p. 49.

17. Herbert Aptheker, *Essays in the History of the American Negro* (New York: International Publishers Co., Inc., 1945), p. 191.

18. Bettersworth, ed., *Mississippi in the Confederacy*, p. 240.

19. Bettersworth, ed., *Mississippi in the Confederacy*, p. 241.

20. Columbus (Georgia) *Daily Enquirer*, December 20, 1863, quoting the Knoxville *Confederate*, n.d.

Confederate Major General banned slave labor near Union lines because bondsmen could not be trusted near the enemy.[21] Reporting a Union raid in the Combahee River region of South Carolina, a Brigadier General claimed that seven hundred Negroes had fled with the Yankee troops "with great alacrity and to some extent with preconceived arrangement." [22] The Canton *Tri-Weekly American Citizen* charged that nine-tenths of the city's black population had deserted because Negro federal cavalrymen had mixed among the slaves and had encouraged defection.[23] According to General Joseph E. Johnson, desertion was rampant whenever federal troops were near.[24]

Southern proponents of slavery had defined the bondsman as an appendage to his master. It followed that if the master was a Confederate, the slave was a Confederate. Therefore, slave defection constituted desertion from the Southern Cause. A bondsman who fled to federal troops committed treason. As a Georgia citizen's committee reported, all blacks who went over to the enemy were traitors.[25] Some slaves were accused of even more dangerous activities. According to a Louisiana planter, "those that did not go on with the [federal] army remained at home to do much worse." [26] A Confederate War Department clerk discovered a "treasonous" attempt to burn the home of President Jefferson Davis.[27] Another planter wrote contemptuously of two local blacks who had treacherously confined a Confederate soldier to the stocks.[28] From Camden and Columbia, South Carolina, came stories of Negro arson and espionage.[29] A joint communiqué issued by Rebel officers of the Army of Tennessee declared that slaves had formed "an omnipresent spy system, pointing out our valuable men to the enemy, revealing our positions, purposes, and resources. . . ." [30] The Richmond *Examiner* and a correspondent for the Knoxville *Confederate* found blacks even more aggressively anti-Confederate; they aided the federals as bandits and outlaws.[31] All

21. Wish, *Journal of Negro History*, XXIII, No. 4 (October, 1938), 442.

22. Wish, *Journal of Negro History*, XXIII, No. 4 (October, 1938), 443.

23. Canton *Tri-Weekly American Citizen*, July 13, 1864, quoted in Bettersworth, ed., *Mississippi in the Confederacy*, p. 242.

24. Aptheker, *Essays*, p. 175.

25. Aptheker, *Essays*, pp. 191–92.

26. G. P. Whittington, ed., "Concerning the Loyalty of Slaves in North Louisiana in 1862," *Louisiana Historical Quarterly*, XIV, No. 4 (October, 1931), 491–92.

27. Swiggett, ed., *Rebel War Clerk's Diary*, II, 133.

28. Whittington, *Louisiana Historical Quarterly*, XIV, No. 4 (October, 1931), 492.

29. Williams, ed., *Diary from Dixie*, p. 544; Aptheker, *Essays*, p. 178.

30. James M. McPherson, ed., *The Negro's Civil War: How American Negroes Felt and Acted During the War for the Union* (New York: Pantheon Books, Inc., 1965), p. 242. For other interesting instances of slaves reported as federal spies, see Williams, ed., *Diary From Dixie*, p. 269; Whittington, *Louisiana Historical Quarterly*, XIV, No. 4 (October, 1931), 489–91, footnote 3; Aptheker, *Essays*, pp. 191–92.

31. Richmond *Examiner*, January 14, 1864; Knoxville *Confederate*, n.d., quoted in the Columbus (Georgia) *Daily Enquirer*, December 20, 1863.

such complaints pointed to one conclusion. The Southern Negro was not playing a passive role in the Civil War. Rather, he seemed aggressively anti-Confederate.

Reports on Negro theft, desertion, and aid to the enemy obviously conflicted with commendations for slave loyalty and servility. The former represented the betrayal of a wise and benevolent master; the latter stood for the proper and just behavior of a lower race. But fears of slave insurrections pointed to a more blatant contradiction. Many such fears were vocalized. A New Orleans woman was certain that Negroes would do more than rob and steal. She feared an uprising.[32] From her northeastern Louisiana plantation, another woman equated her worries over black insurrection with those one feels living "on a mine." [33] A Rebel War Department clerk feared that blacks might rise and destroy telegraph wires, railroad bridges, and other vital lines of communication.[34] Some whites claimed that blacks had actually struck. A resident of New Orleans noted disturbances on several nearby plantations: "The assistance of the authorities has been called in to overcome open resistance of the slaves." [35] A Charleston woman wrote of similar activity in her locality: "No general insurrection has taken place, though several revolts have been attempted; two quite recently, and in these cases whole families were murdered before the slaves were subdued." [36] Even where no revolt materialized, some Southerners sensed that life had taken a disastrous turn. "The fears of insurrection," a Richmond editor anxiously declared, "occasioned by the absence of the greater portion of the arms-bearing white population, had produced a leniency and indulgence among the farmers, which has encouraged the natural laziness of the slave, and resulted in a rapid and yearly increased diminution of the crop . . . and the danger is that famine will be superadded to insurrection." [37]

Clearly, white Southerners had reported a vast range of Negro behavior. They saw docile Negroes who loyally continued to serve them. They also detected insolent "militants" who would not hesitate to slit their throats. But blacks were not all Uncle Toms or Nat Turners, for whites sensed that many bondsmen seemed loyal but occasionally stole and might desert or riot.

As a rule, however, Southern images of Negro behavior tended to polarize. The unequivocally loyal and docile were the "good Negroes." All others, thieves together with insurrectionists, were classified as defiant rebels against a benevolent institution. The wartime diary of

32. Rowland and Croxall, eds., *Journal of Julia Le Grand*, p. 94.

33. John Q. Anderson, ed., *Brokenburn: The Journal of Kate Stone, 1861–1868* (Baton Rouge: Louisiana State University Press, 1955), p. 28.

34. Swiggett, ed., *Rebel War Clerk's Diary*, I, 336–37.

35. Aptheker, *Essays*, p. 179.

36. Aptheker, *Essays*, pp. 180–81.

37. Richmond *Whig*, January 1, 1864.

Edmund Ruffin, leading agricultural scientist and radical secessionist, well illustrates the consequences of this polarized perspective. Writing on October 30, 1864, less than eight months before his suicide, Ruffin noted that before the war slaves had behaved with "attachment and affection" toward their masters. After Sumter, blacks occasionally expressed deference and love, he observed, but they generally conducted themselves with "signal ingratitude and treachery" even "to the most considerate and kindest of masters." [38] Although some blacks were loyal, most were treacherous. For Ruffin, there was no middle ground. On June 17, 1865, having learned the news from Appomattox, he made another entry into his diary. Visibly distressed, the old man wrote of his unwillingness to live alongside "the perfidious, malignant and vile Yankee race." [39] Then he picked up his silver-mounted gun, placed the muzzle within his mouth, and put out his life.[40] Though many factors contributed to Ruffin's suicide, racial ills were certainly among them. He could not accept wild, insolent behavior among some blacks, particularly when it was accompanied by servile, respectful conduct in others. The spark of hope that Ruffin saw in docile Negro conduct contrasted sharply with the gloom that black insolence and betrayal represented. The contrast must have provoked frustration and depression.

III

As the war progressed, Ruffin and other white Southerners felt that Negro conduct was increasingly unpredictable. Race relations were "deteriorating" to the point where whites could not tell whether a specific Negro was perpetually docile, occasionally defiant, or continually treacherous. Nor could they predict what new atrocities an insolent Negro might commit. "This war has taught us the perfect impossibility of placing the least confidence in any Negro," a Georgia planter contended. "In too numerous instances those we esteemed the most have been the first to desert us . . . ." [41] A Louisiana planter concurred; owing to wartime developments, *"no dependence is to be placed on the negro—and that they are the greatest hypocrits*

38. "Conduct of Negroes During the War, 1861–1865: Extracts from the Diary of Edmund Ruffin," *William and Mary Quarterly*, XXIII (1913), 258.

39. Avery O. Craven, *Edmund Ruffin, Southerner: A Study in Secession* (Baton Rouge: Louisiana State University Press, 1966), p. 259.

40. Edmund Ruffin, Jr., to his sons, June 20, 1865, in "Death of Edmund Ruffin," *Tyler's Quarterly Historical and Genealogical Magazine*, V (January, 1924), 193.

41. Kenneth M. Stampp, *The Era of Reconstruction, 1865–1877* (New York: Alfred A. Knopf, Inc., 1965), p. 121.

[*sic*] and liars that God ever made . . . ." [42] A South Carolina slaveholder debated at length whether her black body servant could be trusted.[43] A Georgia editor complained that unpredictable Negro behavior was greatly compounded by "too free locomotion by many of them at late hours of the night." [44]

For most white Southerners, particularly slaveholders, the very unpredictability of race relations was intolerable. If one could not anticipate Negro behavior—whether blacks would be docile or defiant, and if the latter, how their defiance would be manifested—one could not be certain that the "peculiar institution" had survived. With options independent of the will of his master, the Negro ceased to be a bondsman. Sensing that emancipation could have been occurring before their very eyes, Southerners were fearful. General emancipation was a development that none had experienced and most had dreaded.

As the war unfolded, white Southerners therefore became extremely anxious over the master-slave relationship. "There is something suspicious in the constant never-ending statement that 'we are not afraid of our slaves'," observed English traveler William Howard Russell.[45] But consternation was not always cloaked behind the rhetoric of assurance. Sometimes whites alluded to their fears in very specific terms. "Not among the Negroes does fear dwell now, nor uncertainty, nor anxiety," claimed a white woman from South Carolina. "It dwells here, haunting us, tracking us, running like an accursed discord through all the music tones of our existence." [46] A white woman from Louisiana dreaded the conduct that could be expected of a runaway slave near her mother's plantation.[47] The Marion *Star* voiced similar fears: fugitive black bondsmen were "lurking about" the area threatening the white population.[48] In the vicinity of Camden, South Carolina, plantation mistresses wondered whether their house servants would assault, kill, or protect them while their husbands were off to war.[49] Particularly in that locality, but elsewhere as well, certain husbands probably worried about the safety of their wives. For decades, many of them had engaged in sexual affairs with their black bondswomen.[50] Recalling how they

42. Whittington, *Louisiana Historical Quarterly*, XIV, No. 4 (October, 1931), 495.

43. Williams, ed., *Diary From Dixie*, p. 84.

44. Columbus (Georgia) *Daily Enquirer*, August 12, 1862.

45. William Howard Russell, *My Diary North and South* (London: Bradbury & Evans, 1863), I, 190.

46. Williams, ed., *Diary from Dixie*, p. 539.

47. Anderson, ed., *Brokenburn*, p. 88.

48. Marion (South Carolina) *Star*, June 18, 1861.

49. Williams, ed., *Diary From Dixie*, p. 140.

50. In Williams, ed., *Diary From Dixie*, pp. 21–22, Mary Boykin Chesnut reported on the frequency of sexual intercourse between white slaveholders and their black bondswomen. She referred to the Camden area. Her words under-

had craved interracial affairs, many of them probably projected their desires upon their black bondsmen: as they had desired Negro females, black males could seek revenge by assaulting white women. Distressed by the interracial sexual ventures of the white male, would the white woman also seek revenge by offering herself to the black man? And if this happened, who could turn back the black "rapist" with so many white men off to war?

People plagued by fear and uncertainty have often tended to behave aggressively. Aggression has often been a vehicle for resisting change and restoring a predictable and desirable mode of life that the aggressor imagined to have existed before uncertainty arose. Perceptive analysts of the Southern social scene like Frederick Law Olmstead, Ray Stannard Baker, W. J. Cash, and Lillian Smith claim that such behavior has been particularly discernible among white Southerners. Throughout much of the region's history, these analysts maintain, aggression has been used to secure peace of mind. It has allowed Southern whites to sense that they were doing their part to resist trying and unpleasant situations and to restore stability. The racial crisis of the Civil War years well illustrates this phenomenon. As the war progressed, many whites began to behave aggressively toward Negroes to ease their fears, remove their uncertainties, and restore racial stability. Striking out at all "impudent" Negroes, they felt that they could halt "irregular" black conduct. The Negroes who survived the purge might become loyal once again; those who succumbed would provide examples to steer other blacks onto the right track. This thinking contributed to the lynching and subsequent prolonged display of the bodies of the leaders of a thwarted slave plot in Adams County, Mississippi. Justifying the exhibit, the lynchers claimed that they were trying to induce docility in the remainder of the Negro community.[51] Local authorities in Richmond, worried over an increase in Negro burglaries, acted similarly. Circumventing legal requirements, they hanged two blacks as examples.[52] Describing how

---

lined acute personal frustrations and merit citation: "Under slavery, we live surrounded by prostitutes, yet an abandoned woman is sent out of any decent house. . . . Like the patriarchs of old, our men live all in one house with their wives and their concubines; and the mulattoes one sees in every family partly resemble the white children. Any lady is ready to tell you who is the father of all the mulatto children in everybody's household but her own. Those, she seems to think, drop from the clouds. My disgust sometimes is boiling over. Thank God for my country women, but alas for the men!" Kenneth M. Stampp, *The Peculiar Institution: Slavery in the Ante-Bellum South* (New York: Alfred A. Knopf, Inc., 1956), and Earl E. Thorpe, *Eros and Freedom in Southern Life and Thought* (Durham: Seeman Printery, 1967) provide considerable data suggesting that the sort of interracial sex that Chesnutt detected was very widespread.

51. Aptheker, *American Negro Slave Revolts*, pp. 365–66.

52. H. J. Eckenrode, "Negroes in Richmond in 1864," *Virginia Magazine of History and Biography*, XLVI, No. 3 (July, 1938), 199.

he had prodded local Negroes back to work after a federal invasion, a planter from northern Louisiana reasoned along these same lines: "things are just now beginning to work right—the negroes hated awfully to go to work again. Several have been shot and probably more will have to be." [53] In response to insolent black behavior, the Provost Marshall at Natchez, Mississippi, recommended violent repression. There "is a great disposition among the Negroes to be insubordinate, and to run away and go to the federals," he wrote. The remedy, serving as a warning to other blacks, was "to hang some 40 for plotting insurrection, and there has been about that number put in irons." [54] Throughout the war, Conferderates dressed as federal troopers went among the blacks asking for aid and information. Slaves assisting them in any way were lynched as a lesson to other bondsmen.[55] The conduct of whites toward blacks sometimes reached unimaginably brutal proportions. Near Saccaptory, Louisiana, a Negro charged with the death of his master was tied to a tree and suffocated by the dense smoke of pitch pine before burning to death.[56] When Confederates attacked a Mississippi fugitive slave settlement, they shut the blacks within their quarters and roasted them alive, leaving young children about the settlement pierced with wounds.[57] Little mercy was shown in the wartime campaign against black defiance; the South was swept by an unprecedented level of anti-Negro violence. Through their aggressive actions, anxious whites hoped that the old and familiar pattern of Negro docility would return.

IV

If white Southerners forcefully and often violently resisted blacks who did not defer to the white hand, they were particularly aggressive against Negro troops in the Union army. Despite the crudity of Civil War casualty statistics, the mortality rate of black federal troopers clearly exceeded the white mortality rate.[58] One of the most important reasons for the high Negro death rate was that Rebel troops fought

53. Whittington, *Louisiana Historical Quarterly*, XIV, No. 4 (October, 1931), 494.
54. Bettersworth, ed., *Mississippi in the Confederacy*, p. 235.
55. Aptheker, *Essays*, p. 173.
56. New Orleans *Tribune*, September 1, 1864.
57. Wish, *Journal of Negro History*, XXIII, No. 4 (October, 1938), 444.
58. Herbert Aptheker, *To Be Free: Studies in American Negro History*, 2nd ed. (New York: International Publishers Co., Inc., 1968), p. 78; George W. Williams, *A History of the Negro Troops in the War of the Rebellion 1861–1865* (New York: Harper & Brothers, 1888), p. 324. The Negro casualty rate was particularly high considering that blacks missed the first eighteen months of combat owing to a ban on Negro enlistment.

most fiercely against black troopers.[59] When black federals fell into their hands, rules of warfare were often suspended. Blacks were exterminated while whites were usually taken prisoner.[60] Certain Rebels admitted that this was "recognized" if not "official" Confederate policy. In June of 1863, a Confederate General noted that officers in command of capturing parties had "recognized the propriety of giving no quarter to armed Negroes and their officers."[61] According to the Richmond *Enquirer*, it was "recognized" policy that *"none will be taken prisoners.* Our troops understand what to do in such cases."[62] A Brigadier General besieging Columbus, Kentucky, in April of 1864 sent a note to his federal counterpart demanding unconditional surrender: "Should you surrender, the negroes now in arms will be returned to their masters. Should I however be compelled to take the place, no quarter will be shown to the negro troops whatever; the white troops will be treated as prisoners of war."[63]

It is not difficult to understand why white Southerners singled out United States Colored Troops for fierce reprisals. Many black troops were fugitive slaves; since they had chosen to fight their masters, slaveholders considered them guilty of treason. Moreover, because they had traditionally claimed that Southern blacks were treated with kindness and humanity, whites could only conclude that blacks had no cause to take up arms against Southern civilization. Those who did were surely ungrateful. Consider, too, that military activity was perhaps the most honored calling in Southern life. Since the Battle of New Orleans, men with arms had been regional heroes and combat was thought to be the preserve of the bold Cavalier gentleman.[64] Because white Southerners unquestioningly assumed that Negroes were racially inferior, it seemed disgraceful that the bold Cavalier —the cream of white civilization—would have to sully his image by fighting a "lowly" black soldier. If Southern gentlemen had to wage a prolonged war against "mere niggers," warfare would lose its pres-

59. Dudley Taylor Cornish's *The Sable Arm: Negro Troops in the Union Army, 1861–1865* (New York: Longmans, Green & Co., Ltd., 1956), the most comprehensive study of black federal troopers, provides extensive documentation of this conclusion. See also, *Official Records of the Union and Confederate Armies of the War of the Rebellion*, Series I, Vol. XXIV, Part 2, 455–57 (hereafter cited as O.R.A.); Williams, ed., *Diary From Dixie*, pp. 234–35.

60. *O.R.A.*, Ser. I, Vol. XXXII, Part 1, 518–40, 586–90; Ser. I, Vol. XXIV, Part 2, 459; Ser. II, Vol. VI, 1022–23; Aptheker, *To Be Free*, pp. 130–31 citing *Official Records of the Union and Confederate Navies in the War of the Rebellion*, Ser. 1, Vol. XII, 647, 651; Vol. XIII, 83–84; Vol. XV, 158–61.

61. *O.R.A.*, Ser. II, Vol. VI, 21–22.

62. Richmond *Enquirer*, December 17, 1863.

63. Aptheker, *To Be Free*, p. 95.

64. For a thoroughgoing exploration of this Cavalier miiltary tradition. see John Hope Franklin, *The Militant South: 1800–1861* (Boston: Beacon Press, 1956).

tige. Hence, black troopers had to be destroyed with all deliberate speed to preserve the image of Cavalier warriors. Finally, the very sight of a black trooper challenged the assumption that the Negro was inherently and properly a slave. "Whenever we establish the fact that they are a military people," Georgia Governor Joseph E. Brown noted, "we destroy our theory that they are unfit to be free." [65] General Howell Cobb concurred: "If slaves will make good soldiers, our whole theory of slavery is wrong—but they won't make soldiers." [66] White Southerners were determined to prove that blacks did not make good soldiers. They would attack Negro federal troopers— those potential rapists of white women—with ferocity. They would prove to themselves and to their Negro adversaries that men of swarthy complexion were fit only to be docile servants. Above all, they would prove to themselves that their white skin made them dominant. The blood of black soldiers would affirm that the white race was supreme.

V

If these were the thoughts of white Southerners between Sumter and Appomattox, the last months of combat were very discouraging. By late 1864 and early 1865, the Confederacy faced a military disaster that would have serious racial implications. Robert E. Lee declared that federal troops would soon "get access to a large part of the negro population" and would use Negroes to hold whites "in subjection." "Whatever may be the effect of our employing negro troops it cannot be as mischievous as this." [67] Lee therefore recommended enrolling blacks as troopers. Significantly, he concluded that those blacks who fought for the Confederacy would have to be emancipated, for without assurances of freedom blacks would have no inducement to fight.[68]

Shocked and alarmed, many whites opposed Lee's proposal. For them, black Confederate troopers symbolized the destruction of Southern civilization. The proposal would create utter chaos in a society which, after nearly four years of combat, was confused, bitter, and exhausted. A North Carolina Representative, J. T. Leach, fearfully predicted that black Confederate troops would assault whites and turn the region into a wild Santo Domingo.[69] Representative

65. Charleston *Courier*, March 9, 1865.
66. *O.R.A.*, Ser. IV, Vol. III, 1009–10.
67. Wish, *Journal of Negro History*, XXIII, No. 4 (October, 1938), 437.
68. *O.R.A.*, Ser. IV, Vol. VIII, 1012–13.
69. Charleston *Daily Courier*, February 4, 1865.

William Porcher Miles of South Carolina concurred, charging that the Lee proposal would overturn a Southern social structure through which whites ruled and blacks obeyed.[70] Leach and Miles did not specify how black men with guns would destroy the social structure but they may have feared that black troopers would do more than to force their way to power with the point of a gun. Unconsciously, they may have seen a phallic implication in the Negro's gun. A black man with a gun could force himself beyond the white man, win access to the white woman, rape her, and thereby overturn Southern hierarchy through pollution of the "superior race." If Leach and Miles had not consciously thought in these precise terms, Texas State Senator Louis T. Wigfall had. If a black man became a trooper, Wigfall argued, he won the right to interracial sex and thus the privileges of a miscegenationist. Blacks would dominate and pollute the white race.[71] The editor of the Charleston *Mercury* shared these fears. If black men were allowed to have guns they would become "Swaggering buck niggers" who would attack white women, precisely the opposite of "what our soldiers are fighting for." Thus, "if the slaves are armed, South Carolina would no longer have an interest in prosecuting the war." [72] Clearly, white Southern males were fighting for a social order where they dominated an obedient black population. A proposal to give black men guns so that they could overpower white men and assault white women seemed to contradict this very purpose. It completely negated all attempts to resist wartime racial changes and to resurrect docile Negro behavior. Somehow an "old order" had to be restored where white men had access to black women but black men kept away from white women.

Advocates of the Lee plan never denied that it could undermine the quest for black docility. Since opponents of the proposal were primarily concerned with this "danger," Lee provoked no genuine debate over the future of white-black relationships in the South. Military expediency, not racial necessity, was the dominant consideration among the General's supporters. "Let it never be said that to preserve slavery we were willing to wear the chains of bondage ourselves. . . . Let not slavery prove a barrier to our independence," insisted the editor of the Natchez *Courier*. We must "save ourselves from the rapacious North, whatever the cost." [73] Blacks would be fighting no matter what Southerners did, President Jefferson Davis asserted. The choice was simply whether they would be aiding or

70. Charleston *Daily Courier*, February 4, 1865.
71. New Orleans *Tribune*, February 15, 1865.
72. Charleston *Mercury*, January 26, 1865.
73. Natchez *Courier*, December 18, 1863, quoted in Bettersworth, ed., *Mississippi in the Confederacy*, pp. 245–46.

attacking their white rulers.[74] In a characteristically expedient defense
of black Confederate troopers, a Mississippian claimed that if Southerners "do not get the negro, the Yankees will. . . ." There was no
real choice in the matter.[75] These were the words of men who tried to
play the part of sober realists. But because they would not deny that
Negroes with guns represented the overthrow of the Southern social
structure, they were no more realistic than their opponents. They
charged opponents of the Lee proposal with an unwillingness to confront military realities. Yet they were unwilling to face up to those
"dangerous" racial realities that they themselves had implicitly recognized. Clearly, Southerners were visionaries whether they favored
or opposed black Confederate troopers.

Proponents of the Lee proposal carried the day. On March 13, 1865,
the Confederate Congress authorized the President of the Confederacy
to request state recruitment of black troops.[76] President Davis implemented this law, and a week before the fall of Richmond the local
citizenry watched with dismay as Negro Confederate soldiers drilled
in Capitol Square.[77] Only a few months before the drill, the editor of
the Richmond *Examiner* had insisted that the very sight of a Negro
trooper would deprive a white Southerner of his "proprietary feeling." [78] If this was a correct assessment, what whites saw in Capitol
Square was the erosion of the traditional master-slave relationship.

Section Five of the slave recruitment law explicitly disavowed any
"change in the relation which the said slaves shall bear toward their
owners, except by consent of the owners and of the States in which
they may reside. . . ." [79] But this language was mere homage to a
disappearing institution and to states' rights theory. Proponents as
well as opponents of the statute admitted that it was a major step
toward the destruction of slavery because a state would be obliged
to free any black man who took up arms for the Confederacy.[80]
"Freedom is given to the Negro Soldier, not because we believe

74. Dunbar Rowland, ed., *Jefferson Davis, Constitutionalist: His Letters, Papers,
and Speeches* (Jackson: Mississippi Department of Archives and History, 1923),
VI, 482. The New Orleans *Tribune*, October 14, 1864, printed a very similar
analysis by Louisiana Governor Henry W. Allen.
75. Biloxi *Advertiser and Register*, October 19, 1864, as quoted in the New
Orleans *Tribune*, November 3, 1864.
76. Charles W. Ramsdell, ed. *Laws and Joint Resolutions of the Last Session of
the Confederate Congress* (Durham: Duke University Press, 1941), pp. 118–19.
77. Robert Penn Warren, *The Legacy of the Civil War* (New York: Vintage
Books, 1964), p. 34.
78. Richmond *Examiner*, January 7, 1865.
79. Ramsdell, ed., *Laws and Resolutions*, p. 119.
80. Robert Cruden, *The Negro in Reconstruction* (Englewood Cliffs, N.J.:
Prentice-Hall, Inc., 1969), p. 8; E. Merton Coulter, *The Confederate States of
America, 1861–1865* (Baton Rouge: Louisiana State University Press, 1950), p. 268;
Swiggett, ed., *Rebel War Clerk's Diary*, II, 327; Wiley, *Southern Negroes*, p. 156.

slavery is wrong," editorialized the Richmond *Enquirer,* "but because we must offer to the Negroes inducements to fidelity which he regards as equal, if not greater, than those offered by the enemy." [81] Howell Cobb concurred; slaves would fight as well for the Confederacy as they had for the federals because they knew that if they took up arms for Dixie "we [would] give them their freedom." [82] An Alabama legislator claimed that the South was deceiving itself if it expected slaves who had served as Confederate soldiers to return to bondage.[83] These remarks suggested that Southerners were unwilling partners in the destruction of their cherished institution.

The slave recruitment statute was obviously promoting a situation where white Southern soldiers would return home to a racial relationship in complete disarray. By the close of the war many sensed that assertive Negro behavior was more pervasive than ever. Despite violently aggressive efforts to turn back racial chaos and to restore white dominance, the end seemed nowhere in sight. As opponents of black recruitment had contended, Lee's proposal had negated all efforts to restore traditional racial relationships.

During the next several decades, white Southerners would refer to the problem of correcting "uppity" black conduct and restoring order as the "Negro problem." More properly, it was a white problem, for it stemmed from the intense desire of white Southerners for Negro servility. Whites would spend many years seeking solutions to *their* "problem." Ultimately, they would conclude that the "problem" sprang from the savage essence of Negro personality. But this conclusion did not resolve the "problem." It could not have. It ignored the fact that because the "Negro problem" was actually the white man's "problem," it was rooted in the white man's limitations.

81. Aptheker, *Essays,* p. 201.
82. Aptheker, *Essays,* p. 202.
83. Aptheker, *Essays,* p. 201.

PART TWO

Finding the Way Out: Southern Solutions to the "Negro Problem"

. . . the problem resulting now from the presence of the freedman entails on us of the white race a question more difficult to solve satisfactorily, than one which formerly proceeded from his presence as a slave.

—Charles Gayarré, 1885

White Southerners who detected a marked deterioration in race relations during the Civil War found little improvement in the years that followed. Throughout Reconstruction, whites fretted over Negro migration to federal military posts, to nearby towns and cities, and sometimes to distant Western and Southwestern states. But they also complained about the inefficiency of the many Negro laborers who remained. Most disheartening, a large number of Negroes seemed to have forgotten that the black race was supposed to defer to the white. The protests of Negroes against deprivations of civil rights made this all too clear. By their "assertive" behavior, blacks were departing from their traditional role of servility. Indeed, race relations during the postwar years often seemed to verge on anarchy.

Because Charles Gayarré equated racial anarchy with the absence of Negro docility, he was particularly disturbed. In 1885 he charged that the "Negro problem" had become more difficult to solve than any racial obstruction antebellum Southerners had ever encountered. A Louisiana historian, a literary critic, and an old man by 1885, Gayarré knew too much about the old order to deny that racial ills had plagued the "peculiar institution." He recalled only too clearly how the antebellum South had experienced serious racial disruptions ranging from slave revolts and abolitionist attacks to "uncontrollable" free Negroes and "impudent" urban slaves. But for Gayarré and for many others, antebellum disorders had been dwarfed by the tumult of Civil War and Reconstruction. The task at hand—the need to cope with an unprecedented wave of Negro "insolence"—was far more demanding. Unlike the antebellum years, Southern whites could not turn back defiance by tightening or reforming the slave system. They no longer had the ability to institute a night patrol or a pass system, or to invoke the traditional threat of the auction block. Legal emancipation had swept away these devices. If a servile pattern of Negro behavior was to be restored—if anarchy was to be resisted—new techniques of racial control were required. Responding to this new and traumatic dilemma, white Southern racial theorists formulated solutions to the "Negro problem."

Chapter Two

"Nigger Here, Nigger There"

Based upon his travels through the South from the summer of 1865 to the spring of 1866, Massachusetts journalist John Richard Dennett wrote a series of articles for *The Nation* that dealt with nearly every aspect of postwar life. Dennett surveyed topics from agricultural stagnation to urban decay and human degeneration. He concluded that the white Southerner had become a bitter and spiteful man who hated the Yankee and all that Yankee society represented. Clearly, there could be no sectional reconciliation. Yet the white Southerner's contempt for local blacks surpassed his hatred of the Yankee. With fresh memories of the war and legal emancipation, the Southerner believed that Negroes had revealed themselves as a vicious, disloyal race which could no longer be trusted. Years earlier the "great" Southerner, Andrew Jackson, had forcefully removed Indians because they had threatened white civilization. Now Southerners had to expel a second "foreign" race. There was no place for Negroes below the Mason-Dixon line. They had to be *excluded* from the region or, at the very least, from the centers of white population.[1]

There was evidence to support Dennett's perception of the white Southern mind. Indeed, by the fall of 1865, the Lynchburg *Virginian* predicted that *exclusionism* would soon become the region's dominant racial ideology.[2] "I am utterly disgusted with the Negro race," an ex-slaveholder from South Carolina proclaimed, "and trust that I may some day be in a land that is purged of them." [3] Residents of the North Carolina town of Gold Hill sought to force local blacks across the state line.[4] A Mississippi politician submitted a resolution to the State Senate reflecting the same spirit: "That in hearkening to the admonition of history, that where two races are thrown together, a

1. Henry M. Christman, ed., *The South as It Is: 1865–1866 by John Richard Dennett* (New York: The Viking Press, 1965), especially pp. 163–72.
2. Lynchburg *Daily Virginian*, October 15, 1865.
3. H. W. Ravenel to A. L. Taveau, June 27, 1865, as quoted in Joel Williamson, *After Slavery: The Negro in South Carolina During Reconstruction, 1861–1877* (Chapel Hill: University of North Carolina Press, 1965), p. 252.
4. Christman, ed., *South as It Is*, pp. 140–41.

natural antagonism has ensued, we do declare in theory that the freedmen of this State are banished from our land. . . ." [5] A Norfolk resident charged that emancipated Negroes had become wretched souls. Shiftless and lazy, they had to be excluded from white society.[6]

In the course of Reconstruction, a number of whites carried exclusionist ideology to its logical conclusion—colonization. Negroes had to be transported to foreign soil. J. D. B. DeBow, prominent as an antebellum proslavery theorist, abandoned his prewar commitment to the "peculiar institution" and charged that colonization was the most effective way to cope with the problem of the emancipated Negro.[7] A North Carolina politician concurred. The freedmen's moral deficiencies were so great, he maintained, that the race would always threaten white civilization. For this reason, blacks had to be removed.[8] From Tennessee, the editor of the Greenville *New Era* declared that race relations had reached the point where free Negroes could not be permitted "to remain in our country." [9] "That child is already born who will behold the last negro in the State of Mississippi," the editor of the Natchez *Democrat* predicted. Colonization would soon eliminate the "Negro problem." [10]

Essays by the fiery and renowned antebellum propagandist, Hinton Rowan Helper, represent the most systematic statement of the Southern exclusionist position in the immediate postwar years. Over and over in *The Negroes in Negroland, Nojoque,* and *Noonday Exigencies in America,* Helper charged that blacks were "pernicious," "inferior," "impure and revolting." With disgusting "swarthy complexions," it was intolerable for them to live near whites. Absolute and permanent separation of the races was imperative. After July 4, 1876, no Negro should be permitted to remain within the United States.[11]

Helper, DeBow, and countless other postbellum exclusionists were doubtless sincere. Nothing seems contrived in their appeals. They despised Negroes and wanted to be rid of them at any cost. But though these Southerners saw exclusion as the solution to the postwar "Negro problem," the idea was not new. Whites of the Reconstruction decade were merely drawing upon a prewar ideology.

5. Jackson *Daily Clarion,* November 11, 1865.
6. Christman, ed., *South as It Is,* p. 6.
7. *DeBow's Review,* I (January, 1866), 58–67 *passim.*
8. Christman, ed., *South as It Is,* pp. 163–65.
9. Greenville *New Era,* n.d., quoted in the Memphis *Daily Appeal,* November 8, 1865.
10. Natchez *Democrat,* January 8, 1866.
11. Hinton Rowan Helper, *Nojoque: A Question for a Continent* (New York: George W. Carleton & Co., 1867), pp. v–vi, 14–15, 65, 284; *The Negroes in Negroland* (New York: George W. Carleton & Co., 1868), p. 238; *Noonday Exigencies in America* (New York: Bible Brothers, Publishers, 1871), pp. vii, 28, 31, 46.

Helper, for example, was elaborating his dramatic 1857 publication, *The Impending Crisis of the South,* an attack upon a slave system that had promoted interracial association. Samuel Mosheim Schmucker was another influential formulator of antebellum exclusionist doctrine, and some Southern exclusionists of the immediate postwar years must have recalled his 1855 novel, *The Planter's Victim,* with its strong condemnation of interracial contacts, particularly sexual contacts. Within the cities of the Reconstruction South, whites shared fresh memories of a campaign to segregate slaves from white society during the immediate prewar decades.[12] Even the colonization idea could be traced to the antebellum Southern mind, for Thomas Jefferson, James Madison, Henry Clay, and other prestigious leaders had often championed the proposal.[13] Finally, many whites continued to recall the way free Negroes had been treated before the war; by law as well as by social proscription, they had faced numerous color lines. Constant and extensive efforts had been made to minimize contact between free blacks and white society.[14]

These were manifestations of an exclusionist ideology that the Old South conveyed to the New. Confronted by a seemingly unprecedented number of insolent and sexually "dangerous" Negroes in the years after Sumter, Helper, DeBow, and others drew upon the familiar. They elected to apply an old idea to a seemingly new problem.

II

Though exclusionism was a popular racial ideology during the Reconstruction decade, it did not go unchallenged. In his remarkably sensitive novel on the Reconstruction South, *A Fool's Errand* (1879), Albion W. Tourgée contended that proslavery ideology had also survived the Civil War: ". . . the bulk of the Southern people believed it then, and believe it now. They regard the abolition of slavery only as a temporary triumph of fanaticism over divine truth. They do not believe the negro intended or designed for any other sphere in life." [15] Throughout his novel, Tourgée cited manifestations

12. Richard C. Wade, *Slavery in the Cities: The South, 1820–1860* (New York: Oxford University Press, 1964), pp. 266–78.

13. Winthrop D. Jordan, *White over Black: American Attitudes Toward the Negro, 1550–1812* (Chapel Hill: University of North Carolina Press, 1968), pp. 546–47, quotes Jefferson on colonization, while P. J. Staudenraus, *The African Colonization Movement, 1816–1865* (New York: Columbia University Press, 1961), pp. 7, 28, quotes Madison and Clay.

14. Jordan, *White over Black,* pp. 414–22.

15. Albion W. Tourgée, *A Fool's Errand* (New York: Harper Torchbooks, 1966), pp. 86–87.

of proslavery thought. Though his characters did not use terms like "slave" or "bondsman," he left no doubt as to what they intended.

Tourgée's claim contained more than a grain of truth, for many Southern whites challenged the exclusionist position. To them, legal emancipation meant little; slavery had survived and it remained the only way to control Negro behavior. In 1866 the editor of the Memphis *Avalanche* openly proclaimed that blacks "are still slaves in fact if not in name." [16] Several months later "Snowden," Petersburg correspondent for the Richmond *Dispatch*, asserted that it was both proper and humane for masters to continue "caring" for their Negro "servants." [17] Another Virginian continued to buy slaves during the fall of 1865 while a prominent Tennessee politician charged that the "negroes are no more free than they were forty years ago, and if one goes about the country telling them that they are free, shoot him. . . ." [18]

Most often, however, the proslavery challenge to the exclusionist doctrine was not voiced so blatantly. Though legal emancipation failed to destroy the proslavery mentality, it nevertheless induced most proponents of black bondage to modify their rhetoric. By 1867, Joseph E. Brown, the Georgia politician, had ceased to remind local blacks that they were naturally and properly slaves. Rather, he now explained how whites had always "been accustomed to think and provide" while the black race "has been raised to depend on others." [19] Another leading Georgian insisted that "the necessity of subordination and dependence should be riveted on their [Negroes'] convictions." [20] According to the editor of the Richmond *Dispatch*, blacks should "fancy themselves once more living in that time when they were happy, although not 'emancipated.' . . ." [21] The editor of the Lynchburg *Daily Virginian* charged that Negroes "must be subordinated to the white man, or—perish." [22] For men such as these, the "peculiar institution" continued in fact if not in name.

Most leading proslavery theorists who survived the war were equally committed to the "peculiar institution," emancipation notwithstanding. They would not subscribe to exclusionist doctrine. George Fitzhugh, perhaps the most original and creative of the lot, continued to argue that the nation's economy required a subservient

16. Memphis *Daily Avalanche*, March 3, 1866.

17. Richmond *Daily Dispatch*, January 15, 1866.

18. The Lynchburg *Daily Virginian*, October 1, 1865, reports the slave-buying incident, while the Knoxville *Whig*, April 24, 1867, quotes the Tennessee politician, Emerson Etheridge.

19. Jackson *Daily Clarion*, June 20, 1867.

20. Quoted in Alan Conway, *The Reconstruction of Georgia* (Minneapolis: University of Minnesota Press, 1966), p. 55.

21. Richmond *Dispatch*, April 13, 1866.

22. Lynchburg *Daily Virginian*, September 20, 1865.

black labor force.[23] Remaining true to the theme of his *Essay on Liberty and Slavery* (1856), Albert Taylor Bledsoe demanded veto rights against any federal legislation so that the South could undercut "pro-Negro" enactments.[24] Two of Edward A. Pollard's postwar publications, *The Lost Cause* (1867) and *The Lost Cause Regained* (1868), represented a less explicit but more vehement defense of slavery than his well-known volume, *Black Diamonds Gathered in the Darkey Homes of the South* (1859). Before Sumter, Alexander H. Stephens had not been an adamant supporter of slavery. After Appomattox, he wrote in unqualified terms on the propriety of a "superior" race controlling the affairs of "inferior" peoples.[25]

Throughout Reconstruction proponents of slavery, like racial exclusionists, drew upon antebellum ideas. They recalled the many arguments of the tumultuous prewar decades justifying black bondage through the sin of Ham, the allegedly underdeveloped Negro brain, and the "misery and destitution" of free Negroes. But these arguments had been invented or contrived to preserve the racial *status quo* within the antebellum South—the integrated and hierarchic racial order that slavery had allegedly required. Fundamentally the antebellum proslavery position was intended to defend a social condition where blacks labored alongside whites in subordinate roles. A Presbyterian minister, John B. Adger, stated the proposition well:

> They [the Negroes] belong to us. We also belong to them. They are divided among us and mingled up with us, eating from the same storehouses, drinking from the same fountains, dwelling in the same enclosures, forming parts of the same families. . . . See them all around you, in these streets, in all these dwellings; a race distinct from us, yet closely united to us; brought in God's mysterious providence from a foreign land, and placed under our care, and made members of our state and society; they are not more truly ours than we are truly theirs.[26]

23. See, e.g., George Fitzhugh, "Camp Lee and the Freedman's Bureau," *DeBow's Review* (October, 1866), p. 346 and Harvey Wish, *George Fitzhugh: Propagandist of the Old South* (Baton Rouge: Louisiana State University Press, 1943), pp. 316–17. For a fascinating commentary on the postbellum continuation of Fitzhugh's critique of free labor in the capitalist North, see Donald B. Meyer, *The Positive Thinkers: A Study of the American Quest for Health, Wealth and Personal Power from Mary Baker Eddy to Norman Vincent Peale* (Garden City, New York: Doubleday & Company, Inc., 1965), pp. 135–36.

24. See, e.g., Albert Taylor Bledsoe, "Draper's History of the War," *Southern Review*, V (January, 1868), 14–15.

25. See, e.g., Natchez *Weekly Democrat*, September 21, 1868; Alexander H. Stephens, *A Constitutional View of the Late War Between the States* (Philadelphia: National Publishing Co., 1868, 1870), I, 540; II, 80–81.

26. Quoted in Ernest Trice Thompson, *Presbyterianism in the South, 1607–1861* (Richmond: John Knox Press, 1963), I, 441–42.

Basically the arguments of the major antebellum proslavery theorists —the Ruffins, the Bledsoes, and the Petigrus—were pleas for precisely the sort of society that Adger had described. Blacks had to live under the "care" and the "direction" of the "superior" race. Close and continuous interracial association was imperative.[27]

The Fitzhughs, the Bledsoes, the Pollards, and other postbellum champions of slavery knew that they had defended and were defending a social order of integrated subservience. The challenge of Helper and other exclusionists served as a constant reminder. Therefore, like the prewar decades, the Reconstruction South was the scene of sharp ideological conflict. The ideas of a Helper or an aging DeBow collided with the thoughts of a Fitzhugh or a Bledsoe. One group required a society of frequent and meaningful interracial contact; another group demanded the expulsion of all blacks from white society. Success for the one implied defeat for the other. Hence two very different ideological traditions borrowed from the Old South perpetuated a fundamental schism between white racial theorists in the postwar decade. Clearly, the Southern response to the "Negro problem" was not monolithically unified.

III

Though proslavery thought and racial exclusionism were predicated upon conflicting assumptions, the two frequently overlapped. Several antebellum champions of colonization had been avid proponents of the "peculiar institution." For many of them, colonization represented a theoretical but impractical alternative to black bondage; it was simply too costly. Still others opposed the importation of Africans while they defended domestic slavery. Fearing that newly arrived African slaves would be wild and insurrectionary, they campaigned to exclude such slaves from American shores as they simultaneously asserted that white contact with domestic blacks was permissible and even essential.[28] Yet the white man's relationship to his domestic bondsmen was not entirely integrated. As several proslavery theoreticians freely acknowledged, field hands on large plantations seldom associated with the master and his family. Most slaves were required to live in cabins at a distance from the "main house." But the

27. Avery O. Craven, *Edmund Ruffin, Southerner* (Baton Rouge: Louisiana State University Press, 1966), p. 135; Albert Taylor Bledsoe, *An Essay on Liberty and Slavery* (Philadelphia: J. B. Lippincott & Co., 1856), p. 267; *DeBow's Review*, XXV (September, 1858), 293, quotes Petigru.

28. Ronald T. Takaki's "A Pro-Slavery Crusade: The Agitation to Reopen the African Slave Trade" provides an excellent discussion of this point. The manuscript is scheduled to be published in the near future.

mixture of segregation and bondage was most detectable in the urban setting, where proponents of slavery had systematically promulgated segregationist measures in a frantic effort to control "disobedient" slaves.[29]

Hence, there were probably few "pure" exclusionists or uncompromising champions of integrated subservience. Rather, exclusionism and proslavery ideology marked out broad guideposts to Southern racial thought. Concrete issues—the slave trade, the organization of the rural plantation, the intricacies of urban life—blurred distinctions between the two ideologies. A man raised in a nonslaveholding region of the South may have felt a visceral repugnance for blacks, seeking to isolate them from white society. Another man who had been born on a plantation and reared by a black mammy might have been unable to conceive of life without interracial contact. But when a specific issue arose, a white Southerner was capable of "contradicting" his basic orientation. In a given instance, considerations other than proximity of white to black could assume the highest priority.

The fact that exclusionist and proslavery ideas were not always mutually exclusive—that they often overlapped—pointed to a third ideological possibility. A white Southerner who lacked a strong doctrinal commitment to either ideology could borrow from both, formulating a position that was responsive to segregated as well as integrated features of Southern life.

During the Reconstruction decade the Governor of Tennessee, William Gannaway Brownlow, was perhaps the only prominent proponent of this third ideology. He resided in nonslaveholding East Tennessee where exclusionist sentiment ran high. In the antebellum decades, whites of the region had lobbied the state legislature for Negro colonization and in the years that followed Appomattox, desires to rid the region of blacks became even more intense.[30] A nonslaveholder, a newspaper editor who wanted readers, and a nervous and calculating politician who desperately sought popularity, Parson Brownlow was not able to isolate himself from widespread local sentiment against interracial association. But he secretly harbored the desire to become a slaveholder, with insufficient funds his only drawback.[31] Thus, the man articulated local aspirations for ridding

---

29. Wade, *Slavery in the Cities*, pp. 266–77.

30. See, e.g., Willis D. Boyd, "Negro Colonization in the Reconstruction Era, 1865–1870," *Georgia Historical Quarterly*, XL (1956), 369; Walter L. Fleming, ed., *Documentary History of Reconstruction* (New York: McGraw-Hill Book Company, 1966), I, 81; Kenneth M. Stampp, *The Era of Reconstruction, 1865–1877* (New York: Alfred A. Knopf, Inc., 1965), pp. 162–63; James Welch Patton, "The Progress of Emancipation in Tennessee, 1796–1860," *Journal of Negro History*, XVII, No. 1 (January, 1932), 76–77.

31. William B. Hesseltine, "Methodism and Reconstruction in East Tennessee," *East Tennessee Historical Society's Publications*, III (January, 1931), 44.

East Tennessee of Negroes while he simultaneously retained hopes of owning Negroes. Slaveholding aspirations detracted from his exclusionist sentiments while local values and political expediency precluded full commitment to any ideology that smacked of integration. His only choice was to steer some sort of a middle course. Finding this course well before Sumter, he continued to propound it in the decade after Appomattox.

Brownlow therefore represented more than a crude, belligerent politician of the Reconstruction era; he was a leading spokesman of a racial ideology that was neither exclusionist nor proslavery. Though he led no crusade, he presented an ideological alternative to both the Helpers and the Fitzhughs. Owing to East Tennessee exclusionist sentiment, however, the politically ambitious parson tended to disguise his personal ambivalence on the crucial issue of Negro proximity to white society. His rhetoric more closely paralleled the exclusionist Helper than the proslavery Fitzhugh. Because "loyal" Tennesseans hated "niggers," he insisted that blacks had to be kept away.[32] In January of 1865, as the Civil War was drawing to a close, he proclaimed that the "nigger is the rebellion and the rebellion is the nigger, and to put down the one we have to get rid of the other." [33] If Negroes were to remain anywhere near white society, he subsequently asserted, they would have to content themselves with separate restaurants, theaters, cemeteries, churches, and schools.[34] The provision within Charles Sumner's Civil Rights Bill [35] requiring integrated schools was "the sum of villainy and the quintessence of abominations"; it would destroy the "whole fabric of education in Tennessee. . . ." [36]

Remarks such as these suggest that Brownlow would not sanction interracial association of any sort. Like Helper and DeBow, he expressed doubt that the "Negro problem" could ever be solved by segregating blacks from whites within Southern society. That would not remove the "greasy" and "odorous" Negro from the white man's visions, much less from the white woman's bed.[37] From time to time, Brownlow therefore demanded a more extreme form of exclusionism—colonization. Sometimes he proposed completely separate white

32. New York *Times*, January 8, 1866.

33. Knoxville *Whig*, January 11, 1865.

34. Knoxville *Whig*, September 27, 1865; Knoxville *Whig and Chronicle*, March 10, 1875.

35. After amendment, this bill became the Civil Rights Act of 1875.

36. *Congressional Record*, 43rd Cong., 1st Sess., 4144. See also Felix A. Reeve, "W. G. Brownlow," an unpublished essay in the Manuscript Division of the Tennessee State Library, for comment on Brownlow's general reaction to Sumner's Civil Rights Bill. The manuscript is dated August 6, 1878.

37. The Knoxville *Whig*, February 15, 1865, and April 15, 1868, printed remarks pointing to Brownlow's deep distaste for interracial sexual relations within the South.

and black communities "on Southern soil." On other occasions he called for removal of blacks to "a suitable country" of their own. At times he requested separate "territory" for Negroes "within such degree of latitude as are adopted to their nature. . . ." [38]

Helper or DeBow could have disseminated exclusionist pronouncements such as these, for they were totally discordant with the integrated subservience premise of proslavery thought during the Reconstruction decade. Yet unlike the theorists of black removal, Brownlow also lauded the traditional master-slave relationship. When he did, he seemed directly at odds with the exclusionist tradition he so adamantly championed.

The antislavery rhetoric that Brownlow mouthed but never really believed obscured this conflict. Like the leading proslavery theorists of the postwar decade, he tried to avoid words like "slave" and "bondsman." Moreover, he publicly endorsed the Thirteenth Amendment and claimed that he had no love for slavery.[39] But the endorsement must not be taken seriously. Expediency often required a Southerner who wanted power in the Reconstruction period to endorse federal law even if he would not abide by it. Like Fitzhugh, Bledsoe, and Stephens, Brownlow viewed the Emancipation Proclamation and the Thirteenth Amendment as legal provisions but no more; they required no concrete changes in the traditional white-black relationship. They proved that the black bondsman had become a "person" who had "the right to enter into contracts, and to enforce them in courts; to sue and be sued, and to prosecute those who may injure him in person or property." [40] But these legalities did not rule out *de facto* slavery. On a few occasions Brownlow substituted the word "slave" for "Negro" as if nothing of profound importance had happened since Sumter.[41] For him, Roger B. Taney's landmark decision in the Dred Scott case of 1857 remained the law of the land; blacks had no rights that whites were bound to respect.[42] The white man was and

38. Robert H. White, ed., *Messages of the Governors of Tennessee, 1857–1869* (Nashville: Tennessee Historical Commission, 1959), V, 465, quotes the separation "on Southern soil" proposal while the Knoxville *Whig*, April 4, 1866, prints Brownlow's call for "a suitable country." Brownlow's remark on territory of the correct "latitude" for Negroes is quoted in White, ed., *Messages*, V, 465–66 and in the Knoxville *Whig*, October 11, 1865. For a similar and revealing Brownlow remark, see the Knoxville *Whig*, April 19, 1865.

39. The Knoxville *Whig*, July 25, 1865, prints Brownlow's praise of the Thirteenth Amendment. For his sarcastic remarks toward slavery, see Knoxville *Whig*, March 15, 1865; April 12, 1865; and May 8, 1867.

40. White, ed., *Messages*, V, 466.

41. See, e.g., Knoxville *Whig*, September 27, 1865; E. Merton Coulter, *William G. Brownlow: Fighting Parson of the Southern Highlands* (Chapel Hill: University of North Carolina Press, 1937), pp. 291–92; Nashville *Daily Press and Times*, July 3, 1865.

42. *Congressional Record*, 43rd Cong., 1st Sess., 4143.

always had been on a higher "level" than the Negro. Thus, he was duty-bound to "control" the Negro, to "look after" and to "cultivate" him, to see that the Negro remained sober, diligent, and loyal.[43] Kind and persistent compulsion by whites would cure blacks of the false implications of legal emancipation and restore them as efficient laborers.[44]

When proslavery pronouncements like these are contrasted with Brownlow's many exclusionist remarks, it becomes obvious that the Reconstruction Governor of Tennessee was on both sides of the Southern racial debate. He seemed to be operating within the ideological tradition of the Fitzhughs as well as the Helpers. But the Fitzhughs seldom defended exclusionism and the Helpers never propounded slavery. Thus, Brownlow was distinguishable from both. His racial pronouncements represented a third type of racial mind trying to come to grips with the postwar "Negro problem." Along with an exclusionist tradition and a proslavery tradition, there was a "Brownlow tradition."

Like the ideological traditions represented by the Helpers and the Fitzhughs, the "Brownlow tradition" took root during the antebellum decades. But whereas the Helpers had drawn upon a rich vein of Old South exclusionist thought and the Fitzhughs upon a richer vein of proslavery ideology, the "Brownlow tradition" drew upon both. A Methodist circuit-rider turned newspaper editor during the prewar decades, Brownlow had frequently voiced exclusionist remarks. Long before Sumter, he charged that "niggers" had disgusting physical features and animalistic propensities—that they had been the epitome of "sin and wickedness." [45] But there were whites who associated on intimate terms with these wretched creatures.[46] To preserve the "purity" of the white race, he therefore insisted upon separation of the races, with demands ranging from segregation within Southern society to colonization abroad.[47] Interspersed among these exclusionist statements was the parson's defense of the "peculiar institution." *Ought American Slavery to be Perpetuated?*, the report of an 1858 public debate between Brownlow and a New York abolitionist, con-

43. Memphis *Daily Avalanche*, March 29, 1866; Knoxville *Whig*, June 28, 1865, and July 30, 1867; Knoxville *Whig and Chronicle*, June 21, 1876.

44. White, ed., *Messages*, V, 413.

45. See, e.g., Jonesboro *Whig*, August 17, 1842; William G. Brownlow, *Ought American Slavery to be Perpetuated?* (Philadelphia: J. B. Lippincott & Co., 1858), p. 204.

46. Tennessee *Whig* (Elizabethtown), October 24, 1839; William G. Brownlow to T. A. R. Nelson, November 29, 1844, Nelson Papers, Lawson McGhee Library, Knoxville, Tennessee; Brownlow, *Ought Slavery Be Perpetuated?*, pp. 109, 170, 220; Coulter, *Brownlow*, p. 111.

47. William G. Brownlow, *Helps to the Study of Presbyterianism* (Knoxville: F. S. Heiskell, 1834), pp. 107–11; Brownlow, *The Great Iron Wheel Examined* (Nashville: William G. Brownlow, 1856), p. 314; Coulter, *Brownlow*, p. 94.

tained numerous exclusionist remarks. Yet the volume doubled as a textbook for "orthodox" proslavery arguments.[48] In this and other publications, Brownlow cited interracial association as one of the most beneficial features of the Southern slave system. Writing to the *National Anti-Slavery Standard,* for example, he voiced unquestioning preference for integrated subservience over life in the segregated North: "Here in the South, the negroes crowd the galleries and back seats in our Churches—they ride with us in our stage coaches, and upon Railroads—stand on the corners of our streets when they are at leisure, and converse with gentlemen . . . ." [49] Under slavery, "the superior mind of the Caucasian" could "direct his [the Negro's] labor" and accelerate his general development. Blacks were "least perfect" when they were "most distant from the Caucasian." [50]

Like exclusionism and the proslavery thought of the Reconstruction decade, the "Brownlow tradition" was therefore of undisputed antebellum origins. Brownlow had espoused the racial ideas of the Helpers and those of the Fitzhughs long before Sumter and merely continued his double advocacy in the decade after Appomattox. He seemed incapable of devising new concepts to meet new racial realities. Like the Helpers and the Fitzhughs, the Brownlow example testified to a rigid, inflexible quality within the white Southern mind in the aftermath of the tumultuous Civil War racial experience.

IV

In sum, white Southerners of the Reconstruction decade confronted the "Negro problem" by calling upon three antebellum ideologies. The two popular ideologies, exclusionism and proslavery thought, were simple and to the point. Exclusionists would have kept the races apart while proponents of slavery sought to couple black subordination with interracial association. But the "Brownlow tradition" was not so readily delineated. Because it stood for removal of blacks from white society as well as for integrated subservience, it appeared to rest upon an internal contradiction. The essential demand, it seemed, was for Negroes to be in two places at once—distant from, yet near to whites.

Close scrutiny of the parson's words resolves the apparent contradiction, revealing that the "Brownlow tradition" was based upon

48. Hesseltine, *East Tennessee Historical Society's Publications,* III (January, 1931), 43, comments on the widespread influence of this book within proslavery circles.

49. Knoxville *Whig,* December 5, 1857.

50. Knoxville *Whig,* February 27, 1858; Brownlow, *Ought Slavery Be Perpetuated?,* p. 214.

altogether consistent logic. Within a great many of his pronouncements, Brownlow distinguished between servile Negroes and "insolent,
independent" blacks. Before the Civil War he frequently maintained
that uncontrollable blacks would have to be removed to some distant
region. Unregulated Negro behavior was unpredictable behavior. It
was therefore extremely dangerous to white society.[51] Addressing the
Tennessee legislature in the fall of 1865, the parson proposed colonization of the state's black population. "But if the colored man," he
hastily added, "after looking over the whole ground, shall still ask
to stay in the land of his birth, to till the soil and labor in the work-
shop, and to fill positions of usefulness under the bright skies that
smiled on his infancy, I say, in all conscience, let him remain." [52] In
the same speech, Brownlow proposed exclusion of Negroes from
political life but went on to note "a class of them I would be willing to
see vote at once." These were the "slaves" who had remained "faithful" and "loyal" to whites despite the tumult of the Civil War and its
aftermath.[53] A decade later, Brownlow continued to distinguish the
insolent from the servile. "Uppity" Negroes like Frederick Douglass
and John Mercer Langston who dared to threaten whites with their
demands for civil rights had no place near white society. To interact
with whites, Negroes had to avoid "everything calculated to array the
prejudices of the whites against them . . . ." They had to behave
with deference and docility.[54]

Thus, the "Brownlow tradition" was based upon an internal logic
as consistent as exclusionism or the proslavery tradition. It merely
applied different principles to different Negroes. Unlike the exclusionist, Brownlow would permit docile Negroes to remain near whites.
Unlike the proslavery theorists, he explicitly demanded the exclusion
of all insolent, disrespectful blacks. His racial ideology was therefore
predicated upon the search for docile Negro behavior—a fact easily
overlooked because of the parson's inability to tailor his language
more closely to his thoughts.

Calling for the exclusion of "uppity" Negroes and for association
with the servile, Brownlow had developed an ideology remarkably
compatible with the realities of Southern life. Despite the rhetoric
of either the Helpers or the Fitzhughs, relations between white and
black in the nineteenth-century South were at once intimate and distant, integrated and segregated. Servile Negroes had usually been
able to dwell near whites while defiant blacks were kept apart. Under

51. See, e.g., Knoxville *Whig*, May 8, 1858, and February 25, 1860; Brownlow,
Presbyterianism, p. 111.
52. Knoxville *Whig*, October 11, 1865; White, ed., *Messages*, V, 466.
53. White, ed., *Messages*, V, 460.
54. Knoxville *Whig and Chronicle*, March 10, 1875.

the "peculiar institution," the "safest" were traditionally selected as house servants for the large plantation while the potentially dangerous Negro was usually confined to the fields. In the cities, the servant's backyard shack was surrounded by a large wall so that he could not escape to the streets without passing through the master's house. He therefore remained under the watchful eye of the white man. But once the slave made his way to the street and consorted with other blacks against his master's will, segregationist measures were hastily implemented.[55] Though segregationist pressures increased at the end of the nineteenth century, "good" Negroes continued to be sought after as domestics in white homes; black nurses and body servants rode in white railroad cars; and the white man often closed his eyes when a well-known "old-time darkie" crossed the color line. Only defiant blacks were allegedly sent to the chain gang, and Judge Lynch claimed to sentence only the most vicious and hopelessly depraved to permanent isolation from Southern society.[56]

Because he was not oriented toward the specific issues of integration or segregation so much as toward the quest for Negro docility, Brownlow was able to explain these practices. Fitzhugh and Helper could not. If a proslavery theoretician acknowledged that certain slaves were segregated from their masters, he undermined one of the basic tenets in his argument; he denied that slavery had allowed a wise white master to elevate a savage black barbarian through constant supervision. By the same token, if an exclusionist admitted that he craved the presence of servile blacks, he, too, lost his credibility. Brownlow's ideology posed neither of these problems, demanding no evasion of the actualities of Southern racial existence.

In a sense, then, most Southern racial theorists subscribed to the "Brownlow tradition." But in the chaotic postwar decade, few could admit it. On the rhetorical level, most remained wedded to one of the two dominant ideologies of the antebellum decades—ideologies

55. Wade, *Slavery in the Cities,* especially pp. 54–79, 266–78, provides an excellent discussion of these points.

56. See, e.g., A. Eugene Thomson to Woodrow Wilson, October 20, 1913, N.A.A.C.P. Papers, Library of Congress; Philip A. Bruce, *The Plantation Negro as a Freeman* (New York and London: G. P. Putnam's Sons, 1889), pp. 45–46; Charles E. Wynes, ed., *Southern Sketches from Virginia 1881–1901 by Orra Langhorne* (Charlottesville: University Press of Virginia, 1964), pp. 34, 36–37, 86; George W. Cable, *The Silent South together with The Freedman's Case in Equity and The Convict Lease System* (New York: Charles Scribner's Sons, 1895), pp. 21–22, 85–87, 91; Winfield H. Collins, *The Truth About Lynching and the Negro in the South* (New York: Neale Publishing Co., 1918), p. 105; and many scenes within Charles W. Chesnutt, *The Marrow of Tradition* (Boston and New York: Houghton, Mifflin Company, 1901). Stephen Graham's *The Soul of John Brown* (New York: The Macmillan Company, 1920), especially pp. 216–27, explains which Negroes Southerners preferred to lynch and why.

that obscured the racial realities of everyday life. Brownlow was probably the only prominent white Southerner of the Reconstruction period who had escaped this trap and that was no small achievement.

V

A crude and often inarticulate Tennessee editor-politician may have
been the most realistic Southern racial thinker of the Reconstruction
decade. But if one explores the personal motives behind the Ten-
nessean's racial pronouncements, one discovers that like the Fitzhughs and the Helpers, he evaded fundamental facts.

Like the others, the parson spent his adult life in a tumultuous and
anxious America of transportation revolutions, rapid industrial development, sectional tensions, insatiable status aspirations, and acute
Victorian emotional repressions. Though Brownlow's East Tennessee
was somewhat provincial, it was never isolated from the tense conditions of life in the middle decades of the nineteenth century that
Alexis de Tocqueville described so vividly in *Democracy in America*.
Indeed, Brownlow was a prime example of Tocqueville's "nervous
American"—one who desperately sought wealth, power, and popularity but persistently feared that they would escape him. Unsatisfied
with the limited audience and meager financial rewards of a Methodist
circuit-rider, he turned to journalism. Moving from Elizabethtown to
Jonesboro and from there to the more populous Knoxville, he became
one of the most well-known editors in Southern Appalachia. His
limited success notwithstanding, the parson remained unsatisfied. A
devout Whig, he had yet to hold public office; a man who had yearned
to become a slaveholder, he could not afford a bondsman. He joined
the Know-Nothing Party for a time and intensified his political activity, but wealth and recognition continued to elude him. Finally, as
a staunch wartime unionist, he was elected Reconstruction Governor
of Tennessee. Hated by many and loved by few, he failed to build a
political base but managed to win a seat in the United States Senate
before Tennessee's Reconstruction experiment was completely overthrown. Physically ill by then and still unable to command respect or
power, he could not even afford a Negro house boy and died in 1877.
Life had been one constant, anxious, and unsatisfying quest for wealth,
status, and personal power.[57]

If Brownlow had been black, he might have escaped the fate of the
"nervous American." In the North as well as in the South, in Tennessee as well as in Mississippi, Negroes were largely excluded from the

57. Coulter's *Brownlow* provides these and most other essential details concerning the parson's life.

anxious quest for wealth and status. The tense currents that ran through American society in the middle decades of the nineteenth century most profoundly affected white society. Firmly chained to the bottom of the social ladder, blacks remained comparatively undisturbed.[58] Hence, a white man like Brownlow was probably troubled by the accelerating pressures, tensions, and emotional repressions of everyday existence more than any Negro. If the pressures did not overcome him, he could hope for status and recognition, whereas blacks could go nowhere. But for relief from everyday pressures, Brownlow could not turn to anxious, repressed white society. Rather, relief could come through contacts with black society—the more "stable" segment of the population.

The pressures that he felt and the need for relief could explain why the nervous Brownlow constantly depicted blacks as wild African savages who lacked internal restraints.[59] These factors may also explain his assumption that whites were civilized—a cultivated race of a "higher level." [60] They might even help to explain the parson's conclusion that the most effective purgative of Negro barbarity was white contact—to allow white civilization to rub off upon the "lesser" race.[61] The black savage-white redeemer dichotomy and the vision of white civilization uplifting black savagery may have allowed Brownlow, the "nervous American," to justify his contact with Negroes. He could give vent to his frustrations through vicious outbursts against blacks. He could assault the "evil" doctrine "that the chief end of Man is Nigger!" [62] He could scream out "nigger here, nigger there, nigger yonder, and nigger everywhere—nigger in the church, nigger in the social circle, nigger in the wood-pile, . . . nigger at the polls, nigger at the dining-table, black nigger, greasy nigger, odorous nigger, and nothing but grinning, wooly-headed nigger." [63] He could

58. In *North of Slavery: The Negro in the Free States, 1790–1860* (Chicago and London: The University of Chicago Press, 1961), Leon F. Litwack proves that like Southern blacks, antebellum Northern Negroes were firmly chained to the bottom of the social ladder. Leslie H. Fishel, Jr., "The North and the Negro, 1865–1900: A Study in Race Discrimination" (Ph.D. dissertation, Harvard University, 1953) convincingly demonstrates that this condition persisted in the postbellum decades.

59. See, e.g., White, ed., *Messages*, V, 403; Knoxville *Whig*, May 8, 1858; August 30, 1865; September 27, 1865; October 11, 1865; May 20, 1866; Macon *Daily Telegraph*, October 28, 1865; William G. Brownlow to Andrew Johnson, August 31, 1865, Johnson Papers, Library of Congress.

60. See, e.g., Memphis *Daily Avalanche*, March 29, 1866; Knoxville *Whig*, June 28, 1865 and July 30, 1867; Knoxville *Whig and Chronicle*, June 21, 1876.

61. Brownlow, *Ought Slavery Be Perpetuated?*, pp. 98, 101; Knoxville *Whig*, May 8, 1858; White, ed., *Messages*, V, 413; Memphis *Daily Avalanche*, March 29, 1866.

62. William G. Brownlow, *Sketches of the Rise, Progress, and Decline of Secession* (Philadelphia: George W. Childs, 1862), p. 29.

63. Knoxville *Whig*, February 6, 1864.

proclaim the Negro "lying around loose" the cause of all difficulties.[64] The parson could even "lie around loose" with a Negro savage and then confide in her his deepest personal problems and worries.[65] Speaking about and interacting with blacks in these ways, Brownlow could release some of the tensions of life in a nervous, highly competitive, repressed white society. All the while, he knew that whether he yelled profanities at Negroes, struck out at them, confided in them, or fornicated with them, it signified that a member of the civilized race was influencing and therefore elevating black savagery. Thus, as he "broke loose" from the anxieties and repressions of life in white society by treating blacks with various types of unrestrained crudity, he probably felt little if any guilt. After all, he was uplifting the lower race. But there was one requirement. The parson could only ease his personal anxieties by interacting with docile, accepting members of the savage race, for defiant blacks could strike back. Hence, for meaningful relief from the pressures of everyday existence, it was necessary to keep "uppity" black savages at a distance and servile savages close at hand. With the servile black savage, no holds were barred. He could be whipped and then confided in. Whatever gave the white man relief was safe and justifiable if not altogether benevolent.

Clearly, the "Brownlow tradition" was deeply rooted in fantasy. The parson's theory of integration of the docile and exclusion of the defiant was probably the offshoot of the illusion that a Caucasian could treat a Negro savagely and remain civilized. If this were the case, the Brownlow alternative to exclusionist and proslavery ideologies was no proof of realism in Southern racial thought. The Helpers and the Fitzhughs may have been evading the racial realities of Southern society-at-large but the parson in all likelihood evaded personal realities. If he behaved like a savage, then he, not the Negro, was the savage.

64. Knoxville *Whig*, April 12, 1865; May 30, 1866.
65. Knoxville *Whig*, July 30, 1867; Knoxville *Whig and Chronicle*, March 10, 1875.

Chapter Three

Wattersonia: The Road to Autonomy

In 1869 William Brownlow's tottering political regime in Tennessee collapsed. Henceforth he no longer needed the assistance of federal troops to retain power. He was free to propound a notion that might always have been dear to his heart—Southern home rule. On September 15, 1875, the Knoxville *Whig and Chronicle* printed Brownlow's appraisal of race relations in Mississippi. He pleaded against federal intervention to quell an outbreak of racial strife and violence and insisted that Mississippi authorities be conceded complete jurisdiction over all racial matters in the state. By this date, at least, Brownlow had become a champion of home rule.

Local autonomy was no panacea for regional problems. It could not assure rapid economic recovery to a war-ravaged South and guaranteed neither social stability nor the reduction of racial tensions. All that home rule promised was the right of people of the region to determine their own destiny for good or for ill. During the tense debate over Southern particularism in the immediate prewar decades, some Southerners had understood the limitations of local autonomy. Though men like John C. Calhoun and Edmund Ruffin demanded home rule, they knew that it would not automatically remedy the difficulties that the region faced. But they sensed that with continuing federal intervention, Southerners could never even attempt to resolve their problems. Similarly, in 1875 Brownlow had no illusions that racial utopia would arrive if Mississippians were granted autonomy. But without home rule, he knew that it was futile for Mississippians to try to remedy racial ills.

Brownlow was not the only white Southern proponent of home rule in the postwar decade. The powerful South Carolina politician James Hemphill, the popular Virginia journalist Edward A. Pollard, ex-Confederate Vice President Alexander H. Stephens, and countless others had issued the plea.[1] But like the parson, they never elaborated on

1. See, e.g., James Hemphill to W. R. Hemphill, November 7, 1865, James C. Hemphill Papers, Duke University; Edward A. Pollard, *Lee and His Lieutenants* (New York: E. B. Treat & Co., 1867), p. 175; Rudolph Von Abele, *Alexander H. Stephens* (New York: Alfred A. Knopf, Inc., 1946), pp. 293–94.

the nature and potential consequences of home rule. It was a concept that they favored but never spent much time thinking about. They sensed that home rule was only a means to the solution of Southern problems, and amidst the chaos of the postwar decade they wanted something more definite. More than a path to the road out of turmoil, they wanted the road itself.

Nonetheless, white Southerners had to find the path before they could reach the road. They had to retain local power if they were to resolve their difficulties. This meant that they had to prevent meaningful federal intervention in regional affairs. Yet victorious Northerners required at least symbolic manifestations of their hold on the South. Thus, to maintain a surreptitious *de facto* jurisdiction, Southerners had to convince Northerners that they, the Yankees, were indeed reconstructing the South. Only by putting aside their more pressing desires and implementing this difficult strategy could Southerners avoid Northern control of the region and snatch from the North the spoils of victory. But would Southerners have the foresight to implement this strategy?

Henry Watterson, editor of the influential Louisville *Courier-Journal* for half a century, was one of the few white Southerners fully committed to this task. Little is known of his early life and it is difficult to understand his acceptance of the mission. We do know that as a young man he owned only one slave—a young Negro who died in battle against the Confederacy. We also know that in the late 1850's Watterson began his journalistic career as a reporter for the states' rights-oriented Washington *States.* During the Civil War, he accepted the editorship of the Chattanooga *Rebel,* an organ of the Confederate army of Tennessee. Possibly he detected a connection between the disloyalty of his slave and sectional conflict. He might have reasoned that both of these "disasters" had been provoked by Northern interference in Southern internal affairs. Three years after Appomattox, Watterson, deeply committed to the idea of local autonomy, took command of aging George Prentice's Louisville *Journal.* For the young editor, home rule had come to represent more than a potential avenue to the solution of Southern ills. The South would tap her vast cultural and intellectual potentialities if she could develop without outside interference.[2]

Hastily transforming Prentice's *Journal* into a propaganda instrument, Watterson commenced a thoughtful and energetic campaign for

2. Joseph Frazier Wall, *Henry Watterson: Reconstructed Rebel* (New York: Oxford University Press, Inc., 1956), pp. 15, 25–26, 38–40; William E. Beard, "Henry Watterson: Last of the Oracles," *Tennessee Historical Magazine,* Series II, I, No. 4 (July, 1931), 237; Lena C. Logan, "Henry Watterson, Border Nationalist, 1840–1877" (Ph.D. dissertation, Indiana University, 1942), pp. 45–48.

home rule and against Radical Reconstruction. His purpose was to preclude effective federal intervention in Southern affairs, but he realized that this required careful planning. The "head of the South was in the lion's mouth," he wrote some years later, and "the first essential task was to get it out." Open Southern defiance of the federal government and insistence upon home rule would not effect this end; tactics of that sort would only antagonize federal authorities. Success would come if the white Southerner would "stroke the mane, not twist the tail of the lion." He needed to offer friendship to the Yankees so that they would forget sectional antagonisms and permit local government to function everywhere.[3] Certain Northerners had called for federal intervention to assure Southern blacks their civil rights. Responding to this demand, Watterson reasoned that white Southerners would have to take the initiative on civil rights issues. With "this one obstacle to a better understanding" between the sections removed, Northerners would have no choice but to allow the South to run her own affairs.[4]

Clearly, Watterson was interested in home rule, not Negro freedom. He offered to campaign for certain civil rights, but this was not out of empathy for black Southerners. His goal was to eradicate the suspicions of influential Northerners and he calculated that token concessions to local blacks would form a smoke screen, obscuring the realities of the Southern racial situation. Watterson's campaign to repeal a Kentucky statute that barred Negro testimony in state courts must be interpreted in this light. "Negro testimony is right in principle," he charged.[5] It is "a universally admitted rule of evidence in all enlightened courts, essential alike to all men, and to justice." [6] By publicizing such remarks, Watterson was able to reassure certain suspicious Northerners. But these Northerners may have missed statements directed at the planter-controlled Kentucky legislature. "It is the white people that need protection against Federal courts instead of the black people who need protection against State courts," he suggested in one "slip" of the tongue.[7] The ban on Negro testimony in Kentucky courts channeled litigation between white and black into the "pro-Negro" federal tribunals. Unlike Kentucky courts, the federal courts held "a strong partiality for the black over the white race." Therefore, as long as white Kentuckians persisted in excluding Negro

3. Henry Watterson, *"Marse Henry": An Autobiography* (New York: George H. Doran Company, 1919), I, 172.
4. In the Louisville *Courier-Journal*, March 25, 1913, Watterson claimed that this had been his reasoning during Reconstruction.
5. Louisville *Courier-Journal*, May 18, 1869.
6. Louisville *Courier-Journal*, May 27, 1869.
7. Louisville *Courier-Journal*, January 25, 1871.

testimony from state tribunals, they were only hurting themselves.[8]

Successful in his efforts to legalize Negro testimony in state courts, Watterson began to attack Ku Klux Klan operations in Kentucky. Seeking Northern approval, he demanded a ban against the "sudden intrusion of disguised ruffians into the humble home of the Southern negro . . ." [9] "Kuklux are of no political party; they are lawbreakers arrayed against society," he added.[10] Such rhetoric was intended for Northern consumption. But occasional phrases in the Klan fight indicated that Watterson was more anti-Radical than anti-Klan. He did not want to suppress Klansmen because they terrorized Negroes. Rather, the organization had to be destroyed because its terror tactics invited Radical Republican intervention in the Negro's behalf: "Destroy the Kuklux and Radicalism dies." [11]

Watterson's calculations were similar as he campaigned for ratification of the Fifteenth Amendment and for Negro suffrage in Kentucky. Certain that blacks were ignorant and easily misled, he opposed Negro voting in principle. Nonetheless, Northern goodwill could be gained if Southerners initiated campaigns for black enfranchisement.[12] He was sure that the risks were minimal, for there were not enough blacks in Kentucky to influence state elections.[13] On the other hand, if Kentuckians balked on the enfranchisement question, there could be new and regrettable extensions of federal power into state affairs.[14]

By the early 1870's, Watterson began to carry his home rule campaign beyond Kentucky borders. He was instrumental in structuring a tenuous alliance between certain Southern Democrats and Northerners of both parties. He encouraged Southern Democrats to support the Horace Greeley presidential bid in 1872 and the Samuel Tilden candidacy four years later. The hope was that Greeley and Tilden, both respected Northerners, would join Southerners in a national political coalition dedicated to Southern home rule. Through the bait of Southern votes, he planned to move Greeley and Tilden toward the local autonomy principle. White Northerners would not

8. Louisville *Courier-Journal,* July 14, 1869. See also Louisville *Courier-Journal,* May 18 and May 27, 1869.

9. Louisville *Courier-Journal,* November 25, 1874.

10. Louisville *Courier-Journal,* January 25, 1871. See also Louisville *Courier-Journal,* January 15, 1869; December 21, 1870; and March 22, 1871.

11. Louisville *Courier-Journal,* January 25, 1871. See also Louisville *Courier-Journal,* March 1, 1871. A secondary but relevant factor in Watterson's fight against the Klan was his hatred and fear of terrorism *per se.* This becomes apparent from his remarks in the Louisville *Courier-Journal,* March 8, 1871, and November 25, 1874.

12. Louisville *Courier-Journal,* September 17, 1869, September 16, 1874.

13. Louisville *Courier-Journal,* February 2, 1869. See also Louisville *Courier-Journal,* January 28, 1870.

14. Louisville *Courier-Journal,* August 12, 1870.

be very suspicious of a Southern home rule proponent from their own region.[15]

As the Negro testimony issue, the Ku Klux Klan fight, the enfranchisement struggle, and the Greeley and Tilden campaigns demonstrate, Watterson was one of the shrewdest proponents of home rule to emerge from the Reconstruction South. He had done much to spare the region the kind of prolonged foreign occupation that most defeated societies have experienced. There are many reasons why federal occupation was not as burdensome to the white South as it might have been; many factors explain its short duration. Yet Watterson's efforts are important in any explanation. Above all, his tactics illustrated how the white South lost the war but won the peace.

II

Early in 1877 the last federal trooper left the South. Home rule was complete. Even earlier as federal authorities withdrew and the forces of Redemption seized power in one state after another, the home rule argument was fast evolving into a defense of the *status quo*. The passing of Reconstruction simplified the intellectual task of the home rule theorist. Little imagination or projection into the future was required. Mere praise of Southern life became a defense of home rule conditions and an argument against a second Reconstruction.

The ease with which the local autonomy argument could be developed in the post-Reconstruction decades may have helped to persuade white Southerners like Wade Hampton, L. Q. C. Lamar, and Henry W. Grady to join Watterson's home rule crusade. Like the Louisville editor, they sensed that certain powerful Northerners continued to worry about the course of Southern race relations in the aftermath of Redemption. They were adamant in the belief that if the South was to avoid a second Reconstruction, influential Northerners had to be assured that white Southerners treated Negroes properly. The abolitionist Radical Republican tradition, they feared, was still quite viable above the Mason-Dixon line. Like Watterson, they therefore sensed that racial arguments had to be conspicuous among their pleas for home rule.

For more than two decades, from the end of Reconstruction until

15. Louisville *Courier-Journal*, May 17, 1871; Wall, *Watterson*, p. 129; L. C. Logan, "Watterson," p. 210; L. C. Logan, "Henry Watterson and the Liberal Convention of 1872," *Indiana Magazine of History*, XL, No. 4 (December, 1944), pp. 338–39. For some notion of Watterson's influence upon Greeley and Tilden, see Watterson to Horace Greeley, April 24, 1866, Greeley Papers, New York Public Library; Watterson to Samuel J. Tilden, February 16, 1876, Tilden Papers, New York Public Library.

his death in 1902, Wade Hampton of South Carolina devoted great time and energy to preserve local autonomy. In the spring of 1877 he urged President Hayes to remove the last federal troops from his state in order to "establish law" and "insure domestic tranquility." [16] But he emphasized that federal withdrawal was ultimately for the Negro's benefit. The "time is rapidly approaching when the colored people will find their best friends among the thoughtful and considerate whites of the South . . . ." [17] Explaining South Carolina's Red Shirt Redemption movement to an audience in Auburn, New York, Hampton insisted that there was nothing to fear. The Red Shirts had not directed their efforts against the white North and, most important, they had not been antagonistic to the black South. Therefore, there was no reason to suppress the movement through outside intervention. Skillfully, Hampton concluded his plea by wedding his demand for home rule to the theme of sectional reconciliation: "I come to honor my distinguished friend General Shields. He wore the blue and I wore the gray, but we can let the curtain drop over these years, and go back to the time when the flag borne by him waved alike over the men of the South and the men of the North . . . ." [18]

By the end of Reconstruction, Mississippi politician L. Q. C. Lamar had also become a major spokesman for home rule. Even more than Hampton, Lamar exploited the sectional reconciliation theme. For him, the reduction of sectional animosities was absolutely essential; home rule would inevitably follow. Consider, for example, Lamar's famous eulogy of Charles Sumner. A plea for local autonomy was well-concealed within demands for sectional reconciliation: "Charles Sumner, in life, believed that all occasion for strife and distrust between the North and South had passed away, and that there no longer remained cause for continued estrangement between these two sections of our common country." [19]

Like Hampton, Lamar stressed the racial benefits of home rule. He denied that local autonomy led to coercion of Negro voters by white Southerners: what right did anyone have "to assume that whites and blacks are never to vote and act together as citizens of a common country." Interracial harmony and the highest tenets of Americanism rather than intimidation of Negroes were evidenced when blacks voted like their white Southern brethren.[20] Few ills, racial or otherwise,

16. Hampton M. Jarrell, *Wade Hampton and the Negro: The Road Not Taken* (Columbia: University of South Carolina Press, 1950), p. 172.

17. "Ought the Negro to be Disfranchised: Ought He to have been Enfranchised?", *North American Review*, CCLXVIII (March, 1879), 241.

18. *Harper's Weekly,* July 7, 1877.

19. Wirt A. Cate, *Lucius Q. C. Lamar: Secession and Reunion* (Chapel Hill: University of North Carolina Press, 1935), p. 3.

20. Cate, *Lamar,* p. 332. See also *North American Review,* CCLXVIII (March, 1879), 233–34.

could possibly exist under home rule conditions: "Withdraw the disturbing [federal] force, leave our population to the responsibility of local self-government and to the natural operation of social and industrial forces, and all that is now deranged and disorderly will certainly and permanently arrange itself . . . ." Local autonomy promised stability, particularly racial stability.[21]

Much more than Watterson, Hampton and Lamar stressed racial peace and harmony as an inevitable consequence of home rule. But Henry W. Grady, another leading post-Reconstruction exponent of local autonomy, argued the point most convincingly. Grady's argument proceeded on two levels. On one it was abstract and impersonal. He pleaded for home rule through a "New South" philosophy of regional industrialization and commerce. The South, he charged, was departing from her antebellum agrarian ways and would eventually "out-Yankee the Yankee" in capitalist endeavor. This implied that the two sections increasingly resembled each other and would resolve local problems similarly. Hence, the North gained little by interfering in Southern affairs.[22] In a very real sense, this "New South" philosophy was a sophisticated plea for local autonomy.

On another level, however, Grady argued for home rule in a highly personal and sentimental vein. Along with the tough, calculating, cash register mentality of the "New South" philosopher, there was the soft-headed racial paternalist—a mild-mannered Cavalier gentleman. "Nowhere on earth is there kindlier feeling, closer sympathy, or less friction between two classes of society than between the whites and the blacks of the South today," he wrote in *Century Magazine*.[23] "The love we [Southern whites] feel for that race," he told the Boston Merchants Association, "you cannot measure nor comprehend." [24] Southerners assist the Negro "when he is in distress; they advise him when he is in a dilemma. In them, his whole world is centered. Beyond them, and outside of them he had but little knowledge of men or things, and does not care to learn more." [25] Thanks to the whites, Southern blacks were "happy in their cabin homes, tilling their own land by day, and at night taking from the lips of their children the

21. New York *Herald,* January 9, 1875. A similar remark by Lamar is quoted in Stephen Graham, *The Soul of John Brown* (New York: The Macmillan Company, 1920), p. 191.

22. This line of thought is quite evident in Henry W. Grady, "Cotton and Its Kingdom," *Harper's Monthly*, LXIII (October, 1881), especially p. 732. See also Grady's comments in the Atlanta *Herald*, May 5, 1875; Edwin DuBois Shurter, ed., *The Complete Orations and Speeches of Henry W. Grady* (New York: Hinds, Noble & Eldredge, 1910), p. 19.

23. Henry W. Grady, "In Plain Black and White: A Reply to Mr. Cable," *Century*, XXIX (April, 1885), 916.

24. Joel Chandler Harris, ed., *Life of Henry W. Grady Including His Writings and Speeches* (New York: Cassell Publishing Co., 1890), p. 195.

25. Atlanta *Herald*, May 5, 1875.

helpful message their State sends them from the schoolhouse door." [26]
Because Southern whites dwelled in harmony with blacks and supported Negro social development, interference in regional affairs was
unjustified. The black man "must be left to those among whom his
lot is cast . . . ." Local autonomy was imperative.[27] All white Southerners who loved their region knew this and would "appeal to the
world" for home rule.[28] They would argue that the South had traditionally resolved racial difficulties equitably and would continue to
do so.[29]

Others soon joined the crusade. By the turn of the century, many
influential white Southerners had become systematic exponents of
local autonomy. Some, like John Ambrose Price of Arkansas and J. L.
Hall of the College of William and Mary, were scholars.[30] Most were
politicians. Two Mississippians, John Sharp Williams and John M.
Stone, and one Alabamian, John T. Morgan, were perhaps the most
influential.[31] An idea that a Louisville editor had systematically expounded during Reconstruction had become a basic feature of white
Southern thought within only three decades.

III

Though many white Southerners had argued for home rule during
the last years of the nineteenth century and the first decade of the
twentieth, few had introduced new arguments or tactics. Whereas
Henry Watterson had advocated Negro testimony, prohibition of the
Klan, Negro suffrage, and an intersectional political alliance to secure
home rule during Reconstruction, few had argued with imagination
or novelty in the decades that followed. Post-Reconstruction arguments boiled down to a single claim: home rule, the *status quo,* had
to be preserved. Perhaps this was all that one could have expected.
After all, the Redemption movement had restored home rule and
the essential task was to preserve the *status quo.* The obvious way to
perform the task was to describe Southern life under home rule, par-

26. Shurter, ed., *Grady,* pp. 202–3.
27. Shurter, ed., *Grady,* pp. 17–18.
28. Harris, ed., *Grady,* p. 130.
29. Grady, *Century,* XXIX (April, 1885), 916.
30. John Ambrose Price, *The Negro: Past, Present, and Future* (New York and
Washington, D.C.: Neale Publishing Co., 1907), p. 276; J. L. Hall, *Half-Hours in
Southern History* (Atlanta, Richmond, Dallas: B. F. Johnson, 1907), pp. 291–92.
31. George Coleman Osborn, *John Sharp Williams: Planter-Statesman of the
Deep South* (Baton Rouge: Louisiana State University Press, 1943), p. 150; J. M.
Stone, "The Suppression of Lawlessness in the South," *North American Review,*
CLVIII (March, 1894), 501; John T. Morgan, "Shall Negro Majorities Rule?"
Forum, VI (1888), 599.

ticularly racial life, in a favorable light and this was what men like Hampton, Lamar, and Grady had done. Occasionally one of them tried to ease Northern animosity by combining a glowing description of Southern life with praise of Northern society, but innovation went no further.

Against this background of relatively unimaginative argumentation, Watterson's intellectual and tactical accomplishments of the post-Reconstruction decades are particularly striking. Imaginative during Reconstruction when the home rule argument required an alert exponent, he continued to produce new and influential ideas to assure the continuation of home rule during years when most white Southerners had done much less. For this reason, "Marse Henry" ranks among the seminal minds and boldest tacticians of the post-bellum South.

During these decades, Watterson often appealed for continued home rule through the rhetoric of organic nationalism. He charged that a country was a social organism—a "super-person" with a single moral will and purpose. Though Emerson may have propounded this view before the Civil War, it gained popularity among influential Northerners during the postwar decades. Whether one turned to intellectuals like William Graham Sumner, Elisha Mulford, and Francis Lieber, or studied the ideas of powerful Republican politicians like Charles Sumner, Benjamin F. Wade, and George W. Julian, the equation of nationhood with a social organism was strikingly apparent.[32]

Though a number of influential Northerners disagreed with Watterson's goal of Southern autonomy, none openly criticized "Marse Henry." In part, this was attributable to his successful integration of the organic nationalism theme within home rule pronouncements. Addressing the House of Representatives in 1877, Watterson prefaced a call for home rule with a vital message: "There is no sectional line, no air-line or water-line in this country, east or west or north or south, which marks off distinct and separate species. . . . the American people are a homogeneous people . . . ."[33] Terms like "Indiana," "Kentucky," and "New York" had little relevance, he declared; "We are all one people."[34] "No people in the world are more homogeneous than the people of the United States," he stated in a public lecture. "What differences exist are purely exterior."[35] "We are not a nation of sections or factions. We are a singularly homo-

32. Merle Curti, *The Roots of American Loyalty* (New York: Columbia University Press, 1946), pp. 173–99, provides an excellent analysis of this theme.

33. *Congressional Record*, 44th Cong., 2nd Sess. (1877), 1006.

34. Henry Watterson, *The Compromises of Life* (New York: Fox, Duffield & Co., 1903), p. 293.

35. Watterson, *Compromises*, p. 97.

geneous people," he charged.[36] Because remarks like these complimented those of a great many Northerners, Watterson obviously predisposed the Yankee to view him with favor as he went on to demand local autonomy. The organic nationalism rhetoric may have disarmed potential critics. It would have been difficult for a Julian, a Lieber, or a Mulford to criticize him for favoring Southern self-determination, for this was a man who articulated what they considered the essential tenets of American nationalism.

A close student of Northern attitudes, Watterson exploited widely held Northern beliefs in another way. Among Northern intellectuals, there was an unclear, ill-defined fusion between the self-help ethic propounded in the McGuffey readers and Horatio Alger novels and many of the Social Darwinist assumptions of Spencer, Fiske, and Sumner. Through diligence and hard work, a man could rise as far as his God-given capacities would allow. Anglo-Saxons, the most "advanced" racial stock, were capable of the highest achievements, but "lesser" races were fit for some "advancement" if they applied themselves. With remarkable sensitivity, Watterson exploited these ideas precisely at a time when Southern demagogues were promoting violent campaigns to disfranchise Negroes and certain Northerners were correspondingly renewing their calls for federal intervention in Southern affairs. Watterson explained away the disfranchisement campaigns by linking the self-help ethic to Social Darwinism. He charged that Southern Negroes had ample opportunity to become competent voters but the horrid "hot house process" of Reconstruction proved that they were not up to it. Through "the forces of evolution, which are undoubtedly at work, but which in the nature of the case must needs go exceedingly slow," Negroes might eventually become fit for citizenship and the vote, but that day had not yet come. Blacks still lacked the capacities of diligence and perseverance that a responsible electorate required and had to be disfranchised.[37] Many Northerners could agree with this reasoning, for it represented no more than a specific application of their own thought processes.

There was another important feature in Watterson's crusade against a second Reconstruction. From the 1890's until the end of the first World War, he advocated a bellicose policy of national territorial expansion. The white man's burden was to spread American civilization throughout the world. If any dared to interfere with this "great"

36. Henry Watterson, "The South and Its Colored Citizens," *Cosmopolitan*, IX (May, 1890), 113. For similar remarks, see Watterson, "The Reunited Union," *North American Review*, CXL (January, 1885), 25, and Watterson, *Compromises*, p. 289.
37. Watterson, *Compromises*, pp. 446–48; Ray Stannard Baker, *Following the Color Line: American Negro Citizenship in the Progressive Era* (New York: Harper Torchbooks, 1964), p. 305.

task, America's duty was to go to war.[38] Articulating this theme, he condemned President Cleveland for refusing to annex Hawaii.[39] His *History of the Spanish-American War,* published shortly after the end of the conflict, glorified the military campaigns of the war and concluded that America might have to fight in other wars to safeguard her character and vitality. In 1913, Watterson urged United States intervention in Mexico, and by 1915 he espoused a militant anti-German, pro-allied position.[40] In 1914 he posted a large headline atop the front page of the Louisville *Courier-Journal*—"To Hell with the Hohenzollerns and Hapsburgs"—and kept it there until the end of World War I. By 1917 spirited editorials urging American entry into the war won him the Pulitzer award.[41]

As he urged militaristic expansionism, Watterson did not think exclusively of home rule. War itself aroused the man. Battle was man's greatest activity; "Happy he who falls upon the field of glory." [42] But though he gloried in warfare, "Marse Henry" loved home rule more. He knew that foreign dangers diverted attention from domestic issues. He also sensed that when a Southerner fought alongside a Yankee against a foreign foe, it would seem hypocritical for the Yankee to deny the Southerner home rule. Indeed, sectional suspicion and discrimination could be forgotten during a war against a common enemy. As Oscar W. Underwood observed in 1928, "the uniting of the boys of the North and the sons of the South in defense of our flag on the battlefields of two foreign wars has buried the prejudices of the past and united our country as it was never united before." [43] Thirty years earlier, a Northern railroad attorney, George R. Peck, had charged that the Spanish-American War "taught the north and south how truly they are part of a common country." [44] Nathaniel Edwin Harris, Governor of Georgia when America entered the first World War, emphasized how that conflict had completely overshadowed sectional animosities.[45]

38. Louisville *Courier-Journal,* January 29, 1909; February 22, 1913; April 25, 1914; May 18, 1915. See also Watterson's address of August 9, 1898, at the grave of Francis Scott Key, Watterson Papers, Library of Congress.

39. Wall, *Watterson,* p. 240.

40. Louisville *Courier-Journal,* February 23, 1913; Wall, *Watterson,* pp. 299–303.

41. Leonard N. Plummer, "Political Leadership of Henry Watterson" (Ph.D. dissertation, University of Wisconsin, 1940), p. 66.

42. Henry Watterson, "Soldier of the American Union, Lincoln Division," unpublished ms., December 24, 1917, Watterson Papers, Library of Congress.

43. Oscar W. Underwood, *Drifting Sands of Party Politics* (New York: The Century Co., 1931), p. 109.

44. George R. Peck to Henry Watterson, August 11, 1898, Watterson Papers, Library of Congress. See also W. D. Weatherford, *Present Forces in Negro Progress* (New York and London: Association Press, 1912), p. 36, for a similar assessment of the Spanish-American War.

45. Nathaniel Edwin Harris, *Autobiography* (Macon, Georgia: J. W. Burke Co., 1925), p. 463.

Watterson's public pronouncements indicate that he comprehended what Underwood, Peck, and Harris had propounded: foreign conflict undercut domestic sectional tensions and animosities, reducing potential Northern misgivings over Southern home rule. Because the "South rallied with the North" in the Spanish-American War, he wrote, criticism of the region constituted an unjustified denial of Southern patriotism.[46] Foreign war had established the latent nationalism of the Southern people beyond any doubt.[47] Reunited, the nation could oppose the world and it would be tragic if sectional mistrust precluded effective reunion.[48] Clearly, "Marse Henry" was working energetically to assure that conflict abroad eased sectional animosities at home, thus guaranteeing Southern autonomy.

IV

Sixty years old in 1900, Watterson continued as an effective exponent of Southern home rule well into the twentieth century. Keen intellect and an almost obsessive devotion to the cause may explain the superior quality of his argumentation. Hampton and Lamar had been fundamentally concerned with state politics and Grady was a full-time champion of Southern industrialization and commercialization, but nothing diverted Watterson from the home rule issue.[49]

Though Watterson's arguments for local autonomy were obviously influential above Mason-Dixon, it is difficult to measure their precise impact upon Northern society. Only a minority of Northerners penned their thoughts without solicitation, but those who did almost invariably praised the man. Henry Cabot Lodge found Watterson's goals eminently patriotic.[50] Bluford Wilson, another prominent Republican, saw no reason to distrust the South if men like "Marse Henry" provided regional leadership.[51] Robert Lansing, Secretary of State under Wilson, praised Watterson as "the very personification of Amer-

46. Louisville *Courier-Journal*, February 22, 1910.
47. New York *Herald*, June 4, 1917; Watterson's address to troops at Camp Bradley, Lexington, Kentucky, May 27, 1898, Watterson Papers, Library of Congress.
48. Henry Watterson's speech at U. S. Grant Birthday Banquet, New York, April 27, 1898, Watterson Papers, Library of Congress; Louisville *Courier-Journal*, December 25, 1917; draft of Watterson's Louisville speech of May 20, 1899, Watterson Papers, Library of Congress.
49. Comparison of Watterson's writings, public and private, with those of other important home rule theorists like Grady, Hampton, and Lamar reveals that "Marse Henry" wrote about the topic more frequently and at considerably greater length.
50. Louisville *Courier-Journal*, March 2, 1919.
51. Bluford Wilson to James H. Wilson, July 3, 1907, Watterson Papers, Library of Congress.

icanism," and the editor of the Cleveland *Plain-Dealer* charged that the Negro would cease to be a problem if "Marse Henry's" views became more widespread.[52]

One of the clearest indications that Watterson's arguments were captivating is the acclaim he received from certain (though not all) Negro leaders. Booker T. Washington was certain that "Marse Henry" had aided the black man's cause.[53] E. Molyneaux Hewlett, a leading black attorney from Washington, D. C., told Watterson that "the apparent friction between the races can safely be left to men like you." [54] A prominent black minister from the same city thanked "Marse Henry" for his deeply "abiding and unselfish friendship" toward black people and many other Negroes paid him this same compliment.[55]

Those whites who lauded Watterson praised more than an individual. They cheered a cause. By the turn of the century if not earlier, the home rule idea had gained widespread approval throughout the North. Formerly an abolitionist, Lyman Abbott now maintained that the "Southerner understands the Negro better than the Northerner does and likes him better." Hence, the white South had to be allowed to work out the "Negro problem" in its own way.[56] "As to Southern affairs, 'the let alone policy' seems now to be the true course," contended Rutherford B. Hayes.[57] After his widely publicized trip through the region, Charles Nordhoff wrote that "there are no wrongs now in the South which the interference of the Federal Government under the Enforcement acts can reach." [58] "The Southern States have on their hands a race problem of the first magnitude," charged William Graham Sumner; "they will have all they can do to manage it if

52. Louisville *Courier-Journal*, March 2, 1919; Cleveland *Plain-Dealer*, January 21, 1908. See also the New York *Herald*, August 10, 1918.

53. Booker T. Washington to Henry Watterson, February 5, 1901; January 9, 1908; December 5, 1911; Watterson Papers, Library of Congress.

54. E. Molyneaux Hewlett to Henry Watterson, January 18, 1908, Watterson Papers, Library of Congress. A petition by fourteen Louisville Negroes to Watterson, dated October 27, 1908 (Watterson Papers), stated the same essential theme.

55. J. Milton Waldron to Henry Watterson, September 8, 1908, Watterson Papers, Library of Congress. For compliments by other Negroes, see, e.g., W. L. Ricks to Henry Watterson, February 3, 1908, Watterson Papers, Technical Journalism Division, Colorado State University; Ester R. Irving to Henry Watterson, January 22, 1908, Watterson Papers, Library of Congress.

56. Lyman Abbott, *America in the Making* (New Haven: Yale University Press, 1911), p. 217; Thomas F. Gossett, *Race: The History of an Idea in America* (Dallas: Southern Methodist Press, 1963), p. 186.

57. Rayford D. Logan, *The Betrayal of the Negro from Rutherford B. Hayes to Woodrow Wilson*, 2nd ed. (New York: Collier Books, 1965), p. 24. See also Vincent P. DeSantis, "The Republican Party and the Southern Negro, 1877–1897", *Journal of Negro History*, XLV, No. 2 (April, 1960), 72.

58. Charles Nordhoff, *The Cotton States in the Spring and Summer of 1875* (New York: Burt Franklin, 1876), pp. 11–12.

they are left free under the natural social and economic laws." [59] By 1907 Negro leader Mary Church Terrell claimed that "the north has been persuaded to keep hands off"—to steer clear of the Southern racial controversy. From Cleveland, black novelist Charles Waddell Chesnutt made precisely the same appraisal.[60] Clearly, North and South had found the path that Professor Paul H. Buck has called "The Road to Renunion." Essentially, it was an accord between the sections based upon Northern acceptance of the Southern home rule argument. Perhaps more than any other American, Henry Watterson's name had been associated with the concept of local autonomy. When home rule won widespread acceptance, it was only natural that the man would be praised and admired.

V

As home rule became more popular, Watterson could look beyond the question of local autonomy. The continous struggle to win Southern self-determination had become less demanding. Correspondingly, the specific ends to be implemented under home rule conditions became more pertinent. Yet "Marse Henry" rarely commented about those ends. Unlike many, he equated local autonomy with utopia and did not feel compelled to note specific events that might occur under home rule conditions. What he did say was nonetheless revealing. Fundamentally committed to home rule, occasional "slips" of the pen pointed to his severe anxiety over the wrong people ruling at home. Contending that Reconstruction had been a period of "Negro dominance," he feared that history might repeat itself. Certain that Negroes were "the most ignorant and irresponsible portion of each community in the South," he hoped that "the natural order of things" would never be "revoked and reversed . . . ." [61] White Southerners must never again "be reduced to subjection" by a group of "semi-barbarians, ignorant and irresponsible voters, just emerged from slav-

59. R. W. Logan, *Betrayal*, p. 173. For other interesting Northern acknowledgments of the home rule argument, see the Springfield *Daily Republican*, October 5, 1885; the New York *Times*, May 10, 1900; *The Nation*, XLI (1885), 369.

60. Terrell is quoted in the Battle Creek (Michigan) *Enquirer*, November 2, 1907; Chesnutt is quoted in Helen M. Chesnutt, ed., *Charles Waddell Chesnutt: Pioneer of the Color Line* (Chapel Hill: University of North Carolina Press, 1952), p. 193. For similar remarks by Terrell, see the Washington *Times*, October 17, 1907, and the Washington *Post*, October 19, 1905, clippings of which are in the Mary Church Terrell Papers, Library of Congress.

61. Louisville *Journal*, September 28, 1868. Watterson, *North American Review*, CXL (January, 1885), 27, should also be consulted.

62. Watterson, *Cosmopolitan*, IX (May, 1890), 115.

ery." [62] Under proper conditions "the stronger race will govern; the weaker cannot." [63]

If Watterson feared Negro rule in the South, he was almost as disturbed over the possibility of power in the hands of poor whites. He feared poor people generally, white as well as black. Particularly, he fretted over government dominated by a "mob"—"ruffians and rascals" presided over by demagogic "firebrands," murderous Klansmen, "lunatic Populists," or, more generally, "the lower class of white persons." [64] "Intelligence and property," he wrote, "must rule over imbecility and pauperism . . . ." [65] The "conservative intelligence of the South" had to dominate. [66]

When he spoke of "conservatives," Watterson did not refer to prosperous Southerners like Robert Toombs or Alexander Stephens, for these men had provoked sectional antagonism despite their upperclass status. [67] To a striking degree, "conservatives" resembled "Marse Henry." They were propertied but restrained and dedicated to home rule through sectional reconciliation. Above all, "conservatives" were nostalgic, for they were inspired by a "renewal of the old faith" and recalled "the old traditions." [68] They were motivated by " 'the mystic chords of memory' which stretch across the chasm between the present and the past." [69] They were guided by the traditions of the Old South, free of suffragettes, prohibitionists, Social Democrats, federal paternalism, and the other anarchic sources of modern democratic society. The time-tested principles of antebellum civilization preceded chaotic "mass society" and would allow "conservatives" to shape the South's destiny during the turbulent postbellum years. In a biracial society, "conservative" rule was the only alternative to continued anarchy and ultimate disaster. [70]

Though Watterson wanted an elite corps of propertied whites to control Southern affairs, he knew that it was inexpedient to publicize this desire. If blacks or lower-class whites, North or South, had known what he was up to, considerable support for the principle of home rule might have evaporated. It was even risky to inform those upper-

63. Watterson, *North American Review*, CXL (January, 1885), 28.

64. Louisville *Courier-Journal*, August 13, 1870; March 8, 1871; September 3, 1874; November 25, 1874; October 9, 1896; Watterson, "The Tariff," *Harper's Monthly*, LXXVI (January, 1888), 284; Wall, *Watterson*, p. 224.

65. Richmond *Dispatch*, April 26, 1890.

66. Watterson, "The Solid South," *North American Review*, CXXVIII (January, 1879), 54.

67. Arthur Krock, ed., *The Editorials of Henry Watterson* (New York: George H. Doran Company, 1923), p. 41.

68. Louisville *Courier-Journal*, June 8, 1918.

69. Watterson, *North American Review*, CXXVIII (January, 1879), 55.

70. Louisville *Courier-Journal*, March 7, 1918, and March 5, 1919; Washington, D.C. *Woman Patriot*, March 15, 1919, in Watterson Papers, Library of Congress.

class whites who stood to rule under Watterson's plan. Some of them might have differed with him over the principle of elitist rule; some might have been democrats. Thus informed, they too might have repulsed his home rule efforts. Convinced that local autonomy was crucial, Watterson probably concluded that his elitist philosophy simply could not be publicized. Considering his calm, calculating career, these were doubtless the considerations that ran through his mind.

Watterson wanted propertied "conservatives" to control Southern society for several reasons. There was the element of ego gratification. By describing the "natural" leadership of the region, he noted qualities that he identified with himself. Then, too, permanent authority in the hands of "conservatives" represented an end to the threat of class conflict in the South. It left the rednecks powerless. Most important, "conservative" leadership offered the only assurance that the "Negro problem" might some day be solved. As Watterson saw matters, resolution of the "problem" was the most compelling reason for home rule with "conservatives" ruling at home. Surely the rednecks would never solve it; like blacks, they were lower-class and potentially dangerous.

Guided by values of the Old South, Watterson had little doubt that propertied "conservatives" could cope with racial ills. A "conservative" understood that blacks "from the wilds of Africa" had found "redemption" as bondsmen.[71] Through slave labor, the South had "built up great homesteads and homestead affections," [72] and life would have been more humane if slavery had not been abolished.[73] But abolition or no abolition, "the negro is a negro still." [74] He was doomed to be "helpless." Lacking volition, he was a mere "creature of circumstances" and "easily led." [75] Slaveholders had molded the Negro for the good of society before the war, and Southern "conservatives" would assume responsibility for his conduct in postbellum society.[76] They would eliminate "the arrogant and restless, the insolent and trustless" qualities in postbellum Negro behavior.[77] They would remove the black man's "flat and long-heeled foot" from "the white man's neck. . . ." [78] They would force him "to stick close by his hoe-handle" with a "tranquil" mind and "willing hands." [79]

71. Watterson, *Compromises*, p. 450.
72. Watterson, *North American Review*, CXXVIII (January, 1879), 51.
73. Louisville *Courier-Journal*, May 18, 1869.
74. Louisville *Courier-Journal*, April 20, 1915.
75. Watterson, *North American Review*, CXXVIII (January, 1879), 54–55; Louisville *Journal*, July 6, 1868.
76. Louisville *Courier-Journal*, November 14, 1870.
77. Louisville *Courier-Journal*, March 20, 1869.
78. Louisville *Journal*, September 15, 1868.
79. Louisville *Courier-Journal*, February 19, 1870; Montgomery *Advertiser*, June 15, 1907.

Watterson never explained in detail how Southern "conservatives" could transform the "uppity" black man into a servile laborer. Confident that the task would be accomplished, he never gave the matter much thought. On a few occasions, he suggested that the racial scene would improve if Negroes were segregated, deported, or as a last resort, exterminated.[80] But at other times he championed the right of Louisville Negroes to board city streetcars, opposed the Wilson Administration policy of segregation in federal agencies, advised Negroes that they could go nowhere without the guiding hand of the Caucasian, and looked to the day when the dominant and the servile race could interact harmoniously—when "the lion and the lamb shall lie down together" in peace.[81] Like Brownlow, the leading postbellum crusader for local autonomy seemed to vacillate between the exclusionism of a Hinton Rowan Helper and the integration-subordination ideal of a George Fitzhugh. Nonetheless, Watterson's remarks fit within a composite racial theory: "We [Southern whites] want them [Negroes] and they want us. But we don't want them if they are sullen and discontented. We want them as they are industrious and happy." [82] Happy, hard-working Negroes could associate with whites but "conservative" leadership would segregate discontented "uppity" blacks. When "conservatives" called for a rigid exclusionist policy, it was a response to Negro insolence. But when they demanded integration, it was to promote closer contact between docile Negroes and their white overlords. Therefore, Watterson's "conservatives" would solve the "Negro problem" through a differential color line. They would maintain servile Negroes within the white community and keep "uppity" blacks at a distance.

VI

Considering these basic dimensions of his racial solution, Watterson was operating within the "Brownlow tradition." Like the parson, he had argued that differential segregation was the one way to assure

80. See, e.g., Louisville *Journal*, September 25, 1868; Watterson, "Strange Prophecy about Roosevelt: A Midwinter Fantasy," *Cosmopolitan*, XLIV (January, 1908), 304.

81. Wall, *Watterson*, p. 93, tells of the Louisville streetcar protest. "Mr. Trotter and Mr. Wilson," *The Crisis*, IX (January, 1915), 126, quotes an objection to Wilsonian segregation policy which was probably written by Watterson. Watterson, "An Abortive Hero," *North American Review*, CXCIII (January, 1911), 42–43, tells of the need for white guidance while the Augusta (Maine) *Journal*, January 22, 1908, quotes Watterson's "lion and the lamb" remark.

82. Krock, ed., *Editorials*, p. 314. See also a key Watterson racial remark quoted in the Kansas City *Star*, January 18, 1908.

that Negroes would be docile in the presence of whites and that racial stability would prevail. It is true that Watterson stressed local autonomy as an essential prerequisite for differential segregation, but by 1875 Brownlow was also demanding home rule.

Despite these basic ideological similarities, the two men hated one another. Brownlow often wrote mockingly of "Little henry watterson" while Watterson retorted that the parson bore "as near a relation to the devil" as "any other living man." [83] The animosities behind these jibes can be traced, in part, to the Reconstruction experience. Brownlow had demanded intervention by federal troops to retain political power in Tennessee during the years when Watterson had labored most strenuously to nullify federal influence in Southern affairs. Yet tensions between the two were more deeply rooted. Brownlow was a relatively poor, uncouth editor-politician in an impoverished and somewhat isolated East Tennessee society, while Watterson was a prosperous, well-read, and widely traveled "conservative" from Louisville, one of the South's leading commercial centers. Fearing and despising "the lower class of white persons," Watterson doubtless viewed Brownlow as one of them. By the same token, the parson envied and resented upper-class white Southerners, and this combination of emotions would seem to explain his vendettas against Watterson. Thus, despite essential ideological accord on the all-important "Negro problem," class antagonisms probably precluded cooperation between these two highly influential men. Agreeing on the principle of differential segregation, class distinctions became the divisive ingredient in their relationship. Who would rule under home rule conditions? Which class would have the authority to enforce differential segregation? These questions made Brownlow and Watterson antagonists.

Despite deep antagonisms, both men sought Negro docility through a differential color line. Almost entirely preoccupied with the home rule issue, Watterson left few clues concerning the basis of his need for servile black behavior. Drawing together certain of his random comments, however, it becomes clear that his inner need closely paralleled Brownlow's. Like the parson, he viewed the black-white relationship from the broad framework of savagery and civilization. Blacks were "barbarians," "ignorant and degraded" peoples "from the wilds of Africa." [84] But whites, particularly Southern "conserva-

83. Knoxville *Whig*, April 25, 1866; Louisville *Courier-Journal*, November 16, 1868; E. Merton Coulter, *William G. Brownlow: Fighting Parson of the Southern Highlands* (Chapel Hill: University of North Carolina Press, 1937), p. 285; Louisville *Journal*, September 18, 1868.

84. Watterson, *North American Review*, CXXVIII (January, 1879), 54; Watterson, *North American Review*, CXCIII (January, 1911), 39; Watterson, *Cosmopolitan*, IX (May, 1890), 115; Watterson, *Compromises*, p. 450.

tives," represented the height of refinement and cultivation.[85] Hence, whenever whites interacted with blacks, civilization elevated savagery. Like Brownlow, Watterson had justified the right of a white man to deal with a Negro in any way that he chose.

On a few occasions, Watterson admitted that the black savage was not the only person who stood to gain through interracial contact. Whites could also benefit immeasurably through close and constant association with the servile race.[86] Shrewd and calculating in all his pronouncements, he never detailed the precise benefits. Like Brownlow, however, those benefits can be understood in terms of Watterson's life style within white society. Like the parson, he was a "nervous American," anxious over issues of wealth, status, and personal power. And like Brownlow, he was terribly upset over the changes introduced into American life through the Civil War and Reconstruction. Brownlow died in 1877 but Watterson lived until 1921, experiencing what he saw as the increasingly anarchic forces of modern democratic society—the rise of suffragettes, prohibitionists, federal paternalists, and worst of all, "the lower class of white persons." But despite these gross changes in the quality of American life—despite the apparent trend toward anarchy and chaos and the dissolution of the traditional modes of social control—Watterson constantly felt that he had to "hold back." He had to restrain himself and present a calm and confident manner. To assure Southern home rule with "conservatives" ruling at home, he needed all the supporters he could get. He could not afford to make enemies by waging a vigorous public campaign against "the trend of the times." Thus, even more than Brownlow, Watterson had to restrain his inner feelings when he was near other whites.

More than any other factor, this explains Watterson's assertion that whites could benefit by associating with Negroes. He, for one, could benefit immeasurably. Since blacks lacked the power to deter his home rule goals, they represented the only people in the society with whom he could act unrestrained. And since they were savages while he represented the forces of civilization, it followed that by "letting go," he elevated them. He could "wallop" a "nigger," for physical aggression against blacks was altogether "natural"—it was a viable part of Southern tradition.[87] On the other hand, he could visit the happy old Negro pianist, "Blind Tom," and listen with delight to that "chubby little black monkey on the [piano] stool,

85. See, e.g., Louisville *Courier-Journal*, January 29, 1909; February 22, 1913; April 25, 1914; May 18, 1915; Watterson, *North American Review*, CXXVIII (January, 1879), 54.

86. See, e.g., Augusta (Maine) *Journal*, January 22, 1908; Krock, ed., *Editorials*, pp. 313–14; Kansas City *Star*, January 18, 1908.

87. Watterson, *Compromises*, p. 290.

banging away for dear life." Funny "baboons" like Tom were always amusing. Moreover, their apparent happiness proved that their white benefactors were kind and humane.[88] When he was in the mood, Watterson sensed that he could even "lie down" alongside Negroes in "ultimate peace"—something that he could not always do in white society.[89] There was only one qualification. Black savages had to be servile and acquiescent, for if they were defiant, it would be hazardous to "let go" in their presence. Hence the need for differential segregation.

Thus, like Brownlow, Watterson sought out servile Negroes to escape the anxieties of white society. With docile blacks, he could rationalize his crude conduct by thinking that he was civilizing savagery. But though such ideas closely paralleled Brownlow's, Watterson constantly characterized the parson as a crude, unrefined representative of the mob; the man was practically a wild "nigger." This indicates that "Marse Henry" may have been defensive about his own civilized qualities. Far more introspective than Brownlow, he may have sensed that even a solid "conservative" was a wild savage in the presence of Negroes. If the parson was a savage, and if his own racial conduct resembled Brownlow's so closely, then Watterson the "conservative" might also have been a savage. But such a possibility was insufferable to the man's psyche. He had to strike out at the wild parson, for Brownlow had a trait that he could not afford to acknowledge in himself. He chastized the parson for crudity and barbarism and may have hoped, in this way, to distinguish himself from the savagery he accused Brownlow of representing.

On a deeper level, this could indicate that Watterson was struggling to maintain the belief that he, the Southern "conservative," could ward off the crude, chaotic, anarchic conditions of contemporary existence. If his brand of "conservatism" did not stand for civilization but was only wild savagery in disguise, the stability of the old order could never return. For this reason, fantasy may have had to reign supreme in the mind of the shrewdest proponent of home rule in the land. The alternative would have been unbearable.

88. Krock, ed., *Editorials*, p. 209; Louisville *Courier-Journal*, June 17, 1908.
89. Augusta (Maine) *Journal*, January 22, 1908.

Chapter Four

The New Cavalier Literature

In the three decades preceding Fort Sumter, John Pendleton Kennedy, William Alexander Caruthers, William Gilmore Simms, and other important Southern men of letters sensed that the South lagged behind Northern society in economic enterprise, population growth, and national political influence. At once envious and fearful of a powerful, energetic, yet seemingly chaotic North, they tried to convince themselves and others that Southerners had qualities Northerners lacked. They made the attempt through literary imagery. Southern society was characterized in the person of the generous and cultivated cavalier gentleman planter. Boasting ancestry traceable to the most exclusive English stock, holding large estates, and enjoying a seemingly carefree and easygoing life style, the Cavalier stood for a refined, contented agrarian South. Counterpoised was the image of a sly and unscrupulous Yankee devoted exclusively to the pursuit of money. In him, there was neither humanity nor dignity; with him, life was tense and uncertain. A refined agrarian South rooted in the finest Anglo-American tradition was thus pitted against a directionless, coarse, materialistic North. Where would culture and tradition survive? The answer was obvious.[1]

Antebellum Cavalier literature was a weapon in the battle for Southern particularism. Generous and cultivated, the Southern planter could surely manage regional affairs competently. Outside intervention would only be harmful. This was particularly true of racial matters, for the kindly Cavalier planter knew how to care for his blacks. He needed no meddling Northerners to advise him. The Cavalier treated his Negroes compassionately; the Yankee saw them only as a source of wealth. Thus, blacks were better off without Northern intervention. Cruel exploitation of the "lower race" was precluded when Southern autonomy was conceded.

Few readers in the antebellum North were attentive to these pleas

1. This theme is developed in William R. Taylor's brilliant study, *Cavalier and Yankee: The Old South and American National Character* (Garden City, New York: Doubleday & Company, Inc., 1963). It is also thoroughly discussed in David Bertelson, *The Lazy South* (New York: Oxford University Press, Inc., 1967).

for local autonomy. Most never read Cavalier literature. Those who did were instantly repelled by its antagonistic tone and overlooked the special plea for Southern self-determination. As Professor William R. Taylor has convincingly demonstrated, Northerners wished to see themselves as "transcendent Yankees"—people who had shed all but the drive and ambition imbued within Yankee culture and who had assumed the dignified traits of the cultivated Cavalier. But "transcendence" required material sacrifice and, in a sense, self-repudiation. It was easier for a Northern reader to repudiate or ignore the Cavalier writer than to disavow Yankee culture. This may explain why men like Caruthers, Simms, and Kennedy never wrote best sellers.[2]

After Appomattox, Cavalier literature gradually lost its distinctively anti-Northern tone. The writings of prominent South Carolina poet-essayist Paul Hamilton Hayne represent one of the earliest indications of this change. Before the Civil War, Hayne had been a respected Cavalier author. He had been a member of a literary group presided over by William Gilmore Simms and had belonged to the Charleston social elite.[3] Nearly bankrupted by the war,[4] he refused at first to modify his rhetoric or to alter the basic theme of his writings: Cavalier supremacy over scheming Yankees.[5] Because of his reluctance to compromise, Hayne lived in poverty and literary obscurity during the early years of Reconstruction. Fearing adverse reactions from their readers, Northern publishers refused his works while the poorly endowed Southern magazines and newspapers could offer him slight remuneration.[6] Sometime during the early 1870's however, Hayne totally reappraised the nature of American society and his place within it. He needed funds and recognized that the North had become the American author's main source of income. To make his writings marketable above Mason-Dixon, he began to modify Cavalier-Yankee imagery. Ceasing to glorify the South at the expense of the North, he wrote about sectional reconciliation through Northern generosity. While he continued to portray the South as a land of beauty and upright citizenry, he ceased scoffing at Northern society. Yankees were no longer villains.[7]

2. Frank L. Mott, *Golden Multitudes: The Story of Best Sellers in the United States* (New York: The Macmillan Company, 1947), pp. 319–20.

3. Jay B. Hubbell, *The South in American Literature, 1607–1900* (Durham: Duke University Press, 1954), pp. 744–45.

4. Daniel M. McKeithan, ed., *A Collection of Hayne Letters* (Austin: University of Texas Press, 1944), p. xvi.

5. See such early Reconstruction poems by Hayne as "Stonewall Jackson," "Carolina," and "Ode in Honor of the Bravery and Sacrifices of the Soldiers of the South," all of which are printed in Paul H. Hayne, *Legends and Lyrics* (Philadelphia: J. B. Lippincott Co., 1872).

6. Hubbell, *South in American Literature*, pp. 748–49.

7. See, e.g., Paul H. Hayne, *The Mountain of the Lovers: With Poems of Nature and Tradition* (New York: E. J. Hale & Son, 1875), pp. 74–77. See also

Though this modification did not make Hayne rich, it allowed him to survive as a writer. Northern publishers began to award him contracts.[8] Like John Esten Cooke, Richard Malcolm Johnston, and a few other contemporaries, Hayne had learned that a Southern man of letters could not earn his keep by writing as he had before the war.[9]

As early Reconstruction writers like Hayne, Cooke, and Johnston won contracts from Northern publishers, their success encouraged other Southern writers to publish new Cavalier literature. First appearing in 1878 in the pages of the Atlanta *Constitution,* Joel Chandler Harris' Uncle Remus stories exemplified this development. Careful to avoid adverse comments of Northern society, Harris made a special effort to tell Northern readers that they no longer differed with white Southerners on vital issues, particularly racial isues. Yankees could rest content, for Southerners would treat the Negro in a manner any Northerner would approve. Brer' Rabbit (the Negro of the animal world) found no serious problems with Brer' Fox (the Southern white man). Uncle Remus himself acknowledged that "Mars John an' Miss Sally aint got nuthin' das' too good for me." [10] Through Remus, Harris told the Yankee that he had no reason to suspect the Cavalier; after all, the Negro himself was content with Cavalier treatment. By modifying traditional Cavalier literature along these lines, Harris quickly secured national recognition as a leading authority on Negro life.[11] He used the race question to promote, not diminish, intersectional trust, contributing in this way to the cause of home rule. Like Henry Watterson, he helped head off the second Reconstruction that white Southerners had persistently feared.

By the 1880's and the early 1890's, James Lane Allen also began to seek Northern patronage. In his novel, *A Kentucky Cardinal* (1894),

---

Paul H. Buck, *The Road to Reunion, 1865–1900* (New York: Vintage Books, 1937), pp. 146, 207. The reconciliationist spirit is also quite apparent in the letters Hayne wrote during the 1870's to Moses Coit Tyler. They are printed in McKeithan, ed., *Hayne Letters,* pp. 339, 360.

8. Hubbell, *South in American Literature,* pp. 748–49.

9. See John Esten Cooke's *Hilt to Hilt* (New York: Carleton, 1871) and *Mohun* (New York: G. W. Dillingham, 1893). The first edition of *Mohun* was published in 1869. See also Richard Malcolm Johnston, *Dukesboro Tales* (Baltimore, Turnbull Brothers, 1871).

10. Joel Chandler Harris, *Uncle Remus: His Songs and His Sayings* (New York and London: D. Appleton and Company, 1924), p. 251. Besides symbolizing the relationship of Negro to white Southerner, Brer' Rabbit and Brer' Fox may have represented the relationship of the South to the North. Superior in brain power, Brer' Rabbit may have circumvented Northern industrial might (Brer' Fox), nullifying the result of the Civil War and restoring the antebellum state of affairs.

11. *Scribner's Monthly Magazine,* XXI (1881), 961–62; Buck, *Road to Reunion,* pp. 218–19.

he exalted the natural beauty and romantic propensities of rural antebellum Kentucky without even implicitly denigrating the North. Allen also wrote an important article attacking Harriet Beecher Stowe's portrayal of antebellum slavery. Like pre-Civil War pro-slavery theorists, he contended that the master had elevated his slaves through responsible, humane treatment. But unlike most ante-bellum theorists, Allen added that the master probably intended "to liberate them [the slaves] in the end. . . ." [12] Like Cavalier writers of the prewar decades, he acknowledged that "the rapid amassing of wealth" did not motivate the slaveholder. But he departed from them on one significant point, insisting that the slaveholder was not overly concerned with "splendid living." [13] Clearly, Allen's Cavalier gentle-man was not the wealthy planter who wasted away his day sipping mint juleps. Rather, he was a hard worker who treated his slaves kindly but sensed that slavery was on an ebbing tide. Few Northern readers could take offense at this portrayal. It did not mention the Yankee, much less deny Yankee virtue. Reading Allen, a Northerner could perceive a fundamental sectional agreement on Negro slavery; namely, that it had no future. More important, the Northern reader could sense that Cavalier living habits closely resembled his own. Thus, Cavalier and Yankee were not so far apart. Obviously, Allen's was a literature designed to ease sectional animosities—a precondition for Southern home rule.

In the first decade of the twentieth century, Thomas Dixon, Jr. demonstrated another way antebellum Cavalier literature could be reworked to promote sectional reconciliation and prevent the second Reconstruction that Southerners continued to fear. His major novels, *The Leopard's Spots* and *The Clansman,* were true to antebellum literary tradition in that they openly endorsed white Southern rule. But owing to modifications of the prewar Cavalier literary model, they were quite popular nationally. Praise of Abraham Lincoln as the symbol of national unity, endorsement of the intersectional ro-mance between Northerner Elsie Stoneman and Southerner Ben Cameron, and caution in distinguishing "brutal" Northern Radicals like Thaddeus Stevens from a generally humane Northern society all helped to blur the contrast between Cavalier and Yankee. With themes such as these, few white Northerners could have been incensed with a Southern novel.

The limited success of Hayne and the greater popularity of Harris, Allen, and Dixon testified to the success of the new Cavalier litera-ture. It glorified the South, but not at the expense of the North. Fo-

---

12. James Lane Allen, "Mrs. Stowe's 'Uncle Tom' at Home in Kentucky," *Century,* XXXIV (1887), 856.
13. Allen, *Century,* XXXIV (1887), 861.

cusing almost entirely upon a glorious South, it nonetheless hinted at important similarities between the sections, and this made it possible for Northerners to share the glory. It is little wonder that Cavalier writers eventually won over a vast Northern audience without losing their Southern readership. As early as 1888 Albion Tourgée spoke of an American literature that had "become not only Southern in type but distinctly Confederate in sympathy. The federal or Union soldier is not exactly deprecated, but subordinated; the Northern type is not decried, but the Southern is preferred." [14] Five years later, a perceptive Southern literary critic, William M. Baskervill, noted that the South was conducting a successful literary "invasion against the North." [15] The October, 1901, issue of *The Century* reinforced Baskervill's observation; its pages were filled with Cavalier writings. The new literature had such a profound impact upon American *belles lettres* that even black poet-novelist Paul Laurence Dunbar felt obliged to use it as a model.[16] Modified to discount Yankee villainy, postbellum Cavalier writing was far more influential than its antebellum counterpart. It had ceased to be antagonistic and had become the most popular literature on both sides of the Ohio River.[17]

Because the home rule idea had always been implicit within Cavalier writing, the popularity of the literature suggested greater acceptance of the idea. Once a Northerner praised and admired the virtuous Southern planter gentleman of Hayne, Harris, Allen, or Dixon, he was almost compelled to allow the Southerner the right to control local affairs. Tiring anyway by the middle 1870's in their efforts to remake the South, many Northerners probably welcomed this implicit plea within the Cavalier novel and short story as a rationale for abandoning their efforts. There can be no doubt that the new Cavalier writers were as important in the campaign for local autonomy as Hampton, Lamar, Grady, and even Watterson. Perhaps they were more important. Their appeals for home rule were hidden in the sense that they were woven into fiction. A reader who might otherwise have been unsympathetic to the home rule appeal could let down his guard when the appeal was made by a fictional Cavalier gentleman in an "unreal" setting.

14. Albion W. Tourgée, "The South as a Field for Fiction," *The Forum*, VI (December, 1888), 405.

15. *Vanderbilt Observer*, XV (1893), 210, as quoted in Buck, *Road to Reunion*, p. 227.

16. For a good discussion of this point and of Dunbar generally, see Robert A. Bone, *The Negro Novel in America* (New Haven: Yale University Press, 1958), especially p. 39.

17. Sheldon Van Auken, "The Southern Historical Novel in the Early Twentieth Century," *Journal of Southern History*, XIV, No. 2 (May, 1948), 164, 189.

II

Though Hayne, Harris, Allen, and Dixon helped to secure a national audience for the new Cavalier literature, Thomas Nelson Page played the most significant role. Page may have been the most popular novelist in the country at the turn of the century. Americans of all regions eagerly purchased anything that came from his pen.[18] *Red Rock,* his most popular novel, sold over 100,000 copies and was printed in serial form in leading magazines.[19] Copies of *The Old Gentleman of the Black Stock* were ordered well in advance of publication solely upon Charles Scribner's announcement that Page was the author.[20] In 1903, even the hastily composed *Gordon Keith* became the second best selling novel in the country.[21] When Page passed away in 1922, his fiction was basic to the curriculum of English departments in Southern colleges.[22] At his death, Woodrow Wilson referred to him as a great national "ornament," and all of Virginia, Page's home state, went into mourning.[23]

It is not difficult to fathom the secret of Page's extraordinary national popularity. His readers were not overly concerned about literary quality. By the standards of the time, *Gordon Keith* suffered from an abundance of characters and incidents. Almost all of *The Red Riders* dealt with developments peripheral to the novel's central event, South Carolina Redemption. Though the symbolism in *Red Rock* was extremely important, it was not developed with consistency. Frank and Willy of *Two Little Confederates* call to mind Mark Twain's Huckleberry Finn and Tom Sawyer, but they were portrayed with very little color or sophistication. *John Marvel, Assistant* could have been reduced by two hundred pages.

Despite these literary defects, Page was praised by Northerners as well as by Southerners, by laymen as well as by literary critics. Writing to Page, John Sharp Williams suggested the obvious reason:

18. Harriet R. Holman, "The Literary Career of Thomas Nelson Page, 1884–1910" (Ph.D. dissertation, Duke University, 1947), pp. 59–60.

19. Rosewell Page, *Thomas Nelson Page: A Memoir of a Virginia Gentleman* (New York: Charles Scribner's Sons, 1923), p. 185; Holman, "Literary Career," p. 79.

20. Charles Scribner to Thomas Nelson Page, June 4, 1900, Page Papers, Duke University.

21. Holman, "Literary Career," p. 25.

22. W. J. Cash, *The Mind of the South* (New York: Alfred A. Knopf, Inc., 1941), p. 333.

23. Woodrow Wilson to Mrs. Rosewell Page, November 2, 1922, Page Papers, Duke University. Rosewell Page, *Thomas Nelson Page,* pp. 207–8, reports statewide mourning in Virginia.

"You are one of the very few of our Southern men who have been 'lionized' at the North without compromising your character, principles, ideals, and aspirations as a Southerner and your devotions to the traditions of the South." [24] Page's popularity was based upon extraordinarily skillful modifications of the antebellum Cavalier literary model—modifications which retained the allegiance of Southern readers as they won over Northern enthusiasts. He did not modify Cavalier heroism and Yankee villainy enough to disenchant Southerners, but the modifications allowed a vast Northern audience to appreciate his writings.[25] Page was the master among Southern men of letters in altering the old Cavalier literary model.

Red Rock illustrates the nature of Page's modifications. Southern planters who resisted Radical Reconstruction were portrayed as courageous, brave, noble fighters for the just cause. Northerners who sympathized with these planters were also portrayed in noble colors. The villains were Northern carpetbaggers and Southern scalawags. Hence, not all Southerners emerged as bold Cavaliers and not all Northerners were corrupt Yankees. The novel concluded with an intersectional marriage between Steve Allen, the heroic Cavalier gentleman, and Ruth Welch, a kind and understanding Northern woman. It symbolized the union of the good people of the North and the South. The Northern reader could not have resented this Southern hero; through identification with Ruth Welch, he was encouraged to become a partner with that hero.

Intersectional romance also tended to align Northern readers with Southern heroes in Page's *The Red Riders* and *Meh Lady*. In *Gordon Keith*, on the other hand, hero Keith found no lover in corrupt, depersonalized, materialistic Yankee society. He returned to the more level-headed and individualistic South and married a local *belle*. Keith's decision doubtless found favor with the Southern reader though Northern readers were not overlooked. By emphasizing the humanism and sensitivity of two Northerners, Alice Yorke and Norman Wentworth, Page succeeded in blurring the contrast between the virtuous Cavalier and the corrupt Yankee. Yorke and Wentworth emerged as partners with Keith and implicitly called upon Northern readers to join them in that partnership.

John Marvel, Assistant had the same effect. The novel centered in a Western city that had been settled by Northerners. Marvel was the transplanted Cavalier hero living amidst Yankee corruption typified by

24. John Sharp Williams to Thomas Nelson Page, August 29, 1904, Page Papers, Duke University. See, e.g., the Richmond *Times*, April 9, 1893, and the Richmond *Dispatch*, December 4, 1898, for similar expressions of this view.
25. This becomes apparent on survey of the many letters and newspaper articles by Northerners and Southerners praising Page's writings. They are found in the Page Papers at Duke University.

the selfish, scheming Collis McSheen and Sophia Argand. But two Northerners, Leo Wolffert and Eleanor Leigh, and Southerner Henry Glave joined Marvel in his battles against McSheen and Argand and for the underprivileged. This intersectional alliance directed by a Cavalier hero for the well-being of society was developed most strikingly in the last pages of the novel. Yankee Eleanor Leigh explained her allegiance to the Cavalier, John Marvel: "He appears to me the embodiment of truth—rugged and without grace—but so restful—so real—so sincere." [26] Leigh was implicitly calling upon all decent Americans, North and South, to help her to support the bold Cavalier gentleman.

"The Old Planters," a short story in the May, 1909, number of *Century*, reflected still another tactic Page devised to modify and popularize the old Cavalier literary model. A group of white Northerners who "mistakenly" believed that Southerners were a lazy and backward people were stranded in the South. Circumstances required them to lodge for the night with an aging plantation family, and by morning their views had completely changed. Observing their hosts, they saw in them courageous Cavalier planters who knew how to handle "their" Negroes and how to manage other local matters. Subsequently the newly "enlightened" Northerners took pleasure trips to visit their remarkable Cavalier friends. The good people, North and South, had come together and Cavalier virtue had been vindicated.

Page also wrote stories for children—*Among the Camps* and *Two Little Confederates*. They illustrate in yet another way the man's masterful modifications of Old South Cavalier literature. A Southerner could take pride in Page's adventurous Southern children who heroically braved dangerous Civil War battle arenas while the Northern reader could identify with kind Yankee soldiers who treated the children with warmth and sympathy. The stories had no villains. The Cavalier always happened to be the hero, but Yankees who sympathized with the hero were also fine people.

Page was obviously a master at tailoring the old Cavalier model to evoke an enthusiastic response from Northern as well as Southern readers. In this respect, the sophistication of his writing surpassed that of Hayne, Harris, Allen, Dixon, and every other Southern novelist. His writings provided Southern readers with illustrations of Cavalier virtue through hero figures, but he always had some Northern characters aiding the hero's cause to encourage Northern identification. Yankees were permitted and even prompted to align themselves on the side of righteousness.

The extraordinary national popularity of Page's work was charged

26. Thomas Nelson Page, *John Marvel, Assistant* (New York: Charles Scribner's Sons, 1909), p. 382.

with racial significance. If white Southerners could identify with Page's Cavalier hero and Northerners could identify with the hero's ally, readers of both sections would be united behind the hero. In the absence of other variables, they would tend to favor much of what the Cavalier planter-gentleman said or did concerning local Negroes. Because Page commanded a very large national reading audience, the qualities he assigned to his Cavalier hero were therefore bound to have enormous influence upon racial attitudes, North and South. To evaluate the nature of this influence, something must be said of Page's racial outlook.

III

Page's racial ideas were rooted in the Southern past. Like Brownlow and Watterson, he was sure that the Negro had originally been a wild, barbaric African savage. In time, virtuous, responsible Cavaliers —the most civilized people on earth—took it upon themselves to transport the black savage to the American South. There they enslaved him, with bondage providing "the only semblance of civilization which the Negro race has possessed since the dawn of history." [27] This bondage offered the Negro the guiding intellect and "moral support" of the cultivated race.[28] He was "trained to habits of industry, and disciplined to good order." [29] Therefore, slavery lifted the Negro up from savagery.

After a considerable period in bondage, Page believed that the black savage assumed the traits of an Uncle Billy of *Meh Lady* or a Sam of *Marse Chan*. He realized that he could do nothing without white guidance and longed to serve his master in any way possible: "His Master's will controlled him as an officer controls a soldier in battle." [30] According to Page, these slave "controls" were so effective that the Negro felt guilty whenever he tried to circumvent them. This was illustrated by the constant pangs of guilt that plagued fugitive slave Dick Runaway in *On Newfound River*.

Then came the Civil War. Negro conduct during that conflict testified to a remarkable loyalty that the "controls" of slavery had instilled in the savage race. Ignoring the many instances of slave

27. Thomas Nelson Page, *The Negro: The Southerner's Problem* (New York: Charles Scribner's Sons, 1904), p. 57. See also Page, *The Old South: Essays Social and Political* (New York: Charles Scribner's Sons, 1906), pp. 38, 139.

28. Thomas Nelson Page, *On Newfound River* (New York: Charles Scribner's Sons, 1906), p. 266.

29. Thomas Nelson Page, *The Old Dominion: Her Making and Her Manners* (New York: Charles Scribner's Sons, 1908), p. 242.

30. Page, *On Newfound River*, p. 213.

disloyalty during the war, Page charged that blacks remained true to their masters despite opportunities to secure freedom. Hearing Union troops approach his mistress' plantation, Uncle Billy prepared to defend her: "Meh heart jump up in meh mouf. But I step back in meh house and get meh axe." [31] At the close of the war their masters told them that they were free to leave the plantation, but the bondsmen were reluctant to go. "No suh; Marster, you know I don' wan' to be free," Tarquin told Dr. Cary in *Red Rock*.[32] In *Two Little Confederates*, Uncle Balla's response was identical; "Hi, Mistis, whar is I got to go? I wuz born on dis place an' I 'spec' to die here, an' be buried right yonder." [33]

For Page, the Civil War had produced a racial tragedy. It had destroyed the basic institution of a magnificent antebellum Southern civilization—the best of all possible institutions for racial adjustment. With the demise of slavery, "the purest, sweetest life" that civilization could produce had become a thing of the past.[34] The words of Sam, the Negro narrator of *Marse Chan,* summarized the essence of that racial utopia: "Dem wuz good ole times, marster—de bes' Sam uver see! . . . Niggers didn' hed nothin 't all to do—jes' hed to ten' to de feedin' an' cleanin' de hawses, an' doin' what de marster tell 'em to do. . . . Dyar warn' no trouble nor nuttin'." [35]

In "The Old Planters," Page's Cavalier hero remarked that before the Civil War he had "lived" whereas afterwards he had "only existed." [36] The racial instabilities produced by emancipation and Reconstruction destroyed an antebellum Southern utopia and ushered in all of Dixie's racial ills. Daily existence became burdensome in the years that followed Appomattox, providing "an object-lesson which the Southern States can never forget." [37] Led by Thaddeus Stevens, champion of miscegenation, Northern Radicals taught the Negro the erroneous and dangerous doctrine that he was equal to

31. Thomas Nelson Page, *Meh Lady: A Story of the War* (New York: Charles Scribner's Sons, 1904), p. 14. See also Page, *Marse Chan: A Story of Old Virginia* (New York: Charles Scribner's Sons, 1892), p. 48, for a similar example of slave loyalty during the war. In Page, *The Negro,* pp. 184–85 the author claimed that slave loyalty during the Civil War proved that slaves had not been treated cruelly.

32. Thomas Nelson Page, *Red Rock: A Chronicle of Reconstruction* (New York: Charles Scribner's Sons, 1904), p. 41.

33. Thomas Nelson Page, *Two Little Confederates* in *Works of Thomas Nelson Page* (New York: Charles Scribner's Sons, 1906), II, 59.

34. Thomas Nelson Page, *Social Life in Old Virginia* (New York: Charles Scribner's Sons, 1897), p. 101.

35. Page, *Marse Chan*, pp. 13–14.

36. Thomas Nelson Page, *The Land of the Spirit* (New York: Charles Scribner's Sons, 1913), p. 41.

37. Page, *Old Dominion*, p. 323.

the Caucasian and ought to assert himself.[38] These teachings produced horrendous results, for blacks left the fields, refusing to work as
menial laborers.[39] They formed "a wild mob that hooted and yelled
about the village. . . ."[40] Worse yet, they ran Southern government,
performing "like big children playing at something which grown
people do."[41]

Miscegenation, to Page, was the worst consequence of the immediate post-Civil War "erosion" of the white-black relationship. Schooled
to believe false egalitarian doctrines, many Negroes asserted their
equality by "ravishing" white women.[42] Doctor Moses, the educated
Negro community leader of *Red Rock,* was "a hyena in a cage."
Finding the white Ruth Welch, he "sprang at her like a wild
beast. . . ."[43] Despite their uniforms, black troops behaved no better;
white women were their prey.[44] Literally as well as symbolically the
black race was raping the white. Savagery was overturning civilization.

The manhood of the white South responded to this horrid turn of
events. Andy Stamper of *Red Rock* proclaimed: "it's worse than the
war. I never would have surrendered, if I'd thought it ud' a come to
this."[45] Ku Klux Klan-like organizations arose and threw out both
carpetbaggers and scalawags. With the withdrawal of federal troops
from the South, "Negro power, which but the day before had been as
arrogant and insolent as ever in the whole course of its brief authority, fell to pieces."[46] The South had been redeemed; Dixie was "herself again."[47] Black savagery had been overturned by white civilization.

Page was certain, however, that Reconstruction had left an ominous
legacy. Redemption governments could not restore discipline among
the blacks, and the danger of "outbreaks" of the savage Negro impulse
persisted into the twentieth century. The blacks formed "a vast
sluggish mass of uncooled lava . . . which may at any time burst

38. Page, *The Negro,* pp. 54–55. In *Red Rock,* particularly p. 213, Page hinted
that Stevens had engaged in sexual relations with his mulatto housekeeper.

39. Thomas Nelson Page, *The Red Riders* (New York: Charles Scribner's Sons,
1924), p. 169. Page, "Economic Conditions in the Southern Confederacy," unpublished
ms., 1918, Page Papers, Duke University.

40. Page, *Red Rock,* p. 488. See also Page, *Old Dominion,* p. 243.

41. Page, *Red Rock,* p. 223. See also Page, *Pastime Stories* in *Works of Thomas
Nelson Page* (New York: Charles Scribner's Sons, 1906), X, 121–35.

42. Thomas Nelson Page, "The Lynching of Negroes: Its Cause and Its Preven-
tion," *North American Review,* CLXXVII (January, 1904), 26.

43. Page, *Red Rock,* pp. 355, 358.

44. Page, *Red Rock,* p. 193.

45. Page, *Red Rock,* p. 482.

46. Page, *The Negro,* p. 49.

47. Page, *The Red Riders,* pp. 318, 333–34.

forth unexpectedly and spread desolation all around." [48] They remained insolent, "unfit for work," and dangerously unpredictable.[49] The gravest danger was libidinal. Blacks demonstrated enormous sexual appetites; few remained chaste beyond the age of fifteen.[50] Taught the doctrine of social equality during Reconstruction, their dominant passion was to fornicate with white women. Because no civilized white women would ever consent to interracial sexual intercourse, blacks frequently raped them. This provoked retaliation, for the instinct of racial preservation compelled the white manhood of the South to lynch the "barbarians." [51]

Page was not convinced, however, that lynching could end Negro rape or even the danger of miscegenation.[52] There could be no real end to racial strife until white dominance was restored. It "is only where the whites have an undisputed authority that the old relation survives." [53] Where it was lacking, the black man would inevitably revert to his "original type"—the wild African savage.[54]

Page's survey of the history of Southern race relations concluded with this plea for white dominance. Both the survey and the plea were woven into many of his writings. His Cavalier heroes shared Page's historical perspective and were almost invariably pledged to white supremacy. Since a vast reading audience, North and South, payed homage to the Cavalier hero, many were inclined to accept the hero's viewpoint. Even if one's father or grandfather had been an abolitionist, there was a strong temptation to adopt the racial ideology of Page's Cavalier hero; in this way, the reader could be sure that he was on the side of virtue and integrity. Thus, Henry Ward Beecher, the old antislavery agitator, found himself totally in sympathy with Page's *Marse Chan,* a story about the happy and sentimental relationship between a kind white master and a devoted black bondsman.[55] Page's writings also "awakened" Kansas physician Thomas C. Hinkle to the benefits of white dominance. Moreover, Page convinced him that the white Southerner was not as antagonistic to the

48. Page, *The Negro,* p. 64.

49. See, e.g., Page, *The Negro,* p. 54; Page, *John Marvel,* p. 82; Page, *Land of the Spirit,* p. 40.

50. Page, *The Negro,* pp. 83–84.

51. Page, *North American Review,* CLXXVII (January, 1904), 37, 39, 44–45.

52. Page, *North American Review,* CLXXVII (January, 1904), 43.

53. Page, *The Negro,* p. 54.

54. Page, *The Negro,* p. 251. See also Page, "A Southerner on the Negro Question," *North American Review,* CLIV (April, 1892), 403, for a similar remark. Clearly, this contradicted Page's earlier contention that slavery had uplifted the Negro from savagery. But Page did not see the contradiction. Cherishing the memory of the "peculiar institution," he could not admit that it had failed to permanently change the Negro from his "original type."

55. Rosewell Page, *Thomas Nelson Page,* pp. 92–93.

Negro as most Northerners.[56] An editor for *Collier's Weekly* claimed that the "integrity" of Page's writing had converted him to Page's outlook on all aspects of the "Negro problem": "It seems to me that you have left very little, if anything, for anyone else to say." [57] Other white Northerners made similar remarks. If they shared Page's racial ideas before they read his works, reading deepened their commitment.[58]

IV

Because Page was a well-traveled novelist and essayist and quite familiar with the worlds of business and law, one wonders why he devoted most of his writing to the Southern racial situation. A man with his background and interests could have focused upon any number of alternative topics—European history and culture, jurisprudence, Washington high society, or even the American business community. But his early writings on Southern race relations sold well and made him popular, and there seemed to be no point in changing his subject matter. Earning very large dividends,[59] he admitted that the early publications satisfied his burning "desire to see myself in print. . . ." [60] Because he placed a very high premium upon wealth and recognition, Page, like Brownlow and Watterson, was very much the "nervous American," and the success of his early writings may have soothed his status anxieties. On the other hand, he was heir to a vast inheritance, the Page family was venerated throughout the South, and after he married the very wealthy Florence Lanthrop Field in 1893, he was free from any financial worries.[61] Regardless of success or failure as a writer, he seemed assured of the status and the money to satisfy his nervous desires for recognition.

Page's frequent claim that he wrote "from sheer affection" for the values of the Old South bears more directly upon his motivation.[62] He may have written about the South and Southern race relations

56. Thomas C. Hinkle to Thomas Nelson Page, 1904, Page Papers, Duke University.

57. Arthur S. Street to Thomas Nelson Page, February 16, 1903, Page Papers, Duke University.

58. See, e.g., Howard L. Jones to Thomas Nelson Page, August 15, 1899, and James L. Ford to Thomas Nelson Page, April 9, 1902, Page Papers, Duke University; Boston *Daily Advertiser*, January 13, 1892; Hubbell, *South in American Literature*, p. 797.

59. Thomas Nelson Page to William Griffith, December 20, 1912, Page Papers, Duke University. See also Holman, "Literary Career," p. 133.

60. Thomas Nelson Page, "Recollections and Reflections," unpublished ms., n.d., Page Papers, Duke University.

61. Holman, "Literary Career," pp. 36–37.

62. See, e.g., Page, *Social Life in Old Virginia*, p. 5.

for therapeutic reasons. Since he regarded the antebellum slave order as a bygone racial utopia, writing may have helped him to direct his thoughts toward that past. The "hobby" may have cushioned him against adverse racial realities. It may also have safeguarded him from the realities of an urbanizing and industrializing America that contributed to the racial adversities. Literary activity may have had these cushioning effects whether Page wrote of the Old South, Reconstruction, or the "frightful" post-Reconstruction decades, for his stories on postbellum topics always concluded with the heroic Cavalier happily in "control" of "his" Negroes just as he had been before the war. Regardless of the time setting for a story, a pleasant and "natural" antebellum master-slave relation eventually emerged. For Page, the past could always be superimposed upon the present.[63] Thus, he could lose sight of the adversities of contemporary existence. With a pen, he could direct his mind toward the wonderful days of yesteryear—days when life had been "clean and pure and stimulating." [64]

It becomes plausible that Page had immersed himself in literary activity to escape everyday realities when one considers his deep personal attachment to the antebellum South and the slave system. He was descended from an old Virginia family that dated back to the early colonial period and produced many distinguished public figures, including a signer of the Declaration of Independence and two Virginia Governors. He often made proud references to these men.[65] Furthermore, he consistently praised an antebellum literary tradition that centered around George W. Bagby, the Virginia local color novelist. Unlike certain other prewar Southern writers, Page insisted that Bagby had been an independent thinker. He had refused to imitate Sir Walter Scott and had produced, instead, "the most charming picture of American life ever drawn." Bagby wrote so delightfully, Page added, because he was out to preserve "the life of the people he loved," though this appraisal was obviously conditioned by Page's own desire to preserve the life of the Old South.[66]

What touched Page most in his reflections upon the Old South, however, was neither family tradition nor George W. Bagby, but memories of slavery and the bondsmen he had grown up with on his father's plantation. His fiction contained many affectionate references to these blacks.[67] Comments concerning Ma' Lyddy, the ante-

63. This tactic is particularly apparent in *Red Rock* and *The Red Riders*.

64. Page, *Old Dominion*, pp. 383–84.

65. Page's *The Old South* contains many such references.

66. Thomas Nelson Page, ed., *The Old Virginia Gentleman and Other Sketches by George W. Bagby* (New York: Charles Scribner's Sons, 1910), pp. x–xii. See also Page, *Old Dominion*, p. 296, for similar commentary on Bagby.

67. See, e.g., the Negro characters Sam in *Marse Chan*, Uncle Billy in *Meh Lady*, and Ma' Lyddy in "Mam' Lyddy's Recognition."

bellum Negro mammy who had cared for him, were especially moving. She was portrayed as a "mother" who had raised him with "dignity, force, and kindness" and who had taught him "the lessons of morality and truth." [68] The most fulfilling part of his relationship with Lyddy involved intimate physical contact, and he recalled with deep emotion how he had "rocked on her generous bosom, slept on her bed" and had been "fed at her table. . . ." [69] He was a "little charge in her arms, sleeping in her ample lap, or toddling about her. . . ." [70] Page's choice of words suggested more than a close personal relationship with Ma' Lyddy; it pointed to a profoundly satisfying sensual relationship. The white boy had craved physical intimacies with his black "mother." She gave him reason to endure hardship. She was proof that life was worth living.

Page wrote of his relations with antebellum "darkies" so often and with such affection that the writing process must have put him at ease. By jotting down fond memories of childhood relations with Negro slaves, he could direct his mind away from the dangerous trend of postbellum race relations. Writing helped him to escape contemporary racial reality; the pen had definite therapeutic value.

V

However, literary activity did not protect Page at all times. It never gave him total peace of mind against "the trend of the times." Daily, he detected one reminder after another that the Negro was losing respect for the "superior" race. It distressed him profoundly to see "slatternly negro girls . . . run the elevators and whistle all the time." [71] Without "a stern, repressive public opinion among the negroes" in urbanizing, industrializing America, there would be no end to the assaults waged by "black brutes" upon the white womanhood of the South.[72] More and more every day, whites were growing fearful of directing their servants.[73]

68. Thomas Nelson Page, "The Old Time Negro," *Scribner's Magazine,* XXXVI (November, 1904), 525–26.

69. Page, *Scribner's Magazine,* XXXVI (November, 1904), 525.

70. Page, *Social Life in Old Virginia,* p. 26. For similar expressions of a loving and basically physical relationship with Ma' Lyddy, see Page, *The Coast of Bohemia* (New York: Charles Scribner's Sons, 1906), p. 124; Page, *Old South,* p. 179; Page, "Recollections and Reflections," unpublished ms., n.d., Page Papers, Duke University; Page, *The Negro,* pp. 177–78.

71. Thomas Nelson Page to Norval Richardson, November 18, 1919, Page Papers, Duke University.

72. Thomas Nelson Page to Emmett J. Scott, February 25, 1904, Page Papers, Duke University.

73. Thomas Nelson Page to Rosewell Page and Ruth Page, January 25, 1920, Page Papers, Duke University.

When his writings did not divert him from analysis in this vein, Page sometimes sought out the company of "old-time Negroes," usually servile ex-slaves. On a trip to Richmond he saw a black man, old and blind, sitting at the gates of Capitol Square. He deliberately walked over to the Negro, violated local custom by dropping silver in the man's hat, and conversed sympathetically.[74] Sometimes, Page sought out the company of family servants like Sally and "Hannah, the faithful," blacks who continued to live adjacent to the family plantation in Hanover County, Virginia. Six miles away, Reverend John Jasper, the loyal old black defender of the racial *status quo*, was always available for conversation.[75] But Page was particularly fond of Charlotte, a one-time family servant. When she paid him an unexpected visit in 1916, he was very pleased, talked with the old woman for hours, and then insisted on escorting her home.[76] In "Mam' Lyddy's Recognition," it was obviously Page who picked up his beloved black mammy at a Northern railroad station and escorted her through a "surprised" crowd to his home as if she were "the first lady in the land." [77] By associating with docile blacks such as these, Page found some hope for a proper resolution of the race problem. Seeing them, he could believe that not all Southern Negroes were rude and insolent. Not all were disrespectful of the white hand.

As Page sometimes admitted, writing about a glorious antebellum civilization and maintaining contact with a few Negro survivors of that civilization could not solve the South's "Negro problem." When he made this admission, he usually accompanied it with explicit demands for home rule. *The Negro: The Southerner's Problem* was the title of his major nonfictional book on the race issue, and it represented little more than an assortment of pleas for Southern autonomy. "Left alone," Page wrote, "the whites and the blacks of the South would settle their difficulties along the lines of substantial justice and substanial equity." [78] Wherever "Negroes and the Southern whites are left alone, and are not affected by outside influence," he contended, "they, for the most part, live in harmony." [79] Wherever the influence of Northerners was removed, Southern blacks resumed "their old relation of dependence and affection," and racial peace returned.[80] But if Northern whites insisted upon meddling in Southern racial affairs, they too would be plagued by a "Negro problem,"

74. Rosewell Page, *Thomas Nelson Page*, p. 136.
75. Rosewell Page, *Thomas Nelson Page*, pp. 141–43.
76. Rosewell Page, *Thomas Nelson Page*, p. 140.
77. Thomas Nelson Page, "Mam' Lyddy's Recognition," in *Bred in the Bone* (New York: Charles Scribner's Sons, 1904), p. 251.
78. Page, *The Negro*, p. 294.
79. Page, *The Negro*, pp. 300–301.
80. Page, *The Negro*, p. 51.

for the only barrier between "the Negro and the people of the North will be the people of the South." [81]

The basic difficulty with Page's crusade for local autonomy was the same problem that Watterson had encountered. Home rule could not, in itself, solve the "Negro problem" but only open the way to a solution. Once Southern self-determination was assured, whites of the region would have to devise and implement plans for the restoration of an acceptable white-black relationship. Local autonomy could only give them the power to carry out those plans. But Page, like Watterson, rarely looked beyond home rule; when he did, his views seemed contradictory. Like Hinton Rowan Helper, he suggested that "the most dangerous phases of the [Negro] problem would still exist in the mere continuance together of the two races." [82] Also resembling the exclusionist Helper, he wrote that "the Negro race must either remain distinct and keep to itself, or it must be removed to some region, whether within or without the confines of the United States, where it will be substantially separated." [83] But other Page comments pointed to a policy of integration within the old proslavery theoretical framework of subordination. "Where the Negro has thriven it has invariably been under the influence and by the assistance of the stronger race," he charged.[84] For a "proper" white-black relationship, whites had to "steadily keep track" of the blacks about them.[85] Hopefully, "the great Anglo-Saxon race, which is dominant, and the Negro race, which is amiable, if not subservient," would recall "the old feelings of kindliness" and live together again in the natural relationship of master and serf.[86]

Page was therefore arguing that the black man had to be excluded from white society but that he also had to be drawn into an intimate and subordinate relationship with the Caucasian. Sometimes Page drew both contentions together. When he did, he revealed his underlying racial solution: "the Negro race will find its best security in remaining in this country, a people within a people, separate and distinct, but acting in amity with the stronger race and trying to minimize rather than magnify contentions upon those points as to

---

81. Page, *The Negro*, p. 214. For other nonfictional pleas in behalf of home rule, see Page, *The Negro*, pp. 33, 34, 162, 292, and Page, "President Roosevelt from the Standpoint of a Southern Democrat," *Metropolitan Magazine*, XXI (March, 1905), 674.

82. Page, *The Negro*, p. xii.

83. Page, *The Negro*, p. 291. See also the Chicago *Evening News*, January 19, 1892, for another of Page's exclusionist remarks, this time focusing on voting rights.

84. Page, *The Negro*, p. 251.

85. Page, *The Negro*, p. 118.

86. Page, *Scribner's Magazine*, XXXVI (November, 1904), 532.

which the stronger race is most determined." [87] This was to say that black and white should be separated, but not totally. "Good" Negroes acting with amity and deference to whites should obviously be rewarded by contact with whites. Like Brownlow and Watterson, Page was therefore advocating differential segregation as the basic answer to racial difficulties. Because so many blacks had ceased to be deferent to the "superior" white race, segregation was essential. But Negroes who knew their place and deferred to whites, as they had allegedly done before Reconstruction, would be welcomed into a relationship of close physical proximity with whites.

VI

Despite their diverse backgrounds, Page, Watterson, and Brownlow shared a number of ideas. By 1875 each supported home rule. From the standpoint of racial ideology, all were of the "Brownlow tradition" and fundamentally in search of servile Negroes. Moreover, each seemed to need servile blacks for the same reason; a docile Negro invited release from repressive, anxiety-producing contemporary realities. A Charlotte or a Lyddy provided Page with the same relief that "Blind Tom" afforded Watterson and the "grinning, woolyheaded nigger" offered Brownlow.

Though Page, Watterson, and Brownlow thought along similar lines, the three never met. Watterson and Brownlow held each other in contempt while Page did not even acknowledge the "fighting parson." Nonetheless, he frequently read "Marse Henry's" editorials, liked the man, and judged him "about the best political prophet in America . . . ." [88] Watterson was equally complimentary of Page and of Page's literary talents. [89]

It is not difficult to understand why Page and Watterson were on good terms. Both were wealthy, both were at home in Washington high society, both were conversant in European history and culture, and both gloried in memories of the antebellum plantation tradition. Most important, both were restrained and tactful gentlemen and qualified for membership in Watterson's "conservative" elite. Like Watterson, Page was devoted to a South ruled by cautious, cultivated, and propertied Southerners, for these were the qualities of his Cav-

87. Page, *The Negro*, p. 292.
88. The many Watterson editorials that Page clipped from the Louisville *Courier-Journal* (Page Papers, Duke University) suggest that he must have read Watterson somewhat regularly. In Thomas Nelson Page to Henry Watterson, November 18, 1916 (Watterson Papers, Library of Congress), Page praised Watterson as a political prophet. The letter also revealed his warmth toward the man.
89. Watterson's editorials in the Louisville *Courier-Journal* over many decades contained praiseworthy references to Page and to Page's writings.

alier heroes. But Brownlow belonged to the "lower class of white persons"; he was crude, boisterous, poorly educated, and aggressive toward his "betters." Despite firm ideological bonds, "Marse Henry" hated the parson almost as much as he hated "uppity niggers."

Page was thirteen years Watterson's junior. He was a very young man when Brownlow died in 1877, and this probably explains why he had never heard very much about the parson. Had he been older or had Brownlow lived a decade longer, personal animosities would probably have developed. Like Watterson, Page despised assertive lower-class Southern whites; in prose and in fiction, he had made many antagonistic references to them. Ever since colonial times, Page wrote, poor whites had posed a constant drain upon the resources of the "planter class." [90] Through Unc' Gabe, his fictional old-time darkie, he argued that "quality" Negroes had never been owned by the detested "po' white trash." [91] Gordon Keith emerged as the hero of one of Page's best selling novels precisely because he was not of poor-white upbringing—because he had been "the son of a gentleman." [92] In *Red Rock,* Hiram Still, representative of the Southern poor whites, was portrayed as a despicable person. He symbolized the effort of the crude and dishonest lower class to seize control of Southern society during Reconstruction in defiance of the "natural upper-class leadership of the region.[93] In *The Red Riders,* Joe Grease represented poor-white rule in Reconstruction South Carolina and he was portrayed as a coarse, perverse man who aggressively took revenge upon the cultivated, heroic planter gentry. Brownlow, a poor white who held power in Reconstruction Tennessee, was surely the equivalent of the fictional Hiram Still or Joe Grease who Page so detested. For a "conservative" Cavalier gentleman like Page or Watterson, lower-class people, white or black, had to defer to the "better class of white persons." Those who did not represented grave threats, whether their names were Nat Turner or William Brownlow. It did not matter that a specific poor white thought or acted toward blacks like the "conservative intelligence of the South." Racial accord among certain whites simply could not diminish the antagonisms of class.

In a sense, the "nigger" and the poor white served "conservatives" like Page and Watterson in much the same way. In their eyes, the "lowly" Brownlow and the Negro were both crude, uncultivated, and potentially dangerous; they required rigid and forceful direction by "better whites." Hence, much like blacks, the presence of a "lowly"

90. Page, *Old South,* p. 116.

91. Thomas Nelson Page, "Uncle Gabe's White Folks," *Scribner's Monthly Magazine,* XIII (April, 1877), 882.

92. Thomas Nelson Page, *Gordon Keith* (New York: Charles Scribner's Sons, 1903), p. 3.

93. Page, *Red Rock,* particularly pp. 83, 94.

Caucasian helped certain "conservatives" to confirm their sense of personal refinement, eminence, and civilization. They were what blacks and poor whites were not. Considering the coarse way in which they spoke about and sometimes acted towards blacks and poor whites under the pretext of guiding Southern society, they desperately needed that confirmation. They had to think of themselves as civilized, personal conduct notwithstanding. The alternative of giving up their fantasies was too painful.

Chapter Five

From Politics to Purity: The Crusade of the Powerless

In 1938 Professor C. Vann Woodward published a lengthy biography and an article on Thomas E. Watson. He characterized Watson as the leader of a revolt staged by discontented Southern farmers during the early 1890's against the exploitative Bourbon Democratic power structure and its allies within the Eastern big business elite. According to Woodward, Watson argued that Southern Bourbons and Eastern plutocrats had cultivated antagonisms between poor white farmers and Negroes in order to fragment potential opposition to Bourbon and plutocratic domination of the Southern economy. Through an alliance of the exploited of both races, however, the Bourbons and plutocrats could be overthrown and the economic resources of the South could be allocated along more equitable lines. Thinking in these terms, Watson tried to rally poor whites and blacks together under the Populist banner. Woodward claimed that this represented the first time an important Southern politician had ever regarded the Negro "as an integral part of Southern society with a place in its economy." [1] When the Populist crusade was defeated, however, Watson abandoned his efforts to promote biracial cooperation and evolved into a bitter and vicious Negrophobe politician. But this did not nullify the man's historical significance. To Woodward, his crusade during the 1890's proved that a white Southerner was capable, if only for a time, of breaking clear of Southern racist assumptions.

Subsequent to Woodward's biography, historians have appraised Tom Watson as one of the most important racial theorists in the postbellum South. Almost every study of postbellum Southern race relations has included at least passing reference to Watson. These studies have faithfully repeated Woodward's notion that the man was a "great crusader" for biracialism and economic justice.

1. C. Vann Woodward, "Tom Watson and the Negro in Agrarian Politics," *Journal of Southern History*, IV, No. 1 (February, 1938), 24. See also Woodward, *Tom Watson: Agrarian Rebel* (New York: Oxford University Press, 1963), p. 221, for very similar commentary.

There are, however, a number of problems with the Woodward characterization. In the main, Woodward's interpretation rested upon appeals for biracial cooperation within the Populist Party that the so-called rebel made during the early 1890's. Yet Woodward failed to note that these appeals were almost invariably phrased in bland, mechanical prose. Judging from their tone, there seemed to be little heart behind Watson's words. In 1892, for example, Watson proclaimed that good government "does the right thing, whether to the red man, the black man, or the white." [2] "All persons, every man, woman and child, colored or white has a legal right to be protected," he claimed in another call for biracial cooperation.[3] We "shall have a money system that will have regard for the poor man as well as the rich; that will help the white laborer as well as the black; the humble as well as the proud man," he charged in a public debate.[4] Americans of every region should rally with the Populists: "If he be a black man, let us say, come. If he be a brown man, let us say, come. If he be a white man, let us say, come. Let us all come and help to redeem this people and this land." [5]

Clearly, Watson was not singling out the Negro as a comrade. Along with all other members of the human race, blacks were invited into the Populist camp. Rather than genuine appeals for biracial cooperation, Watson's remarks call to mind the traditional American political rhetoric of consensus. "We are all republicans—we are all federalists," Thomas Jefferson proclaimed in his 1801 inaugural address. Since that date, language of this sort has typified the rhetoric of the skillful American politician. He has usually tried to appeal to voters of all sorts by alluding to a variety of races, religions, regions, and occupations. Behaving in this way, the politician has not necessarily demonstrated special concern for any particular segment of the electorate. To be sure, the consensus that most nineteenth-century politicians sought was usually a white consensus; few blacks were enfranchised in either the North or the South. Nevertheless, American political history has witnessed bigoted public figures in constituencies with significant black electorates who have spoken precisely as Watson did, waving the banner for "all Americans of all races, creeds, and colors." Twentieth-century electoral campaigns in major Northern urban centers and in Southern constituencies with large black electorates make this fact glaringly apparent. Hence, Watson's egalitarian slogans do not prove that the man broke from Southern racist assumptions or that he was indeed a rebel.

2. Scrapbook 1892–1894, speech notes of February 17, 1892, Watson Papers, University of North Carolina.
3. Thomas E. Watson, *The Life and Speeches of Thomas E. Watson* (Thomson, Georgia: Jeffersonian Publishing Company, 1916), p. 138.
4. *People's Party Paper*, September 16, 1892.
5. *People's Party Paper*, October 14, 1892.

The qualifications that Watson attached to his appeals for biracial cooperation raise even more serious doubts about his sincerity and compel one to regard Woodward's characterization of the man with even greater skepticism. He consistently told Southern whites that black participation in the Populist Party would never result in "Negro domination." "Existing under such conditions as they [Negroes] now do in this country," he wrote in 1892, "there is no earthly chance for Negro domination, unless we are ready to admit that the colored man is superior in will, power, courage, and intellect." [6] A year later he enlarged upon this theme in a major political address at Douglassville, Georgia. The white race, enriched by centuries of education, military experience, economic activity, and religious training, had become the "dominant" race, and whites could be expected to control any venture in biracial cooperation.[7] In a similar argument advanced decades earlier, George Fitzhugh, Edmund Ruffin, and other uncompromising proponents of slavery had argued that white and black had to cooperate within a context of white rule and black subservience. Because blacks had no vote in the antebellum South, the Fitzhughs and the Ruffins never envisioned cooperation along political lines. But from a broader theoretical perspective, their demands closely paralleled Watson's. Black and white could come together and a beneficial relationship could follow if blacks deferred to white direction.

Watson not only qualified his pleas for biracial cooperation by drawing upon antebellum proslavery thought; he also qualified his pleas along the lines of the exclusionist ideological tradition typified by Hinton Rowan Helper. He continually warned white voters that interracial association within the Populist ranks could never extend beyond the realm of politics. "Socially I want no mixing of the races. It is best that both [races] should preserve the race integrity by staying apart." [8] "Let the whites dwell to themselves and have peace and happiness. We will not have social equality," he told Atlanta Negroes.[9] To blacks from Cedartown, Georgia, he cautioned: "You colored people, as well as the whites, are better apart." [10] In 1894 a correspondent for the *People's Party Paper* assigned to cover Watson's public oratory claimed that the rebel had studiously avoided extending his plea for biracial association beyond the political realm.[11] Two years later, the prominent Negro Populist, H. S. Doyle, stated in

6. Thomas E. Watson, "The Negro Question in the South," *Arena*, VI (October, 1892), 550.
7. *People's Party Paper*, July 7, 1893; Watson, *Life and Speeches of Watson*, pp. 129–30.
8. *People's Party Paper*, July 7, 1893.
9. *People's Party Paper*, May 25, 1894.
10. *People's Party Paper*, October 14, 1892.
11. *People's Party Paper*, June 29, 1894.

a legal deposition: "Mr. Watson's position was that, in politics, the color line should be wiped out. He especially emphasized the word 'politics.' His enemies misrepresented him, and claimed that he was preaching the doctrine of social equality. . . ." [12]

Contrary to Professor Woodward, it is therefore apparent that Tom Watson's biracial venture of the early 1890's was sharply limited. According to his public pronouncements, whites would dominate, blacks would obey, and interracial association would be strictly political. Thus Watson was either a racist, an astute politician catering to the racism of a white constituency, or both. By no stretch of the imagination can the man be characterized as a champion of equal rights.

No doubt political expediency conditioned many Watson pronouncements. In the context of late nineteenth-century Southern politics, a deeply racist white electorate could construe even the blandest of biracial appeals as a concession to black voters. To avoid being stigmatized as a "nigger candidate" and face a loss of white votes, Watson had to qualify biracial appeals with racist undertones. Joining a vague plea for Negro support with blatant appeals to racist sentiment, he was probably out to maximize the Populist electoral appeal: to acquire Negro as well as white racist support.

But more than expediency was at stake. Long before Watson ever launched his venture in biracialism, he had demonstrated racist sentiments. During the 1870's and throughout the 1880's he had often jotted down phrases, sentences, and paragraphs in diaries and personal note pads lamenting black emancipation. Like Brownlow, Watterson, and Page, he had viewed Negro freedom with acute anxiety. Emancipation had released Negroes from the burdens of labor and had allowed them to "get drunk and shout and fight" and to carry on as idlers.[13] He had feared that free black boys would run about nude enticing civilized white girls while black brutes would be tempted to rape refined white women.[14] He lamented that white women were imitating "ignorant, Savage Negresses" by inserting "hideous humps" upon their lower backs to transport babies.[15] The nation's resources were being squandered on ridiculous monuments to "wild" Negro soldiers.[16] Well before the Populist crusade, then, young Watson had viewed emancipated blacks as crude, unrepressed savages who tempted and threatened white civilization.

12. *People's Party Paper,* March 13, 1896.

13. Diary, 1872–1894, contains notes for an October 12, 1872, speech at Mercer University in Macon with this message. See also Diary and Commonplace Book, 1871–1872, entry for October, 1872. Both diaries are in the Watson Papers, University of North Carolina.

14. Diary, 1872–1894, entries for October, 1885, and January 25, 1875.

15. Diary and Commonplace Book, 1871–1872, entry for August 4, 1871.

16. Speech Notes, 1885–1887, Watson Papers, University of North Carolina. The remark is found among speech notes for 1887.

As a leader in the Southern Populist crusade of the early 1890's, the rebel continued to view blacks with fear and contempt. In all probability, he sensed that white votes could be won if he publicized his long-held racist ideas. Thus, beginning in 1892, he started to express his thoughts more openly. Publicly, he contrasted Negro savagery and "black passions" with "pure" and "cultivated" white society.[17] Running for Congress in 1894, he attacked opponent James C. C. Black for "promising to put negroes in the jury boxes." [18] Two years later he charged that Louisiana's Democratic Party had triumphed in a state election with black votes as any mere "Negro Party" could be expected to triumph.[19] In 1895 Watson expressed special alarm because the Governor of Virginia had invited a Massachusetts Negro to dinner. He speculated that the Governor, his white guests, and the Negro "all stretched companionable legs under the same mahogany, and forgot the toils of political war in a feast of brotherly love." [20] President Cleveland's policy of appointing black diplomats to "white countries" was equally reproachable, for the black appointees would enter white hotels, sit in white parlors, and eat at white people's tables.[21] Watson also denounced St. Louis innkeepers. During the Republican National Convention of 1896, he charged that they had allowed Negroes to dine "at the tables with White ladies." [22] At a Populist rally in Lincolnton, Georgia, the Atlanta *Constitution* reported that Watson's racism became so rabid that many Negroes left in disgust.[23]

Contending that Watson had made a sincere and genuine plea for biracial cooperation during the active years of the Populist crusade, Professor Woodward was therefore mistaken. He failed to note that the rebel's biracial pleas were often blandly phrased, that they were linked to racist qualifications, and that they were interspersed among overtly racist remarks. The man could not have represented a liberal "new departure" in white Southern racial thought. He was expedient, contradictory, confused, but above all, the victim of deep-seated racism.

II

Considering Watson's rhetoric during the 1890's and during other years as well, the striking thing about the man is the orthodox, tradi-

17. *People's Party Paper,* September 30, 1892; June 16, 1893.
18. Augusta *Chronicle,* November 22, 1894.
19. *People's Party Paper,* May 29, 1896.
20. *People's Party Paper,* May 22, 1895.
21. *People's Party Paper,* September 22, 1893; September 29, 1893; October 13, 1893.
22. *People's Party Paper,* June 19, 1896.
23. Atlanta *Constitution,* September 1, 1892.

tional quality of his mind. Professor Woodward's rebel rebelled against very little that white Southerners held dear, providing additional grounds to doubt Woodward's characterization of the man. Like Henry Watterson, Thomas Nelson Page, and a great many others, he was always a devout Southern nationalist, solidly committed to Southern interests above national interests. Dixie was the region of promise and potential. "I yield to no man in my profound regard for the integrity of Southern life," he wrote in 1893.[24] Two years later he pleaded with a Georgia audience: "As Southern men, let us think of the South, work for the South, live for the South." [25] Southern children must cease to "look abroad" for heroes and ideals, he warned in 1902.[26] Southerners had founded the national union; with the same creative vigor they would lead the nation out of current ills.[27] Virginian birth notwithstanding, Woodrow Wilson had betrayed the South. His *History of the American People* had neglected the South's great historic achievements.[28] It was necessary for Southerners to build upon those achievements as the true test of "Southern patriotism." [29]

Like Watterson and Page, Watson's Southern identity bound him to the dogma of local autonomy. Confident of the South's potentialities, he was sure that it could remedy its own peculiar problems. At the very least, Southerners could cope with them more adequately than scheming Yankees. Indeed, the South had quite properly seceded and gone to war in 1861 to assert the "universally acknowledged" principle of local self-government.[30] In the mid-1870's "the indomitable white men of the South rose up again amid the ashes of their homes to throw off an alien yoke and to assert the principle of home rule." [31] Again in the 1890's the "infamous" Lodge Federal Elections

24. *People's Party Paper,* February 3, 1893.

25. *People's Party Paper,* March 29, 1895.

26. Notes for a speech, April 25, 1902, Watson Papers, University of North Carolina.

27. Notes for a speech, "Imperialism and Democracy," 1904, Watson Papers, University of North Carolina.

28. Thomas E. Watson, *The Life and Times of Thomas Jefferson* (New York: D. Appleton & Co., 1903), pp. 85–86, footnote 1; Watson, *The Life and Times of Andrew Jackson* (Thomson, Georgia: Jeffersonian Publishing Company, 1917), p. 182.

29. *People's Party Paper,* December 20, 1895. For other remarks pointing to Watson's profound commitment to Southern nationalism, see *People's Party Paper,* September 9, 1892; March 22, 1895; July 31, 1896: Watson, ed., "History of Southern Oratory," in *The South in the Building of the Nation,* IX (Richmond: Southern Historical Publication Society, 1909), p. x; and Diary and Commonplace Book, 1871–1872, entry for August 12, 1871.

30. Watson, *Life and Speeches of Watson,* p. 304; Watson, *Bethany: A Story of the Old South* (New York: D. Appleton & Co., 1904), p. xi.

31. Watson, *Life and Speeches of Watson,* p. 253.

Bill posed the threat of outside intervention.[32] These threats were grave miscalculations; "outsiders must let us alone. We must work out our own salvation. In no other way can it be done. . . . Like all free people, we love home rule, and resent foreign compulsion of any sort." [33]

The Watterson and Page examples suggest that Southern national-ism and the concept of local autonomy were inextricably linked to the "Negro problem." Like the Louisville editor and the Cavalier novelist, Watson was confident that Southern civilization left to itself could remedy racial ills. But neither in the 1890's nor at any other time did he sharply delineate the broad philosophic principles of a racial solution. On some occasions Watson exalted the biracial character of Southern society. Negroes "are here and they are here to stay. They are vested with certain rights and they are the best labor the Southern sun ever saw in our fields." [34] Excellent in the cotton fields, blacks were permanent inhabitants of the Southland.[35] "Plans" to put "all negroes in one place and all whites in another" were absurd.[36] No true Southerner could think of parting from his black mammy.[37]

Yet throughout his life, the rebel also spoke in exclusionist terms. He was always apprehensive about interracial contact. "I do not prophesy that the white and black will war with each other until one is exterminated," he noted in 1872, "but I say if they live together in harmony, History will be searched in vain to furnish a similar ex-ample." [38] Throughout the 1890's, Watson periodically warned of the potential danger of intimate interracial association. Contacts be-tween the races in schools, churches, and other phases of "private" life meant discord.[39] By 1907 he had formulated a lucid philosophic state-ment of this position: there was an "antagonism between the races for which nature is responsible. To multiply points of contact is to increase the provocations for conflict." [40]

Like Brownlow, Watterson, and Page, Watson seemed to be pro-pounding an inconsistent racial ideology. He simultaneously praised and denounced interracial contact. But as the H. S. Doyle incident so well indicates, integration and segregation were not crucial to the

32. *People's Party Paper,* August 12, 1892.
33. *People's Party Paper,* September 16, 1892.
34. *People's Party Paper,* May 25, 1894.
35. *People's Party Paper,* July 13, 1894.
36. *People's Party Paper,* August 11, 1893.
37. Watson, *Bethany,* p. 14.
38. Notes for a speech, October 12, 1872, in Diary, 1872–1894.
39. See, e.g., *People's Party Paper,* September 2, 1892; May 25, 1894; July 13, 1894; June 19, 1896.
40. T. E. Watson, "Editorials," *Watson's Jeffersonian Magazine,* I, No. 5 (May, 1907), 440.

rebel's outlook. A Negro Populist, Doyle came to Watson in 1892 for protection from a lynch mob. Watson ordered Doyle to his "negro house," not to the quarters inhabited by the Watson family, and intimated that Doyle would get no protection but should leave the premises were he defiant, refusing to go to the backyard dwelling.[41] In this way, the rebel made it clear to Doyle that if he were a "good," obedient Negro and accepted his proper station in life, he could remain relatively close to white men, but as an "uppity" Negro he would be sent away. Blacks might have contact with whites if they obeyed white direction; otherwise, interracial contact was unacceptable.

In subsequent years, Watson concisely articulated the viewpoint implicit in the Doyle incident. If his basic racial thoughts had not been clearly expressed at that time, they certainly were by the first decade of the twentieth century. In 1907, he charged that "uppity" Negro behavior was at the heart of all current racial ills. "There are too many surly blacks" who defied white society by elbowing "white girls and ladies to one side on the sidewalk" and performing other obnoxious acts.[42] If defiant blacks are to remain "in the community I would make them behave . . . . And if they did not behave, they would, in some way, get out of that community." Obedient Negroes could be near whites but the defiant could not.[43] In 1908 Watson offered an even clearer statement of his racial position: "There is absolutely no place in this land for the arrogant, aggressive, school-spoilt Afro-American who wants to live without manual labor." [44] "Yes sir! We know Sambo, and we like him first rate, in his place. And he must stay there, too" or move on.[45] Negroes who knew their place could live within white society but those who reverted to their basic instincts and became assertive would have to be removed.

Quite obviously, Watson thought about race during as well as after the 1890's within the framework of the "Brownlow tradition." Docile, cooperative Negroes could associate with whites; this was doubtless what he meant when he praised the biracial nature of Southern society. But insolent, defiant blacks had to be isolated, for they could destroy white civilization. Like Brownlow, Watterson, and Page, dif-

---

41. Watson gave this account of the Doyle incident shortly after it occurred (*People's Party Paper*, October 28, 1892) and fourteen years later (Atlanta *Journal*, August 4, 1906).

42. T. E. Watson, "Editorials," *Watson's Jeffersonian Magazine*, I, No. 2 (February, 1907), 167.

43. Watson, *Life and Speeches of Watson*, p. 279.

44. T. E. Watson, "Editorials," *Watson's Jeffersonian Magazine*, II, No. 4 (April, 1908), 166.

45. Thomas E. Watson, *Socialists and Socialism* (Thomson, Georgia: Jeffersonian Press, 1910), p. 17.

ferential segregation represented the racial policy that he intended to pursue. If the other men stood for a Southern racial orthodoxy, Watson was one of its chief adherents.

III

Deeply racist throughout his life, a devout Southern nationalist, a proponent of local autonomy, and an adherent of the "Brownlow tradition," Tom Watson's mind simply did not operate along the lines that Professor Woodward outlined. Asserting that Watson seriously considered the aspirations of black people during the early 1890's, Woodward misappraised the anti-Negro assumptions that contoured the man's reflections from youth to old age. Only gross distortion results if one overlooks or de-emphasizes the profoundly racist character of Watson's mind. Therefore, it is necessary to transcend the Woodward level of analysis and determine whether Watson, within the context of his deeply racist and rather orthodox ideology, had made a distinctive contribution to the Southern search for a racial solution.

All of his adult life, Watson was impressed with the need for a genuine, workable solution to the South's "Negro problem." Home rule was not enough. Even differential segregation was no cure-all, for the concept could be erroneously implemented. Searching for ways to effectively remove only defiant Negroes from white society, Watson reasoned from an historical perspective. Thoroughly mastering Macaulay, Prescott, Gibbon, Abbott's *Lives of Napoleon*, and Alexander Stephens' *Constitutional View of the Late War Between the States* by the age of fifteen[46] and then going on to write several histories and biographies of his own, he could hardly think along other lines. Like Thomas Nelson Page, he perceived the present only as it emerged from the past. But whereas historical orientation had allowed Page to glory in the Old South as an escape from contemporary realities, it made current racial ills all the more glaring for Watson. As he saw matters, the Negro had "practiced continence and was but slightly contaminated by venereal disease" under slavery but had become "rotten with it now and the constant deterioration is glaringly evident."[47] While the black man had worked regularly and efficiently

---

46. William W. Brewton, *The Life of Thomas E. Watson* (Atlanta: William Brewton, 1926), pp. 42–44.

47. Watson, *Socialists and Socialism*, p. 10. Watson was not alone among Southern whites in the belief that blacks had generally been stricken by venereal disease. It is possible that this notion fortified the exclusionist strain of thought within the "agrarian rebel" and many others. If the Negro was contaminated by an infectious disease, one could conclude that he had to be kept at a distance from white society.

before the war, he had since become a shiftless and careless vaga-
bond.[48] Under the blessings of the "peculiar institution" he had lived
in tidy little cabins; after emancipation he moved into the "big
house" of his former master and allowed the place to decline into
squalor. Guano sacks served as windows and the pretty picket fences
that surrounded the house were converted into kindling wood.[49]

For Watson, the lesson was unmistakable. Blacks were basically wild
African savages lacking in morals, culture, or discipline, given to can-
nibalism and voodoo, and indulging in sexual excess.[50] Their animalistic propensities had to be controlled by white discipline.[51] With the
demise of slavery the savage Negro had re-emerged: "Back, back into
barbarism, voodooism, human sacrifice, social and political anarchy
they have plunged . . . ."[52] Since emancipation, "no city in the
South can have a quiet election or a joyful Christmas . . . . Every
day the traveller is robbed or murdered by his slave, and the shrieks
of violated innocence arise to heavens . . . ."[53] Thus emancipation
represented a "sudden injection into the body politic of a horde of
black savages to create, in public service, the eternal 'Nigger Question' and to overshadow the social world with the ever-present terror
of 'the Black Peril'."[54]

Reasoning along these historical lines, Watson concluded that unless white civilization developed an institution for racial control as
effective as slavery had been, black savagery would overwhelm it. An
adequate replacement for slavery would give whites the machinery to
implement differential segregation. It would allow white civilization
to keep untamed black savages isolated. Only in this way could
whites be assured of an entirely deferent, servile Negro population.

Early in the 1890's when his Southern agrarian crusade was at high
tide, Watson intimated that Southern Populists rather than Watter-
sonian "conservatives" were most capable of forging an institutional
replacement for slavery. The Populist Party itself would provide the
replacement. "It offers the only solution of the color question," he
publicly proclaimed. Like the slave system, the party encouraged

48. Watson, *Life and Times of Watson*, pp. 273–74.

49. *The South in the Building of the Nation*, IX, 468.

50. *People's Party Paper*, October 25, 1895; T. E. Watson, "Editorials," *Watson's Magazine*, I, No. 4 (June, 1905), 394; IV, No. 2 (April, 1906), 165; Watson, *Thomas Jefferson*, pp. 67, 94–95; Watson, *The Roman Catholic Hierachy* (Thomson, Georgia: Jeffersonian Publishing Company, 1912), p. 162; Watson, *Is Roman Catholicism in America Identical with That of the Popes?* (Thomson, Georgia: Jeffersonian Publishing Company, 1914), p. 98.

51. T. E. Watson, "Editorials," *Watson's Magazine*, IV, No. 2 (April, 1906), 165.

52. T. E. Watson, "Editorials," *Watson's Magazine*, I, No. 4 (June, 1905), 393.

53. Diary, 1872–1894, entry for October 12, 1872. As this quotation indicates, Watson continued to equate "slave" with "Negro," emancipation notwithstanding. In this respect, he was similar to Brownlow.

54. Watson, *Jackson*, pp. 205–6.

black and white to "dwell side by side in political harmony instead of political discord . . . ."[55] By drawing Negroes into a white political institution, the Populist Party was offering a new mechanism for control of a savage race.

As he developed this idea, Watson took care to distinguish the Populist Party from the slave system. Unlike that "benevolent" system of racial control, Populism was unconcerned with educational and religious elevation of the savage race, but would take the Negro as he was and ensure that he behaved properly.[56] The antebellum racial experience had proven that blacks could not be elevated, for they were and always would be weak, depraved animals, "ignorant, helpless, and poverty cursed in whose ears the clank of chains have scarcely ceased to sound . . . ."[57] Nonetheless, the Negro was at least "an imitative bird."[58] If he could not be elevated, he could at least be controlled, and he was most susceptible to the controls that political institutions could promote. "We [white Southern Populists] can take the negro to dinner or shoot him away from the polls with equal dexterity and gusto," Watson maintained.[59] If the malleable Negro were fully integrated into the political process, as Southern Populists proposed, he could be controlled much as he had been under slavery. The white race had proven particularly adept at manipulating political institutions. Through their great political skills, whites could draw upon the vast economic resources, education, military might, and religious heritage of the civilized race. They could muster every resource white civilization had at its command, put it to maximum use in the political process, and ultimately force the easily manipulated Negro to toe the mark and defer to white direction or be expelled from white society. If Populists invited blacks into politics, it was only to dominate them the more.[60]

When Watson commented on the politics of racial control, he left a vital question unanswered. If Southern Populists brought blacks into the political process, how would they control Negroes whom they won over? How would they manipulate politicized blacks so that they would either defer to white direction or stay away from white society? Watson's description of the H. S. Doyle affair shortly after it had taken place is again suggestive. Doyle was allegedly told to "take up quarters in a negro house on the lot" of the Watson residence in Thomson, Georgia. The black Populist at first objected to "confinement" in a

55. Thomas E. Watson, *The People's Party Campaign Book, 1892, Not a Revolt: It Is a Revolution* (Washington, D. C.: National Watchman Publishing Company, 1892), p. 350.
56. *People's Party Paper*, May 18, 1894.
57. *People's Party Paper*, July 7, 1893.
58. *People's Party Paper*, September 16, 1892; June 19, 1896.
59. *People's Party Paper*, June 28, 1895.
60. *People's Party Paper*, September 16, 1892; July 7, 1893; September 1, 1893.

"negro house" and to being barred from the Watson family mansion, but Watson was adamant and Doyle gave in: "He is now on Mr. Watson's lot. He is going to stay there." The Populist Party would see to that.[61] A few months before the Doyle incident, Watson had spoken to the blacks of Thomson:

> On my plantation there are some black men working to-day who were my grandfather's slaves, and the foreman on my grandfather's farm was my foreman, and remained there in that position until the old man was too feeble to hold the hoe,—to lead the gang. Does not that speak well for the justice with which I have tried to treat your people? Do you not know that every colored man living on my place feels just as secure when I pass my word for anything as if I had drawn up the bond and signed the paper? [62]

Less than two years after the Doyle affair, Watson stressed the importance of black agricultural labor in the South: "they are the best labor that the Southern sun ever saw in our fields." [63] Interpreted in the light of his account of the Doyle episode, Watson's praise of black labor and his laudatory account of Negro life on the Watson plantation are quite suggestive. He obviously cherished the concept of an old plantation Negro working diligently in the white man's fields precisely as the Negro had labored under slavery. Supported by the Populist Party, he had guided Doyle toward those fields; he had forced Doyle out of the white man's mansion and into the "negro house." With the rise of Populism, he had therefore acquired considerable leverage over blacks. He had been able to resist the Negro's demand for equality and to force the Negro to assume his "proper" station in life. At Populist rallies he had even succeeded in getting blacks to raise their hands in support of a party program that explicitly condemned social equality.[64] Hence, behind his abstract arguments for biracial politics, Watson probably envisioned the forceful restoration of docile, obedient, slave-like behavior. The Populist Party would give whites concerted, systematically directed power to make blacks toe the mark for the first time since emancipation. This seemed to be the core of Watson's politics of racial control.

Clearly Watson, the so-called rebel, placed a high premium upon

61. *People's Party Paper*, October 28, 1892. In the Atlanta *Journal*, August 4, 1906, Watson provided a nearly identical account of the Doyle incident.

62. *People's Party Paper*, August 12, 1892. Watson's language here bore a striking resemblance to the rhetoric used by Henry Hughes, the antebellum proslavery theoretician, as Hughes developed his concept of "Warranteeism."

63. *People's Party Paper*, May 25, 1894. See *People's Party Paper*, July 13, 1894, for a strikingly similar remark.

64. Atlanta *Constitution*, May 17, 1894; *People's Party Paper*, November 3, 1893, May 25, 1894.

the Populist experiment in racial regulation. Other ends, particularly the restoration of rural prosperity and the overthrow of Bourbon Democratic political rule, may have been equally crucial justifications for his Populist experiment, but this does not preclude a link between Populist politics and resolution of the "Negro problem." Watson's economic and political goals and his racial objectives were not mutually exclusive. Negroes within party ranks meant votes; they represented increased political leverage against the Bourbon power structure. Increased political power could, in turn, engender broad economic reforms. Moreover, because a politics of racial control would increase white control over blacks, it could reduce the cost of black labor. Effectively intimidated, blacks would not bargain for higher wages or better working conditions, thus lowering production costs and raising profits for whites who relied upon black workers.

It is difficult to determine whether Southern Populists ever tested Watson's plan for a politics of racial control. During the first decade of the twentieth century when Populism had ceased to be a viable force in Southern life, Watson maintained that he and other Populists had successfully induced servile Negro behavior. "We told those colored people whenever we spoke to them," he reminisced in 1904, "that we do not favor social equality; that we could not surrender the guardianship and keeping of our civilization to any other race whatsoever . . . that we are going to keep control of it in our hands for our benefit and for others . . . . We have said to them [Negroes] . . . when we took hold of you, you were savages from Africa, you knew nothing; we taught you all you know. . . . Social equality? No. Political equality? No." [65] Again, three years later, Watson reflected nostalgically upon the Populist experiment in biracialism: "The negro Populists gave us no trouble whatever. They were docile, they made no demands." Indeed, Watson concluded, "We had him [the Negro] under complete control and meant to keep him so." [66]

Remarks like these must be suspect, for they were made during the first decade of the twentieth century—perhaps the most intense period of anti-Negro hysteria in Southern history. In such a climate, Watson stood to gain politically by claiming that he had discovered how to solve the "Negro problem" a decade earlier—that he had found the way to control black behavior. Unfortunately, we may never know whether his after-the-fact appraisal was an accurate one. In 1903, historian John Spencer Bassett argued that Watson's concept of a politics of racial control had been implemented; Southern Populists had

65. Notes for a speech, November 19, 1904, Watson Papers, University of North Carolina.

66. T. E. Watson, "Editorials," *Watson's Jeffersonian Magazine,* I, No. 11 (November, 1907), 1036.

forced their black associates to be "quietly disposed." [67] Decades later another eminent historian, T. Harry Williams, came to the same conclusion. Lecturing at Mercer University, Watson's *alma mater*, Williams observed that racist Populists like Watson had forced Negroes into minor and segregated roles.[68] In a recent article, Professor Robert Saunders concluded with much the same observation.[69] Yet Saunders, like Bassett and Williams, did not prove his case. Available evidence on the overt behavior of white Southern populists toward Negroes is simply too scant for meaningful conclusions. We know, for example, that blacks had been excluded from the antecedent Southern Alliance, that Negro votes were manipulated at a Populist organizational meeting, that a Populist national committeeman acknowledged that he knew how to "handle the negro," and that certain blacks feared the rowdyism of the Populist rank and file.[70] But these bits and pieces do not really tell us whether Watson's concept of Populist politics as a means of racial control was acted upon in a systematic way. For this reason, the rebel's real importance lies primarily as a racial ideologist. In a vague, imprecise way, he had suggested that political manipulation could replace slavery as a way of restraining black savagery. Concerns that may have been more central—the overthrow of Bourbon Democratic rule and economic relief for the Southern agrarian—certainly commanded a great deal of Watson's attention and may explain why he devoted so little time to the development of his racial solution. But he was perhaps the only significant white Southern racial ideologist in the postbellum decades to theorize about politics as a mechanism for racial regulation, and this fact looms above all else in any evaluation of Tom Watson and Southern racial ideology. This was Watson's genuine "new departure" in race relations.

The concept of Populist politics as a mechanism for the control of blacks contained obvious political and economic benefits, offering as

67. John Spencer Bassett, "Stirring Up the Fires of Race Antipathy," *South Atlantic Quarterly*, II, No. 4 (October, 1903), 302.

68. T. Harry Williams, *Romance and Realism in Southern Politics* (Baton Rouge: Louisiana State University Press, 1966), p. 53.

69. Robert Saunders, "Southern Populists and the Negro 1893–1895," *Journal of Negro History*, LIV, No. 3 (July, 1969), 240–61. Saunders differed from Bassett and Williams in one important respect. He argued that the Southern Populists, by competing with the Democrats for black votes, made both parties somewhat less racist than would otherwise have been the case.

70. Atlanta *Constitution*, February 26, 1892; Columbus *Advocate*, n.d., as quoted in the Topeka *Call*, July 24, 1892; *People's Party Paper*, August 12, 1892; *National Economist*, September 17, 1892; Helen M. Blackburn, "The Populist Party in the South, 1890–1898" (Master's thesis, Howard University, 1941), p. 46; John D. Hicks, *The Populist Revolt: A History of the Farmer's Alliance and the People's Party* (Lincoln: University of Nebraska Press, 1961), pp. 114–15.

well a potential remedy for racial problems. It also provided benefits of a more personal sort. Believing that black savages could be restrained by white civilization through its Populist representatives, Watson could make out a very special case for treating Negroes as he saw fit. The black savage–white civilization dichotomy could allow Watson to break from the repressions of white society and behave in any mode or manner before black people. However crudely he behaved, he was assured by his whiteness that he was civilized. By linking this savagery–civilization dichotomy to the white Populist who, above all others, was destined to restrain black savagery, Watson doubly protected himself from perceiving the true nature of his racial conduct. As the leading light of Southern Populism, Watson could order a frightened black man, H. S. Doyle, to his "negro house," he could brag of the pleasures of "shooting" blacks away from the polls, and he could lose control of himself in a barrage of vicious Negrophobe rhetoric before the blacks of Lincolnton without experiencing excessive pangs of guilt over his vicious conduct. The concept of a Populist politics of racial control encouraged him to believe that no matter how crudely he behaved toward Negroes, his actions as the chosen representative of white civilization were always justified.

In his introduction to *The Story of France* (1899), Watson revealed the importance of the Populist racial mission as a rationalization for personal conduct. He claimed "that civilization is but skin deep and that the savage lurks within us yet." [71] Earlier in the 1890's when the Populist experiment had been viable, Watson had not spoken in this way. He had never verbalized doubts about the superficial quality of white civilization in general and about his own civilization in particular. By 1899, however, the rebel had acknowledged that Populism was no longer a meaningful force in Southern life and had also admitted that a man's skin merely covered a savage interior. No longer able to argue that he was participating in a bold Populist racial crusade to promote white civilization, he may have started to perceive the reality of his racial conduct. He may have become conscious of the savage hidden within himself, white skin notwithstanding.

IV

In the late 1890's Watson began to repudiate politics as a mode of racial control. Still a man of some influence in his native Georgia, he became the state's foremost advocate of proposals to remove Negroes from political life. During Georgia's 1906 gubernatorial campaign he

---

71. Thomas E. Watson, *The Story of France: From Earliest Times to the Consulate of Napoleon Bonaparte* (New York: Dodd, Mead, & Co., 1926), I, xv–xvi.

forced Democratic candidate Hoke Smith to commit himself to Negro disfranchisement by pledging, in return, to deliver the Populist vote to the Smith camp.[72] Smith was elected and Negroes in Georgia soon lost the franchise. By firmly supporting a Democrat, Watson symbolically acknowledged that Populism had ceased to be an independent political movement.

Publicly, Watson tried to explain why he had abandoned biracial politics and had come to favor disfranchisement. The "politicians keep the negro question alive in the South to perpetuate their hold on public office," he charged.[73] A candidate merely had to Negro-bait his opponent and to link that opponent with potential "Negro domination" and fearful whites invariably elected the candidate. Unqualified men thereby rose to power and the political process became unresponsive to the social and economic ills of Southern society.[74] Only if blacks were deprived of voting rights, Watson concluded, could the situation be ameliorated. With no black electorate, political opportunists would find it extremely difficult to accuse sincere Southern statesmen of befriending Negroes.[75]

Explaining his decision to abandon biracialism and to campaign for disfranchisement in these terms, Watson revealed only part of his motivation. Another and more complex reason for his dramatic change in racial posture is detectable from his perception of his opportunistic political opponents. On one level, Watson believed that Democratic Party "regulars" (Bourbons) in the South were the opportunists. He felt that the Bourbons had destroyed his biracial Populist venture through false and irresponsible charges that equated Populism with "Negro domination." And though they had attacked him for appealing to a black electorate during the tumultuous 1890's, they subsequently refused to commit themselves unequivocally to black disfranchisement. Only one conclusion was possible. Bourbons wanted Negroes to vote so that they could continue to exploit the issue of "Negro domination." They were deliberately confusing and enlarging the "Negro problem." [76]

72. Dewey W. Grantham, Jr., *Hoke Smith and the Politics of the New South* (Baton Rouge: Louisiana State University Press, 1958), pp. 139–40; C. Vann Woodward, *The Strange Career of Jim Crow*, 2nd rev. ed. (New York: Oxford University Press, Inc., 1966), p. 90.

73. Quoted in William A. Sinclair, *The Aftermath of Slavery* (Boston: Small, Maynard & Co., 1904), p. 341.

74. Notes for a speech, August 6, 1908, Watson Papers, University of North Carolina.

75. T. E. Watson, "Editorials," *Watson's Jeffersonian Magazine*, II, No. 4 (April, 1908), 166.

76. Notes for a speech, November 19, 1904, Watson Papers, University of North Carolina. See also Watson, *Watson's Jeffersonian Magazine*, I, No. 11 (November, 1907), 1036.

On occasion, as he thought about the problem of political expediency in greater depth, Watson concluded that though the Southern Bourbons were irresponsible, they were not the major culprits. They were mere pawns of the national Democratic Party. Alton B. Parker and William Jennings Bryan, its spokesmen, were the real opportunists of the new century. For black votes, Parker was ready to endorse "social equality." [77] Bryan was considerably more dangerous, for he had expediently refused to condemn Nebraska's integrated school system, even though miscegenation in that state was common.[78] Moreover, Bryan had promised blacks that he would try to remedy *all* their grievances if they voted Democratic.[79] Bidding for Negro support, Bryan was "Africanizing" the Democratic Party and "bringing about the very worst possible danger to the South as well as the entire United States." [80]

Republicans were no better. Like Democrats, they were unconcerned with controlling Negro conduct. Georgia Republicans, who would do anything for black votes, practically allowed Negroes to dominate the state party organization. Incontrovertible "negro influence" upon national Republican leadership explained Theodore Roosevelt's dinner with Booker T. Washington.[81]

Watson occasionally pushed his analysis of political opportunism even further. While Bourbons were puppets of unprincipled national politicians, both Bourbons and national politicians were agents for an Eastern plutocracy. Heirs of the Hamiltonian tradition of special privilege, plutocrats employed politicians to control the nation's agricultural regions, the South and the West, for their own economic benefit. Through these agents, they usurped rich raw materials in the South and West and left hard-working farmers of both regions in abject poverty. Clearly, the Rothschilds, the Belmonts, and the Morgans were out to exploit the South economically but would do no more. They were unconcerned with resolving the all-important "Negro problem." [82]

77. Watson, *Life and Speeches of Watson*, p. 212.

78. T. E. Watson, "Editorials," *Watson's Jeffersonian Magazine*, III, No. 1 (January, 1909), 16–17. See also Notes for a speech, August 6, 1908, Watson Papers, University of North Carolina.

79. Watson, *Life and Speeches of Watson*, p. 307.

80. Thomas E. Watson, "Why I Am Still a Populist," *American Review of Reviews*, XXXVIII (September, 1908), 306.

81. *People's Party Paper*, June 26, 1896; Thomas E. Watson to G. T. Bowers, April 20, 1921, Watson Papers, University of North Carolina; Watson, *Watson's Jeffersonian Magazine*, I, No. 11 (November, 1907), 1036; Watson, *Life and Speeches of Watson*, p. 212.

82. Thomas E. Watson, *Political and Economic Handbook* (Atlanta: Telegram Publishing Co., 1908), pp. 12, 184; Notes for a speech, September 1 and November

Watson's persistent and anxious concern over opportunism suggests that by the early twentieth century he had lost hope in the political process. He knew the plutocracy controlled events. Since politicians used black voters merely to serve Eastern entrepreneurs, and since no viable Populist Party survived to resist this tactic, it followed that black voting threatened the white Southern farmer. Hence, Negro disfranchisement was imperative. Yet disfranchisement was no panacea, for it would not restore responsible politics in the South. Disfranchisement might make it more difficult for the plutocrats and their agents to control Southern politics, but it would not arrest the political power of the plutocracy. Populism represented the only substantial challenge to plutocratic rule, but the party had become weak and directionless. All hope was gone.

Sensing his own impotence in the face of plutocratic opportunism, Watson tended to moralize. If he could not overturn the plutocracy and its political agents, he could at least claim moral superiority over them. If he had little power—if his rantings would not change existing political and economic realities—the rebel could at least prove to himself and to others that he had retained his honor amidst the corruption and chaos of urbanizing, industrializing America. If he was no longer at the helm of a Populist crusade to resolve the "Negro problem" and other modern ills, he was at least a moral man. Watson charged that the plutocracy consisted of "cold," "cruel," and "vile" men who preached brotherhood while exploiting Southern farmers. They were "despots," "thieves," and "lawless corporation plunderers." [83] They employed "mere politicians," "false accusers," and "desperate tacticians" to do their dirty work.[84] By contrast, he knew "that character should outweigh the dollar." [85] He and other Southerners who had participated in the Populist crusade against the plutocracy had always been "principled" and "devoted" men, "guardians of civilization," "liberators," and more generally, Southerners of "conviction." They were brave combatants against the sinister conspiracy to impoverish the Southern agrarian.[86]

19, 1904, Watson Papers, University of North Carolina; Watson, *Life and Speeches of Watson*, pp. 130, 271–72; Watson to R. S. Arlington, November 11, 1905, Watson Papers; Brewton, *Watson*, p. 400.

83. See, e.g., Watson, *Political and Economic Handbook*, pp. 12, 184; Notes for a speech, September 1, 1904, Watson Papers, University of North Carolina.

84. Notes for a speech, November 19, 1904, Watson Papers, University of North Carolina; Watson, *Watson's Jeffersonian Magazine*, III, No. 1 (January, 1909), 16–17; Watson, *Life and Speeches of Watson*, p. 307; Sinclair, *Aftermath of Slavery*, p. 341.

85. Watson, *Life and Speeches*, p. 204.

86. See, e.g., Watson, *Watson's Jeffersonian Magazine*, I, No. 11 (November, 1907), 1035–36; Notes for a speech, November 19, 1904, Watson Papers, University of North Carolina.

Strange as it may seem, Watson had little to say about living conditions of Southern farmers. He displayed little genuine concern about rural poverty, and one can understand why. The rebel was no penniless agrarian. Clad in a large felt hat with long, well-groomed hair, he was instead a very prosperous planter-attorney. By 1908 there were forty-four tenants on his large Georgia plantation.[87] Such wealth suggests that moralizing did more than to compensate Watson for his political impotence. Moralistic rhetoric may have allowed him to hide from himself and from others both the fact that he had little visceral sympathy for those whose cause he purported to champion and the fact that he was not really an agrarian rebel. Constantly exalting his own morality as champion of the lowly farmer, no one could say that he was insincere, that with economic success he had lost touch with the torments and aspirations of those he defended. No one could suspect that the one-time poor farm boy had become another Henry Grady, Southern entrepreneur. Had he ever let his guard down and de-emphasized his moral crusade, others might have sensed that the moralizer was actually the hypocrite. For a man who had abandoned all hope in a Populist politics of racial control and who felt that he had nothing now except his professed principles, such accusations might have been unbearable.

Hence, though Watson had explained his conversion from biracial politics to a program of Negro disfranchisement as a pragmatic move against corrupt politicians, this did not reveal his more fundamental motives. He was only superficially concerned with defeating the Eastern entrepreneur and fostering issue-oriented politics through Negro disfranchisement. When he thought of the problem more deeply, he knew that disfranchisement would not significantly alter the quality of political life—that the plutocracy would continue to control events. Though he might continue to run for and even win political office from time to time, he had resigned himself to minimal political influence; what support he could win did not really matter. Much more than political power, Watson was out to affirm his own morality and to allay guilt for having transcended rural poverty. If he could not do anything of social and political consequence as he had tried to do in the 1890's, he could at least campaign for the integrity of Tom Watson, agrarian rebel—the antithesis of the exploitative entrepreneur. If he could no longer picture himself as the bold leader of white civilization in the crusade against black barbarism, the persona of the moral man would have to do.

87. Francis M. Wilhoit, "An Interpretation of Populism's Impact on the Georgia Negro," *Journal of Negro History*, LII, No. 2 (April, 1967), 121, note 14. See also the *People's Party Paper*, August 7, 1896, for an informative analysis of Watson's expensive dress.

V

Watson's increasing propensity to moralize after the demise of Populism explains more than his abandonment of biracial politics. It reveals the quality of his personal relations with other whites. Though the rebel equated the plutocracy and its political agents with opportunism while he equated Southern farmers with morality, neither equation applied in all cases. There were a number of important exceptions, for moral men could be tricked into compliance with the wishes of Eastern entrepreneurs. Though Democrat James Vardaman of Mississippi had entertained bitter feelings toward the Populist Party throughout the 1890's, Watson felt that the "great white chief" belonged to the virtuous "class" of white persons: "He thinks for himself and is not afraid to say what he believes. He has convictions. . . ." [88] And though Henry Watterson belonged to the Tilden-Cleveland-Parker Eastern Democratic establishment and detested the Populist crusade, Watson classified him among the virtuous. "I glory in the courage in which you stand out for your own convictions," Watson told "Marse Henry." [89] However, though Henry Grady's political affiliations, ideals, and tactics closely paralleled Watterson's, Watson chastised Grady on moral grounds. The "New South" philosopher had deliberately de-emphasized the Southern farmer's problems. Worse yet, Grady had glorified the South when he spoke in the region, but in the North he had praised the Yankee triumph at Appomattox.[90] Thus, Watson attacked Grady on the same grounds as he had criticized the plutocracy and its agents. All were immoral men.

Clearly, Watson perceived an intense conflict within white Southern society. Brownlow, Watterson, and Page had also detected a conflict, but in contrast to these other men, the conflict that Watson perceived did not run along strict class lines. Like the others, he sensed a clash between men of economic power and social status on the one hand and the "lower class of white persons" on the other. And like the others, Watson took sides. He joined Brownlow and supported the poor whites, while Watterson and Page aligned themselves with the upper class. But his willingness to classify a man like Watterson, an agent of the plutocracy, within the principled segment of South-

88. T. E. Watson, "Editorials," *Watson's Jeffersonian Magazine*, I, No. 4 (April, 1907), 443.

89. Thomas E. Watson to Henry Watterson, November 22, 1907, Watterson Papers, Library of Congress.

90. Diary 1872–1894, entry for August 30, 1888, Watson Papers, University of North Carolina; Woodward, *Watson*, pp. 126–28.

ern society suggested that personal morality meant more to Watson than political affiliation or economic status. Unlike the others, he was actually arguing that morality lay at the roots of conflict within white society, and his motives were obvious. As a member of the upper class but a champion of the lower, he could not have applied traditional socio-economic definitions to Southern society. Only by de-emphasizing economics and stressing morality could he avoid having to justify his own wealth on the one hand and the poverty of those he purportedly championed on the other. Only through moralistic sentiment could he allay the guilt that any attempt to understand this disparity would provoke.

Though the example of Tom Watson suggests that certain Southern whites had to perceive conflict within white society from a highly moralistic framework, it suggests even more about the nature of that conflict. During the early 1890's, Watson devoted considerable intellectual and psychic energy to the Populist experiment in racial control. But with the demise of an effective People's Party in the middle 1890's, his orientation changed drastically. Realizing that he had become powerless, he abandoned his crusade to remedy the "Negro problem." Knowing that he could do little, he lost interest in saving the South from the "wild new Negro." He found greater satisfaction in affirming his own moral purity and allaying guilt by presenting the farmer's complaint against the plutocracy. For this reason, his mind was almost exclusively geared to the tensions within white society. Occasional and admittedly vicious Negrophobe rhetoric notwithstanding, the race issue had become secondary. Verbal warfare against whites seemed to give him the sense of self-esteem that his Populist crusade to control black barbarism had formerly provided. Brownlow, Watterson, and Page had also slighted the "Negro problem" as they became embroiled in conflict within white society, but Watson's change in emphasis was more dramatic. It underlined a tendency in postbellum Southern thought that the experiences of the other proponents of the "Brownlow tradition" had evidenced. There seemed to be a distinct connection between tensions among whites and racial ideology. The tensions pressed down upon certain influential Southerners to the point where they ceased to be attentive to the "Negro problem." In part, this explains why the "problem" was never solved, much less understood.

But though conflicts among whites seemed to detract from the concern of certain Southerners for the "Negro problem," both sprang from a common source—a nervous, status-oriented white society. "Conservatives" like Watterson and Page confirmed their sense of cultivation and civilization—the notion that they were the "natural" leaders of the South—by identifying lower-class whites and Negroes alike as crude, lowly barbarians. Recognizing his own powerlessness with the demise of Populism, Watson could not continue to sense his worth and refinement by charging that he was leading a successful crusade to uplift the barbaric black race. Rather, he tried to retain his sense of social and personal eminence by challenging the morality of white plutocrats and their political cohorts. First the Negro and later the upper-class Caucasian gave Watson scapegoats to affirm his self-esteem. Like the others, he exploited distinctions in white society much as he had exploited racial distinctions—to avoid recognizing the crudity and duplicity of his own conduct.

Chapter Six

Heresy in the New South: The Case
for George W. Cable

Perhaps no one better expressed the racial position of the White Savage than the eminently respectable Thomas Pearce Bailey, Dean of the Department of Education and Professor of Psychology and Education at the University of Mississippi. His widely publicized *Race Orthodoxy in the South* (1914) was designed to articulate and defend white Southern efforts to resolve the "Negro problem." Bailey charged that the search for docile Negro behavior was basic to white Southern racial thought: "Individual Southerners look with approbation and sympathy upon the economic improvement of certain negroes, always provided these negroes are 'white men's negroes,' and 'know their place.' As soon as these negroes begin to 'put on style' and express their social *dignity,* even if this exhibition is confined strictly to their own race, mutterings and murmurings begin." [1] Bailey went on to explain how white Southerners hoped to secure docile Negro behavior. *"Contact"* between the races could only take place "on a well-defined basis of 'white supremacy.'" "Assertive" Negro behavior would not be tolerated wherever "contact" was maintained.[2] This was the formula of differential segregation—the essence of the "Brownlow tradition."

Professor Bailey went on to describe and defend several corollaries to differential segregation. One of the most fundamental, the notion of local autonomy, had been systematically developed by Watterson, popularized by Page, and defended by Watson. Since "only Southerners understand the negro question," others must "let the South settle the negro question." [3] Additional corollaries pointed vaguely to Watson's politics of racial control, particularly those warning against "political equality" and suggesting that "in matters of civil

1. Thomas Pearce Bailey, *Race Orthodoxy in the South and Other Aspects of the Negro Question* (New York: Neale Publishing Co., 1914), p. 30. Emphasis added.
2. Bailey, *Race Orthodoxy,* p. 41. Emphasis added.
3. Bailey, *Race Orthodoxy,* p. 93.

rights and legal adjustment" white and black must "co-exist" through white dominance.[4]

If Bailey was correct—if these were the dominant tenets in postbellum Southern racial thought—then Brownlow, Watterson, Page, and Watson had articulated the racial creed of their region. Among the most influential racial theorists in the South, they were important because they enunciated and clarified notions that were dear to many Southern whites.

George W. Cable was one of the few whites of any renown who did not seem to subscribe to this orthodoxy. The New Orleans novelist, historian, and essayist continually argued against racial theories designed to debase black Southerners. When Lura Beam described her travels through the South during the early years of the twentieth century, she recalled that the "only writer I knew about who stood up to the Southern Inquisition after publishing his opinions about race was George W. Cable." [5] Blacks of many persuasions, from Booker T. Washington to W. E. B. DuBois, applauded Cable as the great crusader for Negro rights.[6] William B. Edwards, black president of Connecticut's Sumner Union League, told him that Negroes throughout the nation "look upon you as another Sumner, the founder of all our civil rights." [7]

While these remarks suggest that Cable was a heretic on the race question, one wonders how much this was really the case. The thoroughgoing racism of the men of the "Brownlow tradition" and the propensity toward violent treatment of dissenters below Mason-Dixon makes one wonder whether it was possible for a white Southerner to openly and meaningfully depart from racial orthodoxy. Perhaps more than any other Caucasian of note in the New South, Cable helps to resolve this question. Appraising the quality and degree of his heresy, one can determine whether it was possible for a white Southerner to deviate substantially from the orthodox response to the "Negro problem."

II

In *The Souls of Black Folk* (1903), W. E. B. DuBois suggested a

4. Bailey, *Race Orthodoxy*, p. 93.
5. Lura Beam, *He Called Them by the Lightning: A Teacher's Odyssey in the Negro South, 1908–1919* (Indianapolis: The Bobbs-Merrill Co., Inc., 1967), p. 74.
6. See, e.g., Booker T. Washington to Frederick C. Jones, December 21, 1885; W. E. B. DuBois to George W. Cable, February 23, 1890; Daniel Alexander Payne to George W. Cable, September 4, 1885; J. B. Wells to George W. Cable, April 28, 1888; G. N. Grisham, W. W. Yates, and J. D. Burser to George W. Cable, December 13, 1888; R. S. Lovingood to George W. Cable, August 28, 1890. All of these letters are found within the Cable Papers, Tulane University.
7. William B. Edwards to George W. Cable, March 25, 1887, Cable Papers, Tulane University.

criterion for separating heresy from orthodoxy. Very few white Southerners considered Negroes as individuals, he charged, for most regarded them from the perspective of group stereotypes.[8] Brownlow,
Watterson, Page, and Watson certainly did. To them, every Negro
was either a docile Sambo or a defiant "nigger." They saw no blacks
as complex human beings with personalities that defied simplistic
labels. Even allegedly liberal Southern whites like J. L. M. Curry,
Atticus G. Haygood, Lewis Harvey Blair, and Joel Chandler Harris
conceived of blacks in stereotypes. Negroes were child-like; none could
develop beyond the status of enlightened subordinates.[9] But Cable
could not think along these lines. He had been deeply impressed
with the abilities and the deportment of several Negro intellectuals,
particularly Charles Waddell Chesnutt, George Washington Williams,
and Carter G. Woodson.[10] Sensing that few whites were so cultivated,
he concluded that all Negroes could not be inferior: "It is widely admitted that we [whites] are the vastly superior race in everything—
as a race. But is every colored man inferior to every white man in
character, intelligence, and property? . . . Are there no poor and
irresponsible whites?" [11] Increasingly, Cable maintained, intelligent
white Southerners were learning that individual blacks were "like the
individuals of the white and other races, as possessing among themselves various and widely differing powers of moral and intellectual

8. W. E. B. DuBois, *The Souls of Black Folk: Essays and Sketches* (Greenwich,
Conn.: Crest Books, 1961), pp. 125–26.

9. See, e.g., Charles William Dabney, *Universal Education in the South*
(Chapel Hill: University of North Carolina Press, 1936), II, 127; Atticus G.
Haygood, *Our Brother in Black: His Freedom and His Future* (Nashville:
Southern Methodist Publishing House, 1881), pp. 12, 46, 48; W. J. Cash, *The
Mind of the South* (New York: Alfred A. Knopf, Inc., 1941), p. 178; C. Vann
Woodward, ed., *The Prosperity of the South Dependent Upon the Elevation of
the Negro by Lewis H. Blair* (Boston: Little, Brown and Company, 1964), p. 193;
Joel Chandler Harris, *Uncle Remus: His Songs and Sayings* (New York and
London: D. Appleton and Co., 1924).

10. For data on the Cable-Chesnutt relationship, see Helen M. Chesnutt, ed.,
Charles Waddell Chesnutt: Pioneer of the Color Line (Chapel Hill: University of
North Carolina Press, 1952), p. 50, and the many letters exchanged between Cable
and Chesnutt from 1888 to 1921 in the Cable Papers, Tulane University, and the
Chesnutt Papers, Fisk University. Cable to Adelene Moffat, January 9, 1889,
Cable Papers, Columbia University, and Cable's Diary entry for January 8, 1899,
Cable Papers, Tulane University, contain Cable's most thoroughgoing appraisals of
Williams. See also Philip Butcher, "George W. Cable and George W. Williams:
An Abortive Collaboration," *Journal of Negro History*, LIII, No. 4 (October, 1968),
334–44. Cable's high opinion of Woodson is conveyed in Cable to Carter G.
Woodson, November 7, 1916, and August 20, 1918, Woodson Papers, Woodson
Collection, Library of Congress.

11. Arlin Turner, ed., *The Negro Question: A Selection of Writings on Civil
Rights in the South* by George W. Cable (Garden City, New York: Doubleday &
Company, Inc., 1958), pp. 99–100.

development. . . ." [12] The specific individual, his appearance, manners, and conduct were more significant than racial categories.[13] To a degree, at least, Cable thus departed from the orthodoxy that DuBois had observed—the tendency of whites to stereotype blacks.

Unlike many white Southern racial theorists, especially Watterson, Page, and Watson, Cable also refused to perceive the antebellum master-slave relationship as a racial ideal. He rejected the claim that slavery had produced widespread prosperity and contentment through the direction of happy, docile blacks by kind but stern masters. Rather, he openly contended that "slavery was a dangerous institution." [14] For blacks, it had been "maiming";[15] in "the pathos of slavery" one could detect "the poetry of the weak oppressed by the strong. . . ." [16] More explicitly, "slavery was wrong." [17]

Like Thomas Jefferson, the New Orleans novelist detested the "peculiar institution" most because it had encouraged coarse, barbaric propensities among slaveholders. It had "induced a certain imperiousness of will and temper. . . ." [18] A "crudity and cruelty of criminal laws foreign to the humane spirit of the times" had taken root, causing the South to break "with the world's thought." [19] This failing was apparent in the slaveholder's treatment of bondsmen. In *The Grandissimes,* Cable described how a captured runaway, Bras-Coupé, had been harshly whipped, "his ears shorn from his head, and the tendons behind his knees severed." [20] Cable also described the mob lynching of an elderly female slave. Before death came, she was suddenly released and told to run for her life. As the woman fled, the mob laughed at her limp and somebody in the crowd shot her dead.[21] In "The 'Haunted House' in Royal Street," Cable depicted a beautiful Creole woman, Mme. Lalaurie, who sadistically starved and whipped black slaves concealed within the attic of her home.[22] Such

12. George W. Cable, "Educational Missions in the South," unpublished ms., n.d., Cable Papers, Tulane University. Emphasis added.

13. Turner, ed., *Negro Question,* pp. 64, 178.

14. Turner, ed., *Negro Question,* p. 56.

15. George W. Cable, *The Grandissimes: A Story of Creole Life* (New York: Sagamore Press Inc., 1957), p. 171.

16. George W. Cable, "Creole Slave Dances: The Dance in Place Congo," *Century Magazine,* XXXI (February, 1886), 528.

17. George W. Cable, "We of the South," *Century Magazine,* XXIX (November, 1884), 152.

18. George W. Cable, "Who Are the Creoles?," *Century Magazine,* XXV (January, 1883), 395.

19. George W. Cable, *The Silent South Together with the Freedman's Case in Equity and the Convict Lease System* (New York: Charles Scribner's Sons, 1895), p. 195; Turner, ed., *Negro Question,* p. 15. See also Cable, *Gideon's Band* (New York: Charles Scribner's Sons, 1914), p. 97.

20. Cable, *Grandissimes,* p. 191.

21. Cable, *Grandissimes,* pp. 321–23.

22. George W. Cable, "The 'Haunted House' in Royal Street," *Century Magazine,* XXXVIII (August, 1889), 590–601.

inhumane conduct had encouraged Negro bondsmen to flee for freedom and even to revolt.[23]

Though he was repulsed by the horrors of slavery, Cable was most concerned over the tendency of the "peculiar institution" to promote miscegenation. Slavery had required "close and continual contact" between the white master class and the black bondsmen. These contacts between "powerful and bold" whites and "helpless and sensual" blacks were preconditions for widespread "social confusion." They fostered strong temptations for white and black to copulate, and "pollution" of the races inevitably followed.[24] For this reason, Cable was certain that slavery had done the South great harm. Worse yet, he feared that the spirit of the "peculiar institution" still survived in the South, that it blunted "our sense of the rights of man," and that it would be "sad . . . for our children if we leave it for their inheritance." [25]

Cable's dissent from proslavery assumptions represented a substantial break with the Cavalier literary school characterized by John P. Kennedy, William Caruthers, Paul Hamilton Hayne, James Lane Allen, Thomas Dixon, Jr., and most notably, Thomas Nelson Page. These writers had exalted the improvident but generous-hearted and cultivated Cavalier gentleman planter. In part, the Cavalier gentleman commanded respect because he treated his bondsmen with a proper balance of humanity, courtesy, and discipline. Thus, when Cable wrote of the cruelty and sadism of slaveholders, he did much to undercut the credibility of Cavalier literature. As Cable portrayed the Southern planter, he was an insensitive villain, not a humane gentleman.

If Cable's attack upon slavery was a blow to Cavalier literature, his direct and explicit criticisms of white Southern behavior did even more to challenge the "chivalric" message of writers like Page, Allen, and Dixon. He insisted that even the most exalted of Cavaliers shared "that invincibility of the Southern heart which . . . clad Dixie's every gain in light and hid her gravest disasters in beguiling shadow." [26] Thus the Southerner had boldly seceded and gone to war

23. See, e.g., George W. Cable, *The Creoles of Louisiana* (New York: Charles Scribner's Sons, 1889), pp. 32–33; Cable, *Dr. Sevier* (New York: Charles Scribner's Sons, 1897), p. 403; Turner, ed., *Negro Question*, p. 56.

24. George W. Cable, *The Negro Question* (New York: Charles Scribner's Sons, 1890), p. 45; Turner, ed., *Negro Question*, p. 145.

25. George W. Cable, "A Reply" to John W. Johnston's "The True South vs. the Silent South," *Century Magazine*, XXXII (May, 1886), 170; Turner, ed., *Negro Question*, p. 114. See also Turner, ed., *Negro Question*, p. 45; Cable, *Lovers of Louisiana* (New York: Charles Scribner's Sons, 1918), p. 41; Cable, *John March, Southerner* (New York: Grosset & Dunlap, Inc., 1894), pp. 38–39; Cable, *Creoles of Louisiana*, p. 308.

26. George W. Cable, *Kincaid's Battery* (New York: Charles Scribner's Sons, 1908), p. 242.

in 1861 when all but "children and fools" knew that defeat was certain.[27] A sense of grandeur—a feeling that one could do no wrong—had compelled Southern planters to be guided by their affections instead of by their intellects, to waste their time in idle play, and to subjugate the masses, white and black.[28] It was easy to explain why capital and labor would not locate below Mason-Dixon:

> That she [Dixie] has legislatures a hundred years old, but often no adequate popular reverence for law; that she has judges and courts, but often no patience to wait for their decrees or honor their mandates; that her frightful prisons defend neither the criminal's rights nor those of society; that her provisions for public education will not bear comparison with that of any region bidding successfully for immigration; that her agricultural system is characterized by an ignorance and waste. . . .[29]

Clearly, the Southerner was "an enigma to all the world beside, if not also to himself." [30] He was an "antique" in a modern setting.[31]

When Cable attacked white Southern manners and morals, he singled out Louisiana Creoles, characterizing them as cruel and backward descendants of the "best" blood in France and Spain. From the standpoint of economic development, they kept Louisiana far behind the North and the West, for they "know nothing and care nothing but for meat, drink, and pleasure." [32] They lied, cheated, stole, and gambled with few compunctions.[33] "Show me any Creole, or any number of Creoles, in any sort of contest," he charged, "and I will find you the same preposterous, apathetic, fantastic, suicidal pride. It is as lethargic and ferocious as an alligator." The Creole was immune to rational thought.[34]

Cable's interpretation of white Southern behavior was thus strikingly at odds with the appraisal of those who wrote the new Cavalier literature, for crudity, ignorance, and barbarism typified Cable's Southerner. Breaking from the dominant trend in Southern writing, the New Orleans heretic helped to carve out a place in Southern literature for writers who were critical of white society. He paved a road for Ellen Glasgow, William Faulkner, Erskine Caldwell, and

27. Cable, *Kincaid's Battery*, p. 112.
28. Cable, *Lovers of Louisiana*, p. 307; Cable, *Dr. Sevier*, pp. 448–49; Turner, ed., *Negro Question*, pp. 137–38.
29. Turner, ed., *Negro Question*, p. 208.
30. Turner, ed., *Negro Question*, p. 138.
31. Cable, *Lovers of Louisiana*, p. 307.
32. George W. Cable, "Madame Delicieuse," in *Old Creole Days* (New York: The New American Library of World Literature, Inc., 1961), p. 211.
33. Two stories in *Old Creole Days*, "Belles Demoiselles Plantation" and " 'Sieur George," develop these themes quite clearly.
34. Cable, *Grandissimes*, p. 32.

Lillian Smith. Works like *Absalom, Absalom!* and *Tobacco Road* were the literary heirs of Cable's *Old Creole Days* and *The Grandissimes.*

As Cable strongly disapproved of white Southern thought and behavior, he found little value in the concept of local autonomy expounded by the men of the "Brownlow tradition." A coarse, inflexible, backward society could not manage its own affairs, particularly racial affairs, with humanity and integrity. Over strong Southern objection, he supported the Lodge Bill for federal supervision of local Congressional elections: "It is only a 'Force Bill' to those who cannot be kept from fraud except by force. There is at least one Cotton State whose Electoral System is confessedly calculated to outwit the weakest and most defenseless classes of its lawful voters." [35] Because North Carolina's Democratic Party, after twelve years in power, had inflexibly refused "to share the rights and powers of self-government with the Negro," federal intervention was imperative. Local injustice was "the nation's business." [36] In 1889 he advised Mississippi blacks to publicize incidents of racial violence against them; this could lead to outside intervention.[37]

Cable did more than attack orthodox Southern opinion on home rule, Cavalier literature, the slave system, and Negro stereotypes. He also demonstrated heresy by disputing the sacred and long-standing maxim that "one drop of Negro blood makes a Negro." From the beginning, British colonists in continental America had been reluctant to distinguish Negroes from mulattoes. Legally, they had defined everybody with even the slightest perceptible manifestations of Negro blood as Negro.[38] Unlike the Spanish and the Portuguese in the New World, British Americans thereby flaunted the rules of genetic logic.[39] This view persisted through the nineteenth century. As William Dean

35. Cable penciled this remark on a letter that had been sent to him by Irving Bacheller of the Bacheller Newspaper Syndicate. The letter was dated July 11, 1890, Cable Papers, Tulane University.

36. George W. Cable, "Centralization in North Carolina," unpublished ms., January, 1889, Cable Papers, Tulane University.

37. George W. Cable to Wesley Hoffman, October 25, 1889, Cable Papers, Tulane University.

38. Winthrop D. Jordan, "American Chiaroscuro: The Status and Definition of Mulattoes in the British Colonies," *William and Mary Quarterly*, ser. 3, XIX (April, 1962), 183–85; Winthrop D. Jordan, *White Over Black: American Attitudes Toward the Negro, 1550–1812* (Chapel Hill: University of North Carolina Press, 1968), pp. 168, 178.

39. David Brion Davis, *The Problem of Slavery in Western Culture* (Ithaca, New York: Cornell University Press, 1966), p. 275. See also J. V. D. Saunders, *Differential Fertility in Brazil* (Gainesville, Florida: University of Florida Press, 1958). p. 40, and Gilberto Freyre, *The Mansions and the Shanties* (New York: Alfred A. Knopf, Inc., 1963), p. 411.

Howells' sensitive novel, *An Imperative Duty* (1892), so well demonstrated, the theory that "one drop of Negro blood makes a Negro" remained an essential ingredient in Northern racial thought. In his provocative study, *Following the Color Line* (1908), Ray Stannard Baker came to this same appraisal of white Northerners.[40] But Southerners elevated the maxim even higher, and the frequency of interracial fornication throughout the region may explain why. By acknowledging the existence of mulattoes, Southern whites would have implicitly recognized that interracial fornication had taken place; hence they would have exposed their sexual attraction to the "inferior" race. From Thomas Dixon, Jr., to Virginia industrialist Lewis Harvey Blair and from Father Eastern, the gentle Episcopal priest of Sewanee, Tennessee, to the bellicose Tom Watson, whites of the region adamantly refused to distinguish mulattoes from Negroes.[41] According to Booker T. Washington, this was one of the most salient features of Southern racial thought in the postbellum decades.[42]

Rejecting a principle widely accepted in the North and exalted in his native South, Cable singled himself out as a truly independent thinker. He was far more than an occasional critic of things Southern. In both *The Grandissimes* and *Gideon's Band,* only the crudest and most foolish characters argued that "one drop of Negro blood makes a Negro." [43] Through characters like Olive in "Madame Delphine," Phyllis in *Gideon's Band,* Palmyre in *The Grandissimes,* and 'Tite Poulette in the story " 'Tite Poulette," Cable tried to prove that a mulatto was not a Negro. Yet owing to a "ludicrous" Southern

40. Ray Stannard Baker, *Following the Color Line: American Negro Citizenship in the Progressive Era* (New York: Harper Torchbooks, 1964), pp. 151–74. See also Fanny Garrison Villard to Richard Ely, December 8, 1910, Mary Church Terrell Papers, Library of Congress; Rayford W. Logan, *The Betrayal of the Negro from Rutherford B. Hayes to Woodrow Wilson,* 2nd ed. (New York: Collier Books, 1965), p. 231.

41. Thomas Dixon, Jr., *The Clansman: An Historical Romance of the Ku Klux Klan* (New York: Grosset & Dunlap, Inc., 1905); Dixon, Jr., *The Leopard's Spots: A Romance of the White Man's Burden, 1865–1900* (New York: Grosset & Dunlap, Inc., 1902); Blair is quoted in Charles E. Wynes, *Race Relations in Virginia, 1870–1902* (Charlottesville: University of Virginia Press, 1961), p. 82; Father Eastern is quoted in Ely Green, *Ely: An Autobiography* (New York: Seabury Press, 1966), p. 21; Thomas E. Watson, *Socialists and Socialism* (Thomson, Georgia: Jeffersonian Press, 1910), p. 11. See also "South Carolina Society," *Atlantic Monthly,* XXXIX (June, 1877), 684; Dallas *Express,* August 11, 1917; Helena (Arkansas) *Reporter,* February 1, 1900; J. W. Grant, *Out of the Darkness* (Nashville: National Baptist Publishing Board, 1909), pp. 66, 214.

42. Booker T. Washington, *The Future of the American Negro* (Boston: Small, Maynard & Company, 1900), p. 158. "It is a fact," Washington wrote, "that, if a person is known to have one per cent of African blood in his veins, he ceases to be a white man. The ninety-nine per cent of Caucasian blood does not weigh by the side of one per cent of African blood. The white blood counts for nothing. The person is a Negro every time."

43. Cable, *The Grandissimes,* p. 59; Cable, *Gideon's Band,* p. 282.

dogma, mulattoes had been barred from white society, causing them to suffer enormously for the "misdeeds" of their parents.

Cable's distinction between mulattoes and Negroes proved that he could formulate racial conceptualizations with some reference to genetic logic, and this was rare among white Americans. Yet his thoughts on mulattoes ran deeper. In a letter to Negro novelist Charles Waddell Chesnutt, he acknowledged that his portrayals of the sad life of the mulatto "really ask this question, 'what is a white man, what is a white woman?' " [44] Clearly, Cable worried about more than the distinction between mulattoes and Negroes. Writing so frequently about the plight of the mulatto, he was trying to articulate what the very existence of mulattoes implied—that race is transitory. A darkly complected Negro and a Caucasian could produce a mulatto. Copulating with a Caucasian, that mulatto could produce a lighter mulatto who, in turn, might pass as a Caucasian. Who, then, were the "real" white Americans, North or South?

Although Cable's critique of dominant white Southern ideas and ideals demonstrated that he was unique, his analysis of the psychology of white racism was his most heretical intellectual contribution. Thomas Pearce Bailey had charged that the quest for docile Negro behavior was the basis of Southern racial thought, and the "Brownlow tradition" supported Bailey's claim, but Cable was the only white Southern racial theorist of any significance who systematically tried to explain why whites needed servile "niggers." He recognized that the demand for racial separation tended to cloak the white man's desire for docile Negro behavior. "Separate! No-o-o!" the fictional character, Madame Delphine, declared. Southern whites "do not want us separated: no, no!" [45] Almost always, a desire for racial mastery could be detected behind segregationist slogans. The "moment the relation of master and servant is visibly established between race and race there is a hush of peace." At this point, demands for the color line ceased altogether.[46] Whenever a relationship based on white mastery and black servility was established, Cable maintained, a white Southerner let down his guard. He could relax in the presence of Negroes. He could gratify his deep and profound desire for intimate association with blacks without the fear that the black man might react antagonistically. In the words of Clemence, a slave character in *The Grandissimes*, whites needed servile blacks "fo' dey own cyumfut." [47] But why did Southern whites have such a compulsive need for the "comforts" provided by docile Negroes and what were

44. George W. Cable to Charles W. Chesnutt, June 12, 1889, Chesnutt Papers, Fisk University.
45. Cable, *Old Creole Days*, p. 60.
46. Turner, ed., *Negro Question*, p. 132.
47. Cable, *The Grandissimes*, p. 251. See also p. 315.

the precise "comforts"? Unfortunately, Cable's analysis went no further, leaving these questions unanswered. Nonetheless, the man had probed much deeper than most of his contemporaries, North or South.

III

Though Cable's major intellectual contribution was his unique critique of white Southern racial ideology and the psychology behind that ideology, he gained notoriety as an activist. At a time when the civil rights of Negroes were being curtailed, he spoke out repeatedly for black participation in the political process.[48] To encourage a white Southern crusade for civil rights, he formed an Open Letter Club that published and circulated liberal opinion on the race issue.[49] But Cable was more than a civil rights activist. He publicly rebuked the entire Southern penal system because it had sanctioned barbaric treatment of incarcerated Negroes.[50] He also waged vigorous campaigns to enlarge Negro educational opportunities. In the 1870's he fought to retain integrated schools in New Orleans. He subsequently continued to demand integrated schooling but also assisted Negro industrial colleges in their fund-raising efforts.[51] All such activities in behalf of Southern Negroes reinforced what Cable's theoretical critique of the white South suggested—that he was a thoroughgoing racial heretic.

It may be difficult to imagine that a man who had worked so strenuously for Southern blacks could harbor deep racial prejudices. But within Cable's attacks upon the various Southern orthodoxies, certain intellectual and psychological bonds with other Southern whites could be detected. He attacked the assumption that all blacks were inferior to all whites only to replace it with the dictum that most whites were "far superior" to most blacks. Though he criticized slavery, he failed to demonstrate any genuine concern for the black bondsman, fearing only that a relation of master to slave had desensitized the white ruling class and had encouraged racial "pollution." Like the men of the "Brownlow tradition," Cable even acknowledged

48. See, e.g., Turner, ed., *Negro Question*, pp. 60, 170, 210; George W. Cable to Walter Blair, April 22, 1890, Cable Papers, Tulane University.

49. Turner, ed., *Negro Question*, pp. 179–86.

50. Turner, ed., *Negro Question*, pp. 69–70, 231–32; Cable, "The Convict Lease System in the Southern States," *Century Magazine*, XXVII (February, 1884), 582–99.

51. Turner, ed., *Negro Question*, pp. 26–33 prints Cable's stand during the 1870's for integrated schools in New Orleans. See also G. W. Cable, "Educational Missions in the South," unpublished ms., n.d., Cable Papers, Tulane University. The Montgomery *Advertiser*, May 30, 1907, and the Springfield *Weekly Republican*, February 28, 1907, print statements by Cable proving that he sought to assist Negro industrial colleges.

that blacks were basically wild African savages. In colonial times the black man had been "a most grotesque figure." He was nearly naked. Often his "neck and arms, thighs, shanks, and splay feet were shrunken, though, sinewey like a monkey's." [52] As a slave, he sang a great deal, but his songs did not resemble the songs of white civilization:

> His songs were not contemplative. They voiced not outward nature, but the inner emotions and passions of a nearly naked serpent-worshiper, and these looked not to the surrounding scene for sympathy; the surrounding scene belonged to his master. But love was his, and toil, and anger, and superstition, and malady. Sleep was his balm, food his reenforcement, the dance his pleasure, rum his longed-for nepenthe, and death the road back to Africa.[53]

Cable was certain that the African could never eradicate this basic savage condition. He could never shed his "thick negro tongue" nor his disgustingly ugly lips, nose, ears, and the "black wool" that passed for hair.[54] Nor could he transcend "the feelings handed down . . . through ages of African savagery. . . ." [55] When Negro waiters lost control of themselves and became "holy terrors," this represented a revival of the latent savage impulse.[56] The Negro's disposition to marry a woman he did not love solely to improve his sexual life was another manifestation of the same savage impulse.[57]

Thus, despite his highly critical analysis of Southern race relations, Cable clung to the notion that black and white were essentially unequal: "Yes, the black race is inferior to the white. The Almighty has established inequality as a principle in nature." [58] Whites belonged to "the finer and prouder race. . . ." [59] The Caucasian made up the "high life" on Earth while the Negro represented the "low life." [60] Whites represented civilization while blacks stood for primitive existence.

Paradoxically, it was precisely because Cable believed so strongly in the potentialities of white civilization that he launched his crusade

52. Cable, *Century Magazine*, XXXI (February, 1886), 522.
53. George W. Cable, "Creole Slave Songs," *Century Magazine*, XXXI (April, 1886), 810.
54. George W. Cable, *The Flower of the Chapelaines* (New York: Charles Scribner's Sons, 1918), p. 131 and Cable, *Century Magazine*, XXXI (February, 1886), 525.
55. Cable, *The Grandissimes*, p. 251.
56. George W. Cable to F. B. Adams, November 26, 1912, Cable Papers, Tulane University.
57. Cable, *John March*, pp. 470–71.
58. New Orleans *Bulletin*, September 26, 1875, as quoted in Turner, ed., *Negro Question*, p. 29.
59. Cable, *Silent South*, p. 37.
60. Turner, ed., *Negro Question*, p. 96. See also p. 29.

for civil rights and racial justice, for he feared that whenever whites degraded blacks, they dehumanized themselves. A repressionist policy had a "warping moral effect" upon the repressor.[61] It left whites with "certain conventions which Christianity condemns."[62] Under the "peculiar institution," the results of a systematically cruel and repressive policy were apparent; the white South had departed from the Western humanist tradition.[63] Postbellum segregation policies would have the same effect, Cable predicted. Excluding Negroes from the better public facilities discouraged Negro efforts at self-improvement. Thus, like the policies that had emanated from the slave system, segregation was inhumane. And when whites acted inhumanely to blacks, they invariably brutalized themselves in the process.[64] Another practice that contributed to a hardening of white society, Cable charged, was the inadequate funding of Negro education. White Southerners used black educational facilities as their guidelines and always furnished white children "something a little better. . . ." Hence, if appropriations for black schools were grossly inadequate, the few additional dollars allocated to white schools could not be sufficient.[65] "Whatever we say with regard to the illiteracy of blacks in the South applies to the illiteracy of whites also. . . ."[66] Even by denying blacks a political role, Cable suggested, white Southerners were merely hurting themselves. Totally in control of governmental institutions, whites might assume that only they could rule correctly—that blacks were totally incompetent. This enhanced the possibility of white officials believing that they could do no wrong. As a result, they could rule with carelessness, caprice, and injustice.[67]

Cable thus insisted that the "only way to make the South a good place for white men to come to is to make it a good place for black men to stay in."[68] When whites denied blacks public rights and civil justice, the tragedy was not in what these denials did to the black community. The real tragedy was that the "higher race" became cal-

61. Cable, *Century Magazine*, XXXII (May, 1886), 169.

62. George W. Cable, "Congregational Unity in Georgia." unpublished ms., September 12, 1889, Cable Papers, Columbia University.

63. See Cable, *Grandissimes*, especially pp. 191, 321–23; Turner, ed., *Negro Question*, p. 15.

64. Turner, ed., *Negro Question*, pp. 64–65, 154–55; Cable, *The Negro Question*, p. 51.

65. George W. Cable, "The Public Schools of the South. An Unprofessional Brief in Behalf of Southern Children," unpublished ms., March 25, 1891, Cable Papers, Tulane University.

66. Cable ms., n.d., Cable Papers, Tulane University. See also Philip Butcher, *George W. Cable: The Northampton Years* (New York: Columbia University Press, 1959), pp. 20–21.

67. George W. Cable to Frank Smith, November 12, 1890, Cable Papers, Tulane University; Cable, *Century Magazine*, XXXII (May, 1886), 166.

68. Cable, *The Negro Question*, p. 149.

lous and insensitive and assumed certain degenerate qualities of the "lower race." Civilization became diluted with savagery.

To Cable, the dilution of the superior race with the qualities of the inferior represented more than an empty abstraction. Recognizing the many mulattoes within Southern society, he feared that interracial fornication was widespread. The danger was that sexual intercourse between white and black would ultimately "pollute" and destroy the superior race.[69] Seeing mulattoes all about him, some of whom professed to be white, he tried to discover why whites had been sexually attracted to blacks.

Here, too, Cable concluded that the denial of the black man's civil rights was determinant. This was because civil and private society were separate and distinct. Unlike public life, private life "is personal, selective, assortive, ignores civil equality without violating it, and forms itself entirely upon mutual private preferences and affinities."[70] Therefore, civil rights for black people caused no invasion of private life. Indeed, when black children attended public schools with whites during Reconstruction, it "produced no general intermingling" of the races in their private relations.[71] "Dissimilar races are not inclined to mix spontaneously."[72] There were "ordinary natural preferences of like for like."[73] With equal rights in public life, blacks would naturally and instinctively stay away from whites in private life.[74] Only when they were denied public rights would Negroes dare to invade the white man's private society and "pollute" the superior race. If "our white race does not treat the Negro according to the plain, pure, undistorted principles of Christianity" in public life, "its blood will ultimately be lost in that of the Negro. . . ."[75] Precisely "in proportion to the rigor, the fierceness, and the injustice with which this excommunication from the common rights of man has fallen upon the darker race, has amalgamation taken place."[76] A color line in public life created the very "confusion [of the races] it pretends to prevent," Cable explained.[77] It represented an "arbitrary and cheap artificial distinction" which overpowered the natural

69. Cable, *The Negro Question*, p. 44; Turner, ed., *Negro Question*, pp. 83–84; Cable, *Grandissimes*, p. 134.

70. Cable, *The Negro Question*, p. 44. See also p. 106.

71. George W. Cable, "Overlooked Causes of Southern Illiteracy," unpublished ms., 1891, Cable Papers, Tulane University.

72. Cable, *The Negro Question*, p. 46. See also Turner, ed., *Negro Question*, p. 145.

73. Cable, *The Silent South*, p. 103.

74. Cable, *The Silent South*, pp. 36, 73, 77, 78; Turner, ed., *Negro Question*, p. 95; Cable, *Flower of the Chapelaines*, pp. 121–22.

75. Cable to Editor, Nashville *American*, January 4, 1890, Cable Papers, Columbia University.

76. Cable, *The Silent South*, p. 102.

77. Cable, *The Silent South*, p. 24.

disposition of any society "to hold apart two races which really have no social affinity at all." [78] More specifically, a society that separated and distinguished between blacks and whites in public life encouraged illicit and intimate interracial association. Prohibition against interracial contact in public life turned surreptitious meetings between the races into daring and exciting ventures.[79] As Cornelius Leggett, Negro politician in *John March, Southerner,* told his lover, "Colo' line!—I'll cross fifty colo' lines whenev' I feels like it." For Leggett, the white woman had become an exciting sexual object solely because she represented forbidden fruit.[80] Miscegenation and ruin for the superior race inevitably followed. Hence, if Southerners wished to preserve the white race through separation of black from white on the intimate social level, Negroes had to be granted public rights. These rights constituted "the greatest safeguard of private society that human law or custom can provide." [81]

Therefore, when Cable campaigned for civil rights his aim was not drastically different from the aim of men who opposed these rights—Brownlow, Watterson, Page, and Watson. These four believed that all dangerous, "uppity" blacks had to be isolated from white society and that the color line had to extend into public as well as private life. In this way, they reasoned, none but servile blacks would enter the white man's society. It is true that Cable departed from this approach, contending that a color line in public life did not ward off insolent Negro behavior, that it desensitized the white race, and that it promoted "pollution" of white society. But his very reasons for objecting to public segregation proved that like the men of the "Brownlow tradition," he was primarily out to protect white society against a black population in its midst. Like the others, he sought to perpetuate white supremacy and black servility.

Therefore, Cable was antagonistic to the "Brownlow tradition" only in a technical sense. Unlike Brownlow, Watterson, Page, and Watson, he did not subscribe to the concept of differential segregation. Rather, he sought to remove the color line in all phases of public life to promote across-the-board segregation in private life. Nonetheless, Cable had the same cast of mind as the others. Beyond the issue of segregation he, too, yearned for a servile Negro population. Like the others, he sought to protect white civilization from black savages.

The protection of white civilization was not the only goal of the men of the "Brownlow tradition." When the aggressive, savage essence of the Negro personality had been contained and only docile

78. Cable, *The Silent South,* p. 54.
79. Cable, *The Negro Question,* p. 46; Cable, *The Silent South,* p. 35.
80. Cable, *John March,* p. 99.
81. Turner, ed., *Negro Question,* p. 145.

blacks interacted with whites, the white man stood to gain certain psychological benefits. The presence of servile Negroes allowed Brownlow, Watterson, Page, and Watson to break momentarily from the restraints of a nervous, urbanizing, industrializing, frightening, ever-changing white society. In Uncle Tom's presence, they could release repressed desires while ignoring the consequences of their crudity. The savage essence of any Negro made them, by contrast, civilized even as they treated the Negro with gross crudity. But since Cable was so very sensitive to the barbaric qualities of Southern whites as they dealt with blacks, this black savage–white civilization rationalization for white barbarism did not serve him well. Unlike Brownlow and Watson, the New Orleans novelist could not "break loose" with vicious Negrophobe tirades, and unlike Watterson or Page, he could not dwell upon the pleasures of interacting with comical "old-time Negroes" such as "Blind Tom" and "Hannah, the faithful." Had he ever sought relief through Negrophobe rhetoric, Cable would probably have sensed that he was the crude, barbaric white Southerner he so often rebuked. And had he sought peace of mind by associating with "old-time Negroes," Cable would instantly have realized that he was enjoying the fruits of the old master-slave relationship he so ardently condemned. For a man of his outlook, either course of action was self-defeating. But like the men of the "Brownlow tradition," the New Orleans heretic needed relief, and like the others he was sure that Negroes could provide it. Cable often wrote of friendly and enjoyable relations with cultivated, restrained male Negro intellectuals who looked up to him. He appreciated the fact that Carter G. Woodson had called upon him for assistance in his historical research and for advice in promoting the *Journal of Negro History*.[82] He was also pleased to recall how Booker T. Washington had dutifully supplied him with data for his research on Southern Negroes.[83] The black historian, George Washington Williams, and Negro novelist Charles Waddell Chesnutt made Cable particularly happy. He loved to converse with Williams, "a scholar, a man of affairs, polished, graceful, laborious in life. . . ." Williams was "a *perfect* gentleman" who entertained well and made one feel perfectly at ease.[84] The relationship with Chesnutt was even more pleasurable. The black novelist looked to Cable as his literary adviser and spon-

82. George W. Cable to Carter G. Woodson, November 7, 1916; August 20, 1918, Woodson Papers, Woodson Collection, Library of Congress; Carter G. Woodson to George W. Cable, November 9, 1916, Cable Papers, Tulane University.

83. The Cable-Washington correspondence of 1885–1897 (most of which is in the Cable Papers, Tulane University) makes this more than apparent. See also the Montgomery *Advertiser*, May 30, 1907.

84. Diary, entry for January 8, 1889, Cable Papers, Tulane University; George W. Cable to Adelene Moffat, January 9, 1889, Cable Papers, Columbia University. See also Butcher, *Journal of Negro History*, LIII, No. 4 (October, 1968), 334–44.

sor, and Cable loved to guide the man. He thoroughly enjoyed the conversations that they had together. According to Chesnutt's daughter, Cable "seemed to be having such a delightful time with Papa." The relationship would become even more rewarding, Cable noted, if the Negro writer would only serve as his personal secretary.[85]

Cable's relationship to male Negro intellectuals, particularly to Chesnutt, somewhat resembled Watterson's relationship to "Blind Tom" and Page's association with "Hannah, the faithful." The anxious and intellectually isolated New Orleans crusader sought relaxation and peace of mind by relating to cultivated black men who respected him, sought his advice, and came to his assistance. To be sure, Negroes like Woodson, Washington, Williams, and Chesnutt were not comic "old-time darkies" but respected, restrained members of the black bourgeoisie. Hence, Cable could not laugh at them the way "Marse Henry" could laugh at "Blind Tom," and he could not tell them of his inner personal anxieties as Page could confide in Hannah or Ma' Lyddy. Interaction with Negroes that he could not respect, particularly intimate relations with lower-class Negro women, would only have made Cable fear that he had become the crude, uncultivated white Southerner that he had so bitterly chastised. On the other hand, friendship and constant association with cultivated Negro men dispelled this fear. If the most sophisticated male elements of the savage race were attracted to him, it followed that he had not taken the course of his white Southern contemporaries; he had not become a white barbarian. While association with docile, comic Negroes gave the men of the "Brownlow tradition" peace of mind and helped them feel civilized, relations with cultivated black males probably confirmed Cable's identity as civilized and allowed him to relax. Thus, as in the controversy over public segregation, Cable departed from the proponents of the "Brownlow tradition." But though the departure was important, it was not fundamental. Like the others, the heretic needed agreeable Negroes for a sense of identity and peace of mind.

IV

This basic similarity between Cable and the men of the "Brownlow tradition" is significant, for he drew little reproach from these

<hr/>

85. The Chesnutt-Cable correspondence, 1888–1921, Cable Papers, Tulane University, demonstrates how thoroughly Cable enjoyed serving as Chesnutt's adviser. Two letters in that collection from Chesnutt to Cable (April 10, 1889; May 3, 1889) and one letter from Cable to Chesnutt (April 13, 1889), Chesnutt Papers, Fisk University, reveal Cable's strong desire to have Chesnutt as his personal secretary. In Helen M. Chesnutt, ed., *Charles W. Chesnutt*, p. 50, Chesnutt's daughter notes Cable's fondness for her father.

men or from any other Southerners for his truly heretical ideas. Except for a few mildly worded objections to his criticism of the Southern Cavalier gentleman, he was never really challenged.[86] Nobody attacked him for his objections to racial stereotypes, to slavery, to the home rule idea, or to the principle that "one drop of Negro blood makes a Negro." But Cable was hardly ignored. White Southerners criticized and vilified the man and charged him with heresy where his ideas were most orthodox. Although he had struggled desperately to preserve the purity and morality of the "superior" race and the subordination of the "inferior" race, whites called him a "nigger lover." Grace King, like Cable a New Orleans local color novelist, concluded that he had "proclaimed his preference for colored people over white. . . ."[87] Charles Etienne Gayarré, the prominent Creole historian, insisted that Cable was a "Negro lover" who advocated racial equality and opposed the interests of his white brethren.[88] "Mr. Cable has often urged social equality of the races," the Nashville *Banner* claimed.[89] In his famous essay, "In Plain Black and White: A Reply to Mr. Cable," Henry W. Grady proved that he had entirely misinterpreted Cable's racial essays. The fundamental thrust of Grady's article was that "the South will never adopt Mr. Cable's suggestion of the social intermingling of the races,"[90] though Cable himself would have shuddered at such an eventuality.

Though these and similar criticisms of Cable were vocalized over a period of many years, most came in 1885, shortly after the publication of Cable's most controversial writings. The 1885 criticisms doubtless influenced Cable's decision to leave New Orleans for a permanent residence in Northampton, Massachusetts. Five years earlier, he had told Robert Underwood Johnson that there was "no good reason why I should leave Louisiana. . . ."[91] But in late January of 1885, soon after Southern "warfare" against Cable became intense, he wrote to his wife: "I must admit I shall not from choice bring up my daughters in that state of society. The more carefully I study it the less I expect of it. . . ."[92] By September he told a close friend,

86. Grace King, *Memories of a Southern Woman of Letters* (New York: The Macmillan Company, 1932), p. 60; Charles Gayarré, "Mr. Cable's Freedman's Case in Equity," in Thomas M'Caleb, ed., *The Louisiana Book* (New Orleans: R. F. Straughan, 1894), pp. 198–99; Henry W. Grady, "In Plain Black and White: A Reply to Mr. Cable," *Century Magazine*, XXIX (April, 1885), 909.

87. King, *Memories*, p. 60.

88. New Orleans *Times-Democrat*, January 22, 1885. See also New Orleans *Times-Democrat*, January 11, 1885.

89. Nashville *Banner*, December 6, 1889.

90. Grady, *Century Magazine*, XXIX (April, 1885), 910.

91. George W. Cable to Robert Underwood Johnson, January 24, 1880, as quoted in Jay B. Hubbell, *The South in American Literature, 1607–1900* (Durham: Duke University Press, 1954), pp. 817–18.

92. George W. Cable to Louise S. Cable, January 31, 1885, Cable Papers, Tulane University.

Marion A. Baker, that he had definitely decided to move his family to Northampton, "a school town & college town. There is an atmosphere of intellectual ambition in it such as one is glad to bring his children into." [93] Two years later, he told his wife that "henceforth, more than ever before, my home is in New England. This South may be a free country one of these days; it is not so now." [94]

In large part, Cable left the South over a misunderstanding, for his critics were not irked by his truly heretical ideas, failing even to dispute his claim that public segregation fostered racial integration in private life. Rather, Cable's critics accused him of racial heresy precisely where his thoughts most closely approached orthodoxy.

To a large extent, Cable was misunderstood because white Southerners would not give him a hearing. They charged him with favoring social equality on the basis of his conduct, not his writings. In 1889, for example, the Nashville *American* accused Cable of advocating social equality because he had dined with James C. Napier, a prominent black attorney.[95] Four years earlier, the editor of the New Orleans *Picayune* found conclusive "proof" of Cable's advocacy of miscegenation in Cable's correspondence with a black man from Wisconsin, although the editor never knew what Cable had actually written.[96] In his essay "In Plain Black and White," Henry Grady did not accuse Cable of favoring race mixture on the basis of his writings but from the "fact" that the New Orleans novelist seemed to be at ease when he travelled to the North.[97] Charles Gayarré "proved" that Cable favored race mixing from Cable's alleged arrogance, self-righteousness, and pedagogy.[98] In February, 1885, the New Orleans *Times-Democrat* published an assault by nine Southern newspaper editors upon Cable's "miscegenationist tendencies." To support their charges, the editors cited Cable's behavior but failed to examine his racial ideas.[99]

It is difficult to determine why white Southerners never gave Cable a hearing and turned on him with near unanimity. Charging him with favoring social equality on the basis of his manners and his association with certain Negro men, they may have been projecting their own aspirations upon that unfortunate heretic. By accusing Cable of dangerous racial associations and poor manners, whites may

93. George W. Cable to Marion A. Baker, September 5, 1885, Cable Papers, Harvard University.

94. George W. Cable to Louise S. Cable, June 8, 1887, Cable Papers, Tulane University.

95. Butcher, *Journal of Negro History*, LIII, No. 4 (October, 1968), 337.

96. New Orleans *Picayune*, February 15, 1885.

97. Grady, *Century Magazine*, XXIX (April, 1885), 909.

98. See, e.g., Gayarré's article in the New Orleans *Times-Democrat*, January 11, 1885.

99. New Orleans *Times-Democrat*, February 2, 1885.

have been denying that they shared these qualities. If the seemingly
cultivated, genteel New Orleans novelist was guilty of gross misbehavior, particularly in his relations with black men, his accusers
could think of themselves as civilized and manly Cavaliers. As all
of the men of the "Brownlow tradition" had hoped to affirm their
identities as civilized by trying desperately to convince themselves that
blacks were savages, as Watterson and Page had tried to establish
positive self-identities by degrading poor whites, and as Watson had
tried to affirm his morality by denigrating the plutocracy, Cable's
critics may have been trying to remove doubts about themselves, particularly about their innermost racial fantasies, by calling the New
Orleans heretic an arrogant "nigger lover" and forcing him out of
the South.

PART THREE

Black and White Apart

I charge the Christian white man of the South to mark that the effect of this separation, on which we have insisted, has helped to drive these [Negro] people into a corresponding exclusiveness. . . .

—Thomas Underwood Dudley, 1885

The Negro as a race, considered and acting solidly, may be a burden and a menace. . . .

—Thomas Nelson Page, 1904

Though George W. Cable never quite subscribed to the "Brownlow tradition" of differential segregation, he was sure that the "tradition" dominated Southern thought. In his 1885 essay, "The Freedman's Case in Equity," the New Orleans novelist commented on the general tone of racial life in the postbellum South: "Any colored man gains unquestioned admission into innumerable places the moment he appears as the menial attendant of some white person, where he could not cross the threshold in his own right as a well-dressed and well-behaved master of himself. The contrast is even greater in the case of colored women." [1] Servile Negroes could be near whites, but dignified blacks threatened white society and had to be isolated. Twenty-four years later, Quincy Ewing, the Episcopal minister of Christ Church in Napoleonville, Louisiana, appraised white Southern racial thought and action in these precise terms: "Almost anything the Negro may do in the South, and anywhere he may go, provided the manner of his doing and his going is that of an inferior." The "black nurse with a baby in her arms, the black valet looking after the comfort of a white invalid" could enter areas reserved for whites. But Negroes who were not acting out servile roles could not claim this privilege. [2] Between 1910 and 1914 many Southern cities passed ordinances requiring residential segregation. Harshly

1. George W. Cable, *The Silent South Together with the Freedman's Case in Equity and the Convict Lease System* (New York: Charles Scribner's Sons, 1895), pp. 21–22.

2. Charles E. Wynes, ed., *Forgotten Voices: Dissenting Southerners in an Age of Conformity* (Baton Rouge: Louisiana State University Press, 1967), p. 132.

phrased, the ordinances nonetheless exempted Negro domestics from color lines; they could continue to live in white homes.[3] "Being a servant cancelled all . . . marks of disfavor," wrote Lura Beam, as she summed up her study of black Southerners during the early years of the twentieth century. For the servile, color lines posed few basic problems.[4] In 1885 Tennessee politician-jurist David M. Key charged that differential segregation was systematically implemented on railroad trains below Mason-Dixon: "So long as a colored passenger occupies a servile position, he may ride anywhere." But dignified middle-class Negroes who traveled on their own business were usually forced "into the smoker as repulsive to those aboard the better car."[5] From time to time a cultivated, well-dressed Negro who went out of his way to be courteous to whites found that he could travel freely,[6] but even this was rare. The color line was enforced against John Mercer Langston after he had campaigned for a political party that most white Virginians opposed; he could find no public accommodations in Lynchburg. But when Frederick Douglass spoke out against Negro migrations from the South, a message that white Virginians appreciated, he found that he was suddenly allowed to stay at the best hotel in nearby Staunton.[7] Real efforts were made to send only insolent, defiant blacks off to the chain gang while none but the most vicious and hopelessly depraved were allegedly executed.[8]

The men of the "Brownlow tradition," then, were no isolated, insignificant group of racial theorists. Articulating the concept of differential segregation, Brownlow, Watterson, Page, and Watson had pointed to a procedure that many Southern whites supported. The

3. Gilbert T. Stephenson, "The Segregation of the White and Negro Races in Cities," *South Atlantic Quarterly*, XIII, No. 1 (January, 1914), 7. See also Winfield H. Collins, *The Truth about Lynching and the Negro in the South* (New York: Neale Publishing Company, 1918), p. 105.

4. Lura Beam, *He Called Them by the Lightning: A Teacher's Odyssey in the Negro South* (Indianapolis: The Bobbs-Merrill Company, Inc., 1967), p. 73.

5. Richard Lowitt, ed., "David M. Key Views the Legal and Political Status of the Negro in 1885," *Journal of Negro History*, LIV, No. 3 (July, 1969), 291. James Weldon Johnson, *Along This Way* (New York: The Viking Press, 1933), p. 87, claimed that the "Negro car" on the Southern train carried more than those Negroes who did not labor under patently servile roles. Sometimes it transported insane whites who were under custody.

6. C. Vann Woodward, *The Strange Career of Jim Crow*, 2nd ed. (New York: Oxford University Press, Inc., 1966), pp. 38–41.

7. Charles E. Wynes, ed., *Southern Sketches from Virginia 1881–1901 by Orra Langhorne* (Charlottesville: University of Virginia Press, 1964), p. 34. See also the Raleigh *News and Observer*, November 11, 1898. "Bumptious negro political leaders," the newspaper editorialized, "are being made to leave the town [Wilmington, North Carolina] on almost every train."

8. See, e.g., George W. Cable, "The Convict Lease System in the Southern States," *Century Magazine*, XXVII (February, 1884), 582–99; Stephen Graham, *The Soul of John Brown* (New York: The Macmillan Company, 1920), pp. 216–27.

concept of a differential color line was so attractive to postbellum Southern society that even the heretical Cable could never bring himself to repudiate it. Like many other whites, he craved what differential segregation promised to deliver—a "well-behaved" Negro population that gave the white man pleasure and represented no threat to white civilization.

If Negro servility was the ideal of the postbellum South, however, whites were in for trying times. By the turn of the century, it was becoming increasingly difficult for a white Southerner to associate only with servile Negroes while he avoided the "uppity" ones. Attempts to exclude defiant Negroes were gradually producing an unwieldy system of public segregation. Extensive, complex, and impersonal, the system often unwittingly prevented the docile from crossing color lines. During the early years of the twentieth century, for example, segregation in Alabama had developed to the point where white female nurses were legally prohibited from attending Negro male patients.[9] This sort of ban could not be differentially enforced. A white female nurse could not care for a black man even if the docile qualities of the black man had been apparent. Uncle Tom was thus denied the loving care which had supposedly tamed his savagery and which had been partly responsible for his servile loyalty. To apply a city ordinance segregating white and black prostitutes into separate districts, New Orleans whites encountered perhaps an even more intolerable situation. The black whores that white men preferred had to be declared "off limits" together with feared and detested black whores.[10] The ordinance demonstrated how Jim Crow was becoming increasingly incompatible with certain basic white Southern aspirations.

Black migrations to Southern cities and the growth of those cities also made it difficult to carry out differential segregation. By 1900 twenty-seven per cent of New Orleans' population, forty per cent of Atlanta's, and forty-two per cent of Birmingham's were black.[11] Moreover, in practically every Southern city, the ratio of black to white was rapidly increasing. In nine Southern states, the proportion of Negroes living in urban areas rose from nearly twelve per cent in 1890 to almost fifteen per cent in 1900 and to practically eighteen per cent in 1910.[12] Within these big urban centers, large numbers of

9. Woodward, *Strange Career of Jim Crow*, p. 99.
10. Woodward, *Strange Career of Jim Crow*, p. 102.
11. John Samuel Ezell, *The South Since 1865* (New York: The Macmillan Company, 1963), p. 233, cites urban population figures for 1900. Thomas D. Clark and Albert D. Kirwan, *The South Since Appomattox: A Century of Regional Change* (New York: Oxford University Press, 1967), p. 343, cites black population figures for the same year.
12. Ray Ginger, *Age of Excess: The United States from 1877 to 1914* (New York: The Macmillan Company, 1965), p. 235.

people were seldom on personal terms. Since a Caucasian could not always tell whether a strange Negro was obedient or "uppity," the safest approach was to push all blacks behind the color line. Hence, a pattern of urban segregation that had first begun to emerge in Southern cities in the decades before Sumter intensified.[13] Since urban centers utilized color lines in streetcars, hotels, theaters, parks, colleges, port facilities, hospitals, and other institutions not so common to rural locations, they became the most thoroughly and rigidly segregated areas in the South. In 1901 W. E. B. DuBois took special note of this phenomenon, particularly as it applied to residential housing: "Usually in [Southern] cities each street has its distinctive color, and only now and then do the colors meet in close proximity." [14] As the South urbanized, the flexible, differential segregation of the "Brownlow tradition" became increasingly difficult to apply.

Another deterrent to differential segregation was the widespread belief that Negroes harbored contagious diseases.[15] This myth was deeply embedded in the American mind. Following clinical observations at the Pennsylvania Hospital during the late eighteenth century, Dr. Benjamin Rush concluded that Negroes were black because the entire race had been afflicited with leprosy.[16] Certain proslavery theoreticians had exploited this same myth, claiming that the "peculiar institution" was necessary because free Negroes were impoverished and filthy carriers of disease.[17] In his well-known attack on the slave system, *The Impending Crisis of the South,* Hinton Rowan Helper also drew upon the myth. Blacks had to be emanci-

---

13. Richard C. Wade, *Slavery in the Cities: The South 1820–1860* (New York: Oxford University Press, Inc., 1964), pp. 266–77, provides a thoroughly documented analysis of antebellum urban segregation below Mason-Dixon.

14. W. E. B. DuBois, "The Relation of the Negroes to the Whites in the South," *Annals of the American Academy of Political and Social Science,* XVIII (July–December, 1901), 123. See also DuBois, *Dusk of Dawn: An Essay Toward an Autobiography of a Race Concept* (New York: Harcourt, Brace & World, Inc., 1940), p. 30. Ray Stannard Baker, *Following the Color Line: American Negro Citizenship in the Progressive Era* (New York: Harper Torchbooks, 1964), pp. 26–65, made this same general observation concerning the urban South.

15. In her unpublished 1968 essay, "The Sick Negro: His Segregation and Subordination," Ann Pfaff, a U.C.L.A. undergraduate, brilliantly argued that the myth of the diseased Negro correlated with increasing segregationist sentiments, North and South, during the late nineteenth and early twentieth centuries. Though I take issue with the precise correlation that she drew, I am indebted to Miss Pfaff for her insights.

16. Daniel J. Boorstin, *The Lost World of Thomas Jefferson* (New York: Henry Holt and Company, 1948), p. 90; William Stanton, *The Leopard's Spots: Scientific Attitudes Toward Race in America, 1815–1859* (Chicago: The University of Chicago Press, 1960), pp. 6–7.

17. See, e.g., Wade, *Slavery in the Cities,* pp. 92, 141–42; "Uncle Tom's Cabin: The Possible Amelioration of Slavery," *North American Review,* LXXVII, No. 161 (October, 1853), 477.

pated, he maintained, but they also had to be colonized abroad to safeguard whites from disease and other forms of "pollution." [18]

Legal emancipation intensified white Southern fears of Negro disease. When Mississippi Negroes began to mix extensively with whites in railroad cars, whites objected, charging that the freedmen menaced the health of all white passengers.[19] In 1867 the Richmond *Enquirer* editorialized: "The most iminent [sic] Southern physicians assure us that the post mortem examinations reveal the facts that consumption and scrofula, those scourages [sic] of the Northern negro, have since his liberation marked the [Southern] freedman for their victim." [20] In the 1870's and 1880's, certain white Southerners continued to argue that "filthy negroes" were "foul vermin" and must never ride in Pullman cars occupied by whites.[21]

By the late 1880's the myth of the diseased Negro was rapidly gaining adherents, perhaps because of greater familiarity with the germ theory of disease. According to this theory, germs were associated with filth, and for generations many whites had assumed that free Negroes lived in filth. Thus freedmen had to be isolated. In 1889 South Carolina rice planter-physician James R. Sparks concluded that ever since emancipation, blacks had been plagued by "contagious diseases," particularly "lung diseases." [22] In *Racial Integrity and Other Features of the Negro Problem* (1907), Mississippi scholar A. H. Shannon was most fearful of Negro disease within congested urban areas. Even a black writer, William Hannibal Thomas, charged that Negroes tended to be sick and diseased.[23] Many who spread this myth emphasized venereal disease. In 1910 University of North Carolina social scientist Howard W. Odum wrote that venereal infections, together with pulmonary disorders, were "everywhere on the increase among the negroes to an alarming extent." The real problem, Odum concluded, was that "such afflictions are dangerous not only to negroes, but *menacing to those among whom they dwell.*" [24] That same year, Tom Watson argued that blacks had been "but slightly contaminated by

18. Helper develops this argument throughout *The Impending Crisis of the South: How to Meet It* (New York: Burdick Brothers, 1857), especially on p. 129.

19. Vernon Lane Wharton, *The Negro in Mississippi, 1865–1890* (New York: Harper Torchbooks, 1965), p. 230.

20. Richmond *Enquirer*, November 22, 1867.

21. See, e.g., Claude H. Nolen, *The Negro's Image in the South: The Anatomy of White Supremacy* (Lexington: University of Kentucky Press, 1967), p. 36; Henry W. Grady, "In Plain Black and White: A Reply to Mr. Cable," *Century Magazine*, XXIX (April, 1885), 909–17; Jackson *Clarion*, September 8, 1870.

22. Joel Williamson, ed., *The Origins of Segregation* (Boston: D. C. Heath and Company, 1968), p. 67.

23. William Hannibal Thomas, *The American Negro* (New York: The Macmillan Company, 1901), p. 127.

24. Howard W. Odum, *Social and Mental Traits of the Negro* (New York: Columbia University, 1910), pp. 160, 172. Emphasis added.

venereal disease under slavery," but they were "rotten with it now and the contrast is glaringly evident." [25] Four years later Charles H. McCord charged that the Negro was a "defective animal" because he was highly susceptible to contagious disease, particularly venereal disease.[26]

Stressing venereal infection, the myth of the diseased Negro reduced the incentive for differential segregation. Even docile Negroes like "Blind Tom" or "Hannah, the faithful" could endanger white society. Mere physical proximity to "white men's Negroes" could lead to horrendous consequences. But sexual intercourse between white and black was particularly dangerous, serving notice on white men to abandon their long-standing associations with black women. And now more than ever before, black men had to be kept away from white women. The venereal disease that might result could literally destroy the white race, body and soul. Rigid across-the-board segregation of white from black seemed essential to the health and safety of white civilization.

As inflexible segregation statutes were enacted, as the South urbanized, and as the myth of Negro disease spread, the idea of a differential color line therefore became increasingly difficult to implement. White Southerners who desperately sought the company of docile blacks found it increasingly "dangerous" and even unpopular to have any Negroes around. As James K. Vardaman stated in 1901, "good [Negroes] are few, the bad are many, and it is impossible to tell what ones are . . . dangerous to the honor of the dominant race until the damage is done." [27] The search for black servility entailed considerable worry and frustration, for even if a docile Negro were located, he could still be contagious.

But if white Southerners were becoming frustrated in their search for servile Negro behavior, blacks experienced greater hardships. Where the color line was differentially applied, the black man was pressured to swallow his pride and defer to the white hand—to become a "white man's Negro." But as pleas for across-the-board segregation grew, demands upon black Southerners were hardly less onerous, for money, food, professional aid, and other necessities were on the white man's side of the color line. Moreover, blacks had to face other manifestations of intensified white racism—campaigns for Negro disfranchisement, the convict lease system, the widely heralded racist

25. Thomas E. Watson, *Socialists and Socialism* (Thomson, Georgia: Jeffersonian Press, 1910), p. 10.

26. Charles H. McCord, *The American Negro as a Dependent, Defective and Delinquent* (Nashville: Chas. H. McCord, 1914), pp. 44, 90, 155, 183.

27. Quoted in Albert D. Kirwan, *Revolt of the Rednecks: Mississippi Politics: 1876–1925* (New York: Harper Torchbooks, 1965), p. 147.

theory of Social Darwinism, the "white man's burden" justification for American imperialism, and growing Northern indifference toward the plight of the Southern Negro. The search for Negro docility produced little peace of mind for Southerners of either race.

Chapter Seven

Black Masks, White Fears

The white Southern search for docile Negro behavior was hindered by more than the inherent rigidities of the Jim Crow system, urbanization, and the myth of Negro disease. Changing behavioral patterns of black Southerners presented another major obstacle. Between Redemption and the election of Woodrow Wilson, white Southerners continually lamented the rise of an "obnoxiously assertive" quality in Negro conduct.[1] According to the editor of *The Southern Methodist Review*, a "new generation of negroes is already on the stage of action. They know nothing of the benefits and blessings of their father's estate in time of slavery, and they hear things which the lovers of strife and discord convey to them in a thousand forms of evil." [2] From Virginia, Orra Langhorne, champion of Negro industrial education, complained that Negroes had suddenly become far too concerned with proving that they were no longer loyal, obedient bondsmen.[3] John Ambrose Price, one of Arkansas' leading champions of home rule, was distressed over increasing Negro hostility toward the Southern Caucasian. Black behavior had convinced him that more than local autonomy was required if Southerners were ever to resolve their "Negro problem." [4]

Along with complaints of increasing assertive Negro behavior, some Southern whites began to voice apprehension about secret and exclusive Negro activities. These activities hindered the white man's

1. See, e.g., John Hammond Moore, ed., *Before and After, or The Relations of the Races at the South by Isaac DuBose Seabrook* (Baton Rouge: Louisiana State University Press, 1967), p. 123; George T. Winston, "The Relation of the Whites to the Negroes," *Annals of the American Academy of Political and Social Science*, XVIII (July–December, 1901), 118; Thomas E. Watson, "Editorials," *Watson's Jeffersonian Magazine*, I, No. 11 (November, 1907), 1038; "Letter to the Editor," *Moving Picture World* (August 26, 1911), p. 551; Claude L. Meals, "The Struggle of the Negro for Citizenship in Kentucky since 1865" (Master's thesis, Howard University, 1940), p. 64.

2. *The Southern Methodist Review*, III (November, 1887), 250.

3. Charles E. Wynes, ed., *Southern Sketches from Virginia 1881–1901 by Orra Langhorne* (Charlottesville: University Press of Virginia, 1964), p. 109.

4. John Ambrose Price, *The Negro: Past, Present, and Future* (New York and Washington, D.C.: Neale Publishing Co., 1907), p. 171.

traditional surveillance of Negro life. Hence, whites might never discover how to turn back the "new" wave of black insolence. For this reason, the danger of secretive black cohesion became a constant preoccupation. As early as 1879, a North Carolina politician expressed "uneasiness" over a Negro fair in Raleigh because it symbolized a dangerous "movement" toward "togetherness" and racial self-consciousness.[5] Four years later an influential Alabamian, John T. Morgan, complained that Negroes had begun to "congregate in dense communities."[6] To the Episcopal Bishop of Kentucky, black "exclusiveness" was "diminishing" white understanding of and control over Negro "belief" and "practice."[7] Historian Philip Alexander Bruce was exceedingly distressed, for he feared that the traditionally intimate master-servant relationship would cease altogether. As blacks withdrew among themselves, the natural and proper white-black relationship would pass from the scene.[8]

By the first decade of the twentieth century, whites throughout the region charged that the trend toward black cohesiveness precluded resolution of the "Negro problem." A Houston minister complained that there could be little improvement in the white-black relationship: since "coming to Texas I have not been able to know anything of the Negroes. . . ." Yet, to control blacks, whites had to know where they were and what they were doing.[9] Fretting over "a tendency to racial solidarity in opposition to whites on all questions whatsoever," Thomas Nelson Page contended that black "solidarity" would have to be broken.[10] Mississippi politician John Sharp Williams analyzed the problem with greater cogency: "More and more every year the negro's life—moral, intellectual and industrial—is isolated from the white man's life and therefore from his influence."[11]

Despite these sorts of comments, it was not assertive, secretive, and cohesive behavior, *per se*, that bothered many whites. Rather, without the simple, honest, "old-time Negro" who constantly deferred to white

5. "The Colored Fair at Raleigh, N. C.," *Frank Leslie's Illustrated Newspaper,* XLIX (December 6, 1879), 243.

6. Charles A. Gardiner, *et al.,* "The Future of the Negro," *North American Review,* CXXXIX (1884), 83.

7. Charles E. Wynes, ed., *Forgotten Voices: Dissenting Southerners in an Age of Conformity* (Baton Rouge: Louisiana State University Press, 1967), p. 55. Henry W. Grady, "In Plain Black and White: A Reply to Mr. Cable," *Century,* XXIX (April, 1885), 914, manifested these same apprehensions.

8. Philip A. Bruce, *The Plantation Negro as a Freeman* (New York, London: G. P. Putnam's Sons, 1889), pp. 43, 46, 48, 110, 242, 243; Bruce, "Evolution of the Negro Problem," *The Sewanee Review,* XIX, No. 4 (October, 1911), 397; Bruce, *The Rise of the New South* (Philadelphia: George Barrie & Sons, 1905), p. 356.

9. The Houston minister is quoted in W. E. B. DuBois, ed., *The Negro Church* (Atlanta: Atlanta University Press, 1903), p. 172.

10. Thomas Nelson Page, *The Negro: The Southerner's Problem* (New York: Charles Scribner's Sons, 1904), pp. 156, 159, 160, 194, 195, 304, 307.

11. Quoted in the Springfield *Republican,* December 6, 1906.

direction, escape from the nervous, chaotic and repressed qualities of life in white society became all the more improbable. For this reason, many whites were desperately concerned with the same essential question—how to restore contact and communication with blacks.[12] The question probably lay behind many of their commentaries on seemingly new and adverse Negro behavioral patterns. In a sense, then, the apparent changes in Negro conduct merely drew out and intensified the internal war that anxious Southern whites had been waging within themselves.

II

Daily experiences contributed to the anxiety of Southern whites over supposed black assertiveness and cohesiveness. A white man had only to see a group of blacks conversing in a grog shop to assume black racial cohesion. A Negro had only to forget to address a Caucasian as "mister" for the Caucasian to decry Negro assertiveness. But everyday experiences such as these were often ambiguous. The white man did not know for certain that Negroes in the grog shop were acting in concert; they could have been engaged in a divisive argument. And he was not always sure when a Negro failed to treat him respectfully. A particular Negro may not have been "insolent" but inadequately trained in the imperatives of Southern racial etiquette.

But though many Negroes could be "excused" for their improper conduct, one group could not. These were racial activists of the Negro middle class. Like other members of the black bourgeoisie, they tended to be independent professionals, white-collar workers, or small proprietors who made a living from economic ventures that were not competitive with whites. These ventures usually involved services to "black folk" as the poor black masses were called. Unlike the folk, they did not have to worry about the necessities of everyday existence. Yet unlike other members of the black middle class, they were not totally oriented toward a Horatio Alger ethic that equated success with capital assets.[13] Enjoying some economic security, Negro activists devoted themselves to more than materialistic self-gratification. In the novels and poetry that they wrote, in the histories that they narrated,

12. For particularly striking examples of whites posing this question, see Benjamin F. Riley, *The White Man's Burden* (Birmingham: B. F. Riley, 1910), p. 60, and the Atlanta *Journal*, November 8, 1906.

13. E. Franklin Frazier, *Black Bourgeoisie: The Rise of a New Middle Class in the United States* (New York: Crowell-Collier Publishing Company, 1962), especially pp. 31-41, provides the best available analysis of the development of Negro middle class ideology.

in the political speeches that they delivered, and in their sociological investigations, they were concerned with one purpose above all others: they sought to understand and to overcome the dilemmas of being Negro in the postbellum South. More disturbed by the effects of white racist pressures upon Negro life than any other element within the black population, they tried to attack white racism through concerted and sometimes secretive activity. But though they did not all agree on tactics or ideology, whites nevertheless saw in their campaigns the most telling proof of an aggressive and cohesive black population. Their deliberate and systematic attempt to resist racist pressures obscured underlying conflicts of motive and method in the eyes of most whites. To the Caucasian who sought servile behavior, all activitists confirmed the existence of an unsolved "Negro problem." Hence, vital distinctions among them usually went unnoticed.

As activists studied Southern race relations, certain of them concluded that aggressively anti-white rhetoric was the least debilitating way for blacks to resist white racist pressures. Unconsciously perhaps, they gambled upon the possibility that aggressive speech habits by one person toward another can foster or enlarge a communications impasse between them. They may have sensed that indulgence in anti-white outbursts could detract from everyday pressures generated by life in a white-controlled society. Most important, denigration of whites implicitly fostered a pride in things black.

Though anti-white rhetoric was extremely dangerous and perhaps suicidal in the postbellum South, activists sensed that it was worth the risk and began to castigate whites. They warned fellow Negroes that white characteristics precluded meaningful interracial cooperation. A Caucasian was inherently devious and would trick or betray a Negro in any biracial venture. Since blacks were innocent and principled while whites were corrupt and sly, a mutually beneficial relationship was impossible.

As early as the Reconstruction decade, several activist newspapers, particularly the New Orleans *Tribune* and the *New National Era*, printed such attacks.[14] But they became more widespread in subsequent years. In the 1880's the editor of the Jackson *People's Advertiser* argued vigorously and emotionally that whites could no longer be trusted to fight black people's battles.[15] An Atlanta editor charged that the "Southern white man, as a unit, is against us politically. And when he calls upon us for a vote, it is for a selfish end, and not for our good." [16] By the end of World War I, the scholarly historical pub-

14. See, e.g., New Orleans *Tribune*, February 1, 1865; *New National Era*, January 27, April 28, 1870. See also black leaders quoted in the Knoxville *Whig*, May 1, 1867.

15. Jackson *People's Adviser*, n.d., as quoted in the Savannah *Weekly Echo*, August 26, 1883.

16. Atlanta *Independent*, November 11, 1905.

lications of Carter G. Woodson echoed this message: it was "a delu-
sion" for Negroes to think that they could have the sincere cooperation
of Caucasians. Whites might profess to offer their assistance but they
were invariably doing so for their own ends. A white man was
incapable of empathizing with a Negro.[17]

The case against the Caucasian was sometimes stated more acidly.
"You know what I think of white people," a black artisan from
Alabama proclaimed, "They are no good." [18] An editor from Richmond called whites "degenerates" while a black novelist described
them as "an ignorant, narrow and childish people." [19] A black
minister from Baltimore insisted that white pigmentation was "anti-
natural." [20] By way of contrast, all of these activists proclaimed that
Negroes were "good," "intelligent," and "natural."

Some activists boldly singled out specific white Southern leaders
for special attack. Sutton E. Griggs, Kelly Miller, and Charles W.
Chesnutt were the most daring. Joined on occasion by other activists,
they chastised white racists of all varieties. William Brownlow, Thomas
Nelson Page, Tom Watson, and even George W. Cable were among
their victims. These whites were characterized as crude, scheming,
insensitive foes of black America.[21]

For many activists, all such contentions led to one conclusion.
Whites, particularly Southern whites, had little to offer blacks. "I
think that the time has come," one wrote, "when that race should
cease to set themselves up as a standard for the colored race." [22]
Some insisted that they had to reverse the traditional scheme of
things, with blacks ruling and civilizing the crude white race. Since

17. Carter G. Woodson, *The Education of the Negro Prior to 1861* (Washington.
D. C.: The Associated Publishers, Inc., 1919), p. 287; Woodson, *The History of the
Negro Church* (Washington, D. C.: The Associated Publishers, 1921), pp. 312–13.

18. Quoted in Ely Green, *Ely: An Autobiography* (New York: Seabury Press,
1966), p. 53.

19. Richmond *Planet*, August 25, 1888; Helen M. Chesnutt, ed., *Charles Waddell Chesnutt: Pioneer of the Color Line* (Chapel Hill: The University of North
Carolina Press, 1952), p. 195.

20. Harvey Johnson, *The Nations from a New Point of View* (Nashville: National Baptist Publishing Board, 1903), p. 138.

21. Sutton E. Griggs, *The Hindered Hand* (Nashville: Orion Publishing Company,
1905), pp. 259, 303–33; Kelly Miller, *Race Adjustment* (New York: Neale Publishing Company, 1908), pp. 40, 53; Miller, "A Reply to Tom Watson: Is the Negro
Inherently Inferior?" *Voice of the Negro,* II (August, 1905), 543; Montgomery *Advertiser,* June 16, 1906; Charles W. Chesnutt to George W. Cable, March 28, 1890,
Chesnutt Papers, Fisk University; *People's Party Paper,* September 16, 1892; Emmett J. Scott to Thomas Nelson Page, February 12, 1904, Page Papers, Duke University; W. E. B. DuBois, "The Southerner's Problem," *The Dial,* XXXVIII (May
1, 1905), 316; Nashville *Union and Dispatch,* April 17, 1867; Nashville *Daily Press
and Times,* August 12, 1868; William A. Sinclair, *The Aftermath of Slavery* (Boston: Small, Maynard & Co., 1905), p. 9.

22. Harvey Johnson, *The Nations,* p. 203.

Negroes had "a better heart than white people," one activist suggested, blacks could help to make whites "free." [23] A Nashville physician charged that he was trying to uplift Southern whites—to inculcate in them that "full sense of justice" which they so desperately needed.[24]

Thus, racial activists waged verbal warfare against the Caucasian. As white racial theorists had debased them, they in turn invoked similar racist myths to debase whites and exalt blackness. To be sure, white Southerners did not hear all of their charges; some of their cries never passed beyond the black community. But many did. For example, the popular Neale Publishing Company printed activist writings, and many reached white hands. Nor were the activist writings published by less well-known houses like the National Baptist Publishing Board restricted to a black readership. Moreover, the white press reprinted certain activist editorials from Negro newspapers; sometimes it featured stories about Negro activists. Finally, whites learned about racial activists through rumor and hearsay. Tom Watson, for instance, had never read *The Voice of the Negro*. But through conversation, he learned that a "vicious" Negro had published an article in that journal charging him with racism. Activist writing therefore had its impact. Its fiery, aggressively anti-white tone did much to convince white Southerners that blacks were dangerously cohesive and self-conscious. It made whites all the more anxious to regain servile Negro behavior.

III

Most Southern whites never realized that few activists had the power to implement their rhetoric. So long as whites possessed the wealth of the South, blacks of all classes and ideologies had to be concerned about their livelihood. If whites chose to use economic power, the most prosperous Negro could have been destroyed. Intensive competition could force the Negro out of business. Governmental authorities could be bribed to charge recalcitrant Negroes with criminal violations. If the white man elected to invoke his immense financial power, activists would find it difficult if not impossible to realize their anti-white slogans.

Certain black leaders grasped the consequences of the race's economic weakness. Realizing that money in the black community could reduce pressures upon the black man to become a white man's "nigger," they waged an energetic campaign to augment black

23. Henry McNeal Turner as quoted in the Augusta *Colored American*, January 13, 1866.
24. Charles V. Roman, *American Civilization and the Negro* (Philadelphia: F. A. Davis Company, 1916), p. 123.

financial resources. Activist newspapers frequently urged blacks to establish and patronize black enterprises.[25] "Patronize Negro Business" became the motto printed on all stationery of the Alabama State Negro Business League.[26] In an advertising leaflet, a Negro bank in Virginia asked in bold type: "ARE YOU DOING ANY BUSINESS WITH A COLORED BANK?"[27] And at Atlanta University's 1899 conference on "Negro Problems," a delegate pleaded: "Let us keep our money among ourselves. Let us spend our money with each other. Let us protect each other, as the other races do."[28]

This program was not entirely in vain. By 1907 there was a proliferation of black-owned insurance companies, cemeteries, grocery stores, and general merchandise stores throughout the South.[29] The growth of black business was particularly striking in the large cities of the region, notably Columbia, Houston, Lexington, Mobile, and Charleston.[30] Writing of black Durham and black Atlanta on the eve of World War I, W. E. B. DuBois contended that a Negro could go from morning to night eating, sleeping, and working among blacks in black-owned enterprises.[31]

Yet Negro economic development within the South was not as impressive as these initial observations suggest. Activist propaganda for black business enterprise and for "buying black" may even have indicated dissatisfaction with the existing state of Negro economic resources. In 1911, Booker T. Washington, always the optimist when it came to black economic activity, predicted that Negroes *could*

25. See, e.g., Helena (Arkansas) *Reporter*, February 1, 1900; Dallas *Express*, January 13, 1900; *Paul Quinn Weekly* (Waco, Texas), January 27, 1900; Lexington (Kentucky) *Standard*, n.d., quoted in the Raleigh *Gazette*, November 6, 1897; Brandon (Mississippi) *Free State*, January 20, 1900; Houston *Western Star*, January 27, 1900.

26. Correspondence in which this stationery was used may be found in the Booker T. Washington Papers, Library of Congress.

27. Several copies of this 1909 leaflet, "Black Stock is the Money-Making Investment," are in the Booker T. Washington Papers, Library of Congress. It was printed for the Crown Savings Bank of Newport News.

28. Quoted in W. E. B. DuBois, ed., *The Negro in Business* (Atlanta: Atlanta University Press, 1899), p. 61.

29. August Meier, *Negro Thought in America, 1880–1915* (Ann Arbor: University of Michigan Press, 1963), pp. 145–50 and the Greensboro *Daily News*, September 14, 1910, contain data on black insurance enterprises; W. E. B. DuBois, ed., *Economic Cooperation among Negro Americans* (Atlanta: Atlanta University Press, 1907), p. 131, has information on Negro cemeteries; observations on black groceries and general merchandise stores are found in DuBois, ed., *Negro in Business*, p. 12.

30. George B. Tindall, *South Carolina Negroes 1877–1900* (Baton Rouge: Louisiana State University Press, 1966), p. 143; DuBois, ed., *Negro in Business*, pp. 29–33.

31. W. E. B. DuBois, "The Upbuilding of Black Durham," *World's Work*, XXIII (January, 1912), 338, and "The Social Evolution of the Black South," *American Negro Monographs*, I, No. 4 (March, 1911), 7–8.

form "a nation within a nation" in the South. Nonetheless, he cautioned, they were a long way from achieving that end. Before economic self-sufficiency was possible, Washington calculated that blacks would have to create at least thirty thousand additional businesses—an enormous task.[32] The authoritative Atlanta University study, *The Negro in Business* (1899), reported that most Southern blacks continued to be unskilled agricultural laborers and that Negroes owned and operated only four banks in the entire nation.[33] Of all gainfully employed Southern blacks, only 2.5 per cent were in the professions, with the black community particularly short on doctors and lawyers. In 1908 sociologist-mathematician Kelly Miller calculated that one black doctor practiced for every 24,000 Negro inhabitants in Alabama and one black lawyer for every 52,000. The ratios in South Carolina and Texas were only slightly less.[34] The message was clear: most blacks had to rely upon whites for medical and legal services.

Lacking financial resources and professional counsel, blacks had little chance of success in any direct economic confrontation with Southern whites. Yet some Negro activists openly challenged white power. In several Southern cities they tried to circumvent segregated white streetcar lines by organizing lines of their own. But deficient financial resources told the story. White bondholders foreclosed, electric companies sometimes refused to furnish electricity, and in certain cases blacks simply lacked the funds to purchase carriages.[35] In 1919 Louisville was the site of an even more pitiful economic confrontation. Several women's shops refused to permit blacks to try on garments before making purchases. Protests were voiced but a boycott was out of the question, for the discriminating stores were the only shops in the city where Negro women could buy clothing. "Won't somebody please open a store, a first-class store, catering particularly and especially to Colored women, so that they may at least spend their money free from insult? Please," pleaded the editor of the Louisville *News*.[36] Against white economic power, exorcisms of Negro activists counted for little.

After repeated failures, some activists began to perceive the probable consequences of direct white-black economic confrontation. They

32. *Southwestern Christian Advocate* (New Orleans), August 10, 1911.

33. DuBois, ed., *Negro in Business*, pp. 10, 13. See also Frazier, *Black Bourgeoisie*, p. 39.

34. Meier, *Negro Thought*, p. 207, reports the 2.5 per cent figure. Kelly Miller, *Race Adjustment*, pp. 184–85 cites doctor and lawyer ratios.

35. DuBois, ed., *Economic Cooperation*, pp. 164–65; August Meier and Elliot Rudwick, "The Boycott Movement against Jim Crow Streetcars in the South, 1900–1906," *Journal of American History*, LV, No. 4 (March, 1969), 764; D. B. Jefford to Whitefield McKinley, October 19, 1904, McKinley Papers, Woodson Collection, Library of Congress.

36. Louisville *News*, October 18, 1919, as quoted in Robert T. Kerlin, ed., *The Voice of the Negro 1919* (New York: E. P. Dutton and Company, 1920), pp. 162–63.

chose to avoid direct confrontation until blacks could accumulate greater wealth and thus greater power. Some began to promote ventures that whites would not interpret as a direct challenge, hoping in this way to accumulate funds and to cultivate racial pride. They tried to establish black theaters where Negro patrons could sit in boxes as well as in the galleries and where the black face did not always stand for a servant, a clown, or a petty criminal—the happy, docile, erring "nigger" that white Southerners loved.[37] They also tried to remove stove-black "nigger" dolls and white dolls from Negro homes and encouraged black production and distribution of true-to-life, dignified Negro dolls.[38] Excluded from white library facilities, several black churches and women's clubs even attempted to organize Negro libraries and reading rooms.[39]

Convinced that only the most vicious white racist—the Hinton Rowan Helper or the Tom Watson—felt threatened by Negro education, some activists calculated that the black community could augment its economic resources if it controlled Negro educational facilities. Since the facilities were funded and could employ black teachers, they represented economic assets. Moreover, if black students at these schools could acquire a sense of racial loyalty, they could be motivated to accumulate capital for the race. Accordingly, a number of activists campaigned for a black educational experience that was oriented toward the Negro's psychological and intellectual needs, charging that if a school was to provide education of this sort, it would have to be black controlled.[40] This usually translated into demands to hire black teachers. Under the slogan "Colored Teachers for Colored Schools," campaigns were launched in Baltimore, Washington, D. C., and other cities for the recruitment of black faculty.[41]

Though they were profuse, most activist efforts to increase black control over Negro schools yielded meager results. Charles Dudley Warner concluded from his Southern tour of 1886 that "scarcely anywhere can the colored people as yet have a private school without

37. See, e.g., the Chicago *Conservator*, November 24, 1906, and the *Praiseworthy Muse* (Norfolk), September, 1919, as quoted in Kerlin, ed., *Voice of Negro*, pp. 166–67.

38. W. D. Weatherford, *Present Forces in Negro Progress* (New York, London: Association Press, 1912), pp. 42–43; Stephan Graham, *The Soul of John Brown* (New York: The Macmillan Company, 1920), pp. 196–97.

39. Meier, *Negro Thought*, p. 136.

40. Miller, *Race Adjustment*, p. 273; New York *Globe*, January 20, 1883; Ridgely Torrence, *The Story of John Hope* (New York: The Macmillan Company, 1948), p. 201; Henry A. Bullock, *A History of Negro Education in the South from 1619 to the Present* (Cambridge: Harvard University Press, 1967), p. 147; Nashville *Banner*, August 5, 1911.

41. Virginia *Star* (Richmond), September 27, 1879; Tindall, *South Carolina Negroes*, pp. 220–21; "Address of R. H. Terrell," unpublished ms., June 12, 1899, Robert H. Terrell Papers, Library of Congress.

white aid from somewhere." [42] *Economic Cooperation Among Negro Americans,* the 1907 Atlanta University study, maintained that schools for "higher training" and industrial institutions continued to be financed by white money.[43] Until at least World War I, Negro colleges were almost entirely sustained, manned, and administered by whites striving to "cultivate" an "unenlightened" race.[44] Moreover, as Southern legislatures reduced the flow of funds to Negro educational institutions, black educators at all levels of instruction became increasingly dependent upon wealthy Northern philanthropists. Unfortunately, these philanthropists tended to regard blacks as inferiors whom they were "ordained" to "elevate." [45] Thus, as a black educator from Mississippi maintained, black school officials were wisest if they raised as much money as possible from the Negro community before they approached whites.[46] The problem was that the Negro community had very little money.

The failure of most economic confrontations with whites, direct and indirect, caused a few activists to explore the concept of the all-black town. "If we can come together, build up communities of our own, promote them into towns and cities," a Raleigh editor predicted, "we shall do well." [47] By moving to areas where there were no whites, blacks would be free to accumulate wealth and foster pride-in-race without interference. Certain black leaders proceeded to organize these communities. Beginning in the late 1880's, they established all-Negro settlements in such diverse locations as Eatonville, Florida; Columbia-Heights, North Carolina; Hobson City, Alabama; Grambling, Louisiana; Boley, Oklahoma; and Mound Bayou, Mississippi.[48]

42. Quoted in James P. Shenton, ed., *The Reconstruction; A Documentary History of the South after the War: 1865–1877* (New York: G. P. Putnam's Sons, 1963), p. 289.

43. DuBois, ed., *Economic Cooperation,* p. 88.

44. S. P. Fullinwider, *The Mind and Mood of Black America: 20th Century Thought* (Homewood, Illinois: The Dorsey Press, 1969), p. 92.

45. Booker T. Washington, *The Story of the Negro* (New York: Doubleday, Page & Company, 1909). II, 344–45, and John Samuel Ezell, *The South Since 1865* (New York: The Macmillan Company, 1963), pp. 251–52 provide information on fund and facility limitations set by Southern governments. Louis R. Harlan, *Separate and Unequal: Public School Campaigns and Racism in the Southern Seaboard States 1901–1915* (Chapel Hill: University of North Carolina Press, 1958) offers one of the best analyses of the racism of Northern educational philanthropists. Harlan also provides a cogent assessment of the Northern philanthropist's role in financing black Southern education.

46. Elias Cottrell to Mary Church Terrell, February 1, 1908, Mary Church Terrell Papers, Library of Congress.

47. Raleigh *Independent,* April 28, 1917.

48. Booker T. Washington, *The Negro in Business* (Boston and Chicago: Hertel, Jenkins & Company, 1907), pp. 74–76, 77–80, 89–93, supplies data on the all-Negro towns of Columbia-Heights, Eatonville, and Mound Bayou. Alan Boles, " 'Black Power' Since 1899," *The Southern Courier* (October 7–8, 1967), p. 3, tells of the founding of Hobson City. Harold M. Rose, "The All-Negro Town: Its Evolution

With the possible exceptions of Mound Bayou and Hobson City, however, the all-black town afforded little refuge from the crushing power of white financial resources. After seventeen years, blacks in Columbia-Heights continued to transact *all* their business in nearby Winston-Salem.[49] Negroes in Kowaliga failed to sustain enough enterprise to export a single product or raw material.[50] Twenty years after its founding, Eatonville had only two hundred and fifty inhabitants, one church, and one school.[51] Life was not pleasant in poor, economically stagnating settlements such as these. As DuBois emphasized, poverty tended to create a frustrating "veil" in the all-black community between the Negro inhabitants on the one side and opportunity on the other.[52]

Clearly, black activists lacked the economic resources to implement their fiery rhetoric. Almost everywhere they turned to increase the race's economic resources—whether to the black streetcar line, the black public school, or the black town—they met with little success. In large part, those who controlled the economic resources of the South—the Wattersons, the Gradys, and the Pages—assured the failure of all such black separatist economic ventures. Determined to secure a servile black race that could never become independent of the Caucasian, powerful whites opposed black separatist economic activity. Had the white owners of Southern electric companies furnished power for black electric-carriage ventures, had Southern legislators increased rather than reduced appropriations for black schools, and had white Southern investors permitted low interest loans to the founders of all-black towns, genuine economic power might have developed within the black community. But white anxieties could only be increased by blacks who became financially independent. Negro economic success would contradict white Southern assumptions concerning the primitivism and indolence of the black race. Even a "liberal" like Cable could not allow himself to be contradicted on this score. If Negroes succeeded on their own without white guidance, his "liberalism" would have become irrelevant. Psychologically, whites could ill afford black economic progress.

and Function," *Georgia Review*, XIX (July. 1965), 368–69, comments on the origins of Grambling, Fairmont Heights, and Glenarden. Washington, *Story of the Negro*, II, 248–50, notes Boley. For other informative evaluations of all-black towns, see Miller, *Race Adjustment*, pp. 166–67; Winfield H. Collins, *The Truth about Lynching and The Negro in the South* (New York: Neale Publishing Company, 1918), p. 103; Washington, *Story of the Negro*, II, 253.

49. Washington, *Negro in Business*, pp. 74–76.

50. W. E. D. DuBois, ed., *The Negro Artisan* (Atlanta: Atlanta University Press, 1902), p. 86.

51. Washington, *Negro in Business*, pp. 77–80.

52. W. E. B. DuBois, "A Negro Schoolmaster in the New South," *Atlantic Monthly*, XCIII (January, 1889), 102.

IV

Failing in most of their economic endeavors, Negro activists sought other ways to counter white racist pressures and to promote black self-awareness. If they could not nullify white racist pressures through economic activity, they could try to rescue the black psyche through myth. If the activist could repudiate the pervasive white Southern interpretation of Negroes as savages—if he could formulate and disseminate an alternative myth—he could help blacks to "pull together." Refuting the traditional white Southern myth of the Negro past as a barbaric past, he could supplant it with mythology that might compensate for the economic weakness of the race. If economic ventures failed him, historical invention could afford the activist strength to endure. History could become therapy. In the words of Daniel Augustus Straker, one of many activists who took up the study of the Negro past: "There is enough history of the Negro race to make a Negro proud of his race. Why not then teach the Negro child more of himself and less of others, more of his elevation and less of his degredation [*sic*]. This only can produce true pride of race, which begets mutual confidence and unity." [53] Other activists heartily concurred.[54] Officers of Nashville's Phyllis Wheatley Woman's League carried this logic to the point of consciously equating "the history of the Negro Race" with the Negro's "grand achievements." [55]

Activists were demanding consciously partisan and therefore essentially mythological history. Cold, dispassionate narrative of historical facts would not meet the needs of the frustrated black psyche. Joseph T. Wilson, a native Virginian and a Union trooper during the Civil War, was one of the first activists to reconstruct the Negro past along these therapeutic lines. His widely publicized book, *The Black Phalanx* (1890), simultaneously vindicated the black man's past and Wilson's personal history. He portrayed black soldiers in the Revolutionary War, the War of 1812, and particularly the Civil War as gallant fighters who drew their strength from a sense of racial pride. South Carolina physician William A. Sinclair's *The*

53. Daniel Augustus Straker, *The New South Investigated* (Detroit: Ferguson Printing Company, 1888), p. 207.

54. See, e.g., Sutton E. Griggs to Carter G. Woodson, May 28, 1918; Charles W. Chesnutt to Carter G. Woodson, January 3, 1917, both in the Woodson Papers, Woodson Collection, Library of Congress; Mary Church Terrell as quoted in the Galesburg (Illinois) *Evening News*, August 1, 1901; Clement Richardson to Mary Church Terrell, November 14, 1916, Mary Church Terrell Papers, Library of Congress.

55. L. A. Davis and M. B. Jackson to National Association of Colored Women, September 15, 1897, Mary Church Terrell Papers, Library of Congress.

Aftermath of Slavery (1905) was another volume illustrating the development of a partisan, mythological historical tradition. It was little more than an annotated list of black heroes from Crispus Attucks to the "honest" and "brave" black politician of the Reconstruction decade. Booker T. Washington deliberately subtitled his book, *The Story of the Negro* (1909), with the phrase *The Rise of the Race from Slavery* in order to emphasize his central theme—the bond between the black man's past glories and his future potentialities. Benjamin Griffith Brawley's *A Short History of the American Negro* (1913) was designed to meet this same end. As Brawley narrated the black man's past, he omitted the debilitating aspects of Negro life, offering a story of continuous black progress in the arts, the sciences, and the military. Even Carter G. Woodson, father of modern Negro historiography, gave in to this trend toward partisan, mythological historical scholarship. In *The Education of the Negro Prior to 1861* (1919), Woodson accumulated a vast array of evidence to "prove" that a heroic struggle for knowledge was the central theme of Negro history. He sought to demonstrate that "the accounts of the successful strivings of Negroes for enlightenment under the most adverse circumstances read like beautiful romances of a people in an heroic age." [56]

Confronted by white racist pressures and lacking the economic resources to fight back, certain black historians thus strove to recreate a Negro past that could heal tormented black psyches. To them, black history could do more than disseminate knowledge; it could help blacks to "pull themselves together." Indeed, the development of a mythic past of Negro activism and heroism had definite therapeutic value.

Searching for signs of heroic activism, black historians encountered numerous instances of Negro passivity. Usually they chose to ignore this data, for evidence of Negro weakness contradicted the basic thrust of their message. But some chose to confront the data. Like evidence concerning Negro activism, they could use it to prove the heroic qualities of the race. The humble Negro beaten to the ground by a coarse Caucasian could be praised for his bravery. Unlike members of the crude white race, he had the strength to endure.[57] Black leaders like Frederick Douglass and Hiram R. Revels were characterized as men who had patiently and courageously withstood white racist pressures; they had therefore triumphed over the invidious Caucasian.[58] In *The History of the Negro Church,* Carter Woodson

56. Carter G. Woodson, *The Education of the Negro Prior to 1861,* p. iii.

57. For a brilliant analysis of the uses of this image in postbellum Negro writing, see Fullinwider, *Mind and Mood of Black America,* pp. 1–71.,

58. See, e.g., *New National Era,* June 23, 1870; Booker T. Washington, *The Future of the Negro* (Boston: Small, Maynard & Company, 1900), p. 180; Phil Waters to Robert H. Terrell, February 18, 1914, and E. D. W. Jones to Robert H. Terrell, March, 1914, both in the Robert H. Terrell Papers, Library of Congress.

emphasized that blacks had traditionally displayed remarkable endurance in the face of adversity. Others dwelled upon the same theme, always equating survival in the face of hardship with the heroic.[59]

That black historians drew proof for the heroic qualities of the race from opposite behavioral patterns—passivity as well as activism—underlined the partisan and mythic nature of their writings. Evidence for an interpretation of the past that could help black people to cope with the present had to be "illuminated" by a preconceived conclusion. But even partisanship and myth-making had its limitations. Though the activist as historian was capable of interpreting any data on the Negro past to prove heroism, the data was not always available. He often found himself exploring a great mass of important detail about whites before uncovering even a small quantity of information concerning Negroes. As a result, the writings of many activists could almost be called white history. Conflict between whites led to the great events of the American past—the Revolution, the War of 1812, and World War I. In *Emancipation: Its Course and Progress* (1882), the fiery black intellectual, Joseph Wilson, had little to say about Negro Americans. They seemed to have played no crucial role in their own liberation. Ironically, John R. Lynch's *The Facts of Reconstruction* (1913) suggested that Negroes had played a smaller role in Southern Reconstruction than even the racist William A. Dunning school of historians had indicated.[60]

Thus, though Lynch, Wilson, and other activist historians drew strength and pride from what they uncovered in the black past, their research no doubt impressed upon them the comparatively greater influence of white Americans. Moreover, as they published their findings under titles like *The Black Phalanx* and *A Short History of the American Negro*, they probably conveyed this impression to black readers. Many of their histories inadvertently taught literate blacks more of white power than of the Negro's past glory. Therefore, the quest for a black past did not always reinforce the black psyche. At times, it may have fostered sharp doubts concerning the Negro's capacities, fortifying the white racist stereotype of blacks as lowly, coarse barbarians.

59. See, e.g., John Mercer Langston, *Freedom and Citizenship* (Washington, D. C.: Rufus H. Darby, 1883), p. 116; Edward A. Johnson, *A School History of the Negro Race in America, from 1619 to 1890. With a Short Introduction as to the Origins of the Race; Also a Short Sketch of Liberia* (Chicago: W. B. Conkey Company, 1893), especially pp. 9–10, 14; Joseph T. Wilson, *The Black Phalanx: A History of the Negro Soldiers of the United States in the Wars of 1775–1812, 1861–1865* (Hartford: American Publishing Company, 1890), p. 96.

60. See also John R. Lynch to Carter G. Woodson, October 30, 1917, Woodson Papers, Woodson Collection, Library of Congress, for proof that Lynch viewed Southern Reconstruction as essentially white history.

In 1897 a black editor from Raleigh complained that Negro children could recount the major names and events in white history but knew virtually nothing about the black experience in America.[61] Through some research and considerable invention, Negro activists published books that may have somewhat improved the status of black history. But until successful confrontations with the white community became part of the black past, Negroes who looked to history ran the risk of becoming disenchanted with their race. When history was exploited for therapy, white racists like Page and Watson ran fewer risks than any black activist.

V

As a device for activists to protect blacks from white pressures, historical myth-making had limited value. Desperately seeking to cultivate a sense of black worth and dignity, some activists turned to debate whites over the relationship between race and sexual "misconduct." What provoked them were the humiliating charges that blacks assaulted or craved to assault white women. Southern whites had regularly proclaimed that because the Negro was a savage, he was a potential rapist and had to be controlled in the interests of white civilization, Activists attempted to refute this assertion simply by reversing its assumptions, contending that whites, not blacks, were the rapists. The real danger was an assault by the white male upon the black female. One activist charged that Negro girls had difficulty retaining their virginity because they were constantly molested by white men.[62] Another insisted that the white Southern male was a "rapist." The white South could be forgiven for most of its faults, but blacks could never forget "its wanton and continued and persistent insulting of black womanhood which it sought and seeks to prostitute to its lust." [63] Because a "corrupt" Southern judiciary had sanctioned crude sexual assaults upon Negro females, an angry black woman charged that it was nearly impossible for a black girl to grow to womanhood unviolated.[64] Clearly, the savages of the region were white. By implication, civilization became linked to blackness.

61. Raleigh *Gazette*, October 23, 1897.

62. Griggs, *Hindered Hand*, pp. 96, 140.

63. W. E. B. DuBois, *The Souls of Black Folk: Essays and Sketches* (Greenwich, Conn.: Crest Books, 1961), p. 84; DuBois, *Darkwater: Voices from Within the Veil* (New York: Harcourt, Brace & Howe, 1920), p. 172.

64. The woman, Mary Church Terrell, is quoted in the Washington *Post*, October 19, 1905; the Topeka *Daily Capitol*, February 21, 1907; and the Charleston *News and Courier*, November 14, 1907. For similar charges by other activists, see J. W. Grant, *Out of the Darkness* (Nashville: National Baptist Publishing Board, 1909), p. 27; Galveston *New Idea*, October 25, 1919; Louisville *News*, October 18, 1919.

Male activists were particularly vehement in their attack on the sexual improprieties of white men toward black women. To an extent, they sought to have black women protected against white aggression because they saw in the Negro female the essence of black beauty. Free from white violation, she was the Athena of the race. An N.A.A.C.P. organizer claimed that "the most virtuous creature in the United States of America is the Negro woman. Her resisting and enduring powers are of the highest order." [65] According to a black physician, "the most accurately proportioned human form I ever examined was a 17-year-old black girl. The symmetry of her body was perfect," while her color and her hair were Negroid and hence beautiful.[66] Commentaries in DuBois' *Darkwater* were strikingly similar. Women distinctly "black or brown and crowned in curled mists" represented "the most beautiful thing on Earth." [67]

Phrases like "resisting and enduring power," "symmetry of her body," and "curled mists" underlined the sexual attractiveness of the black female. Hence, though the black men who exalted her obviously wanted to protect her from the white male, they may also have wanted exclusive rights to her body. In this way, they could fuse themselves with the essence of black beauty. This possibility is quite plausible, for efforts to protect black women were elements in a broader campaign for racial integrity—for blacks to fornicate exclusively with other blacks. In his novel, *Out of the Darkness* (1909), J. W. Grant called for the protection of black womanhood within a more general plea for racial purity.[68] Equally fearful of white sexual assaults upon black women, another black activist concurred: "Fellow Negroes, for the sake of the world interests, it is my hope that you will maintain your ambition for racial purity. So long as your blood relationship to Africa is apparent to you the world has a redeeming force. . . ." [69] The commentary of a black editor from Houston was the most revealing. The black community would be well off, he charged, if it could keep itself "100 per cent pure." This meant that all Negroes, *particularly women*, should not be " 'hossing' to be the social companions of white people." [70] Like others, the editor saw collateral benefits in racial purity. He knew that emphasis upon Negro purity helped black males to eliminate white competition for black females. It would reduce the tendency for black women to "hoss" with white men.

65. William Pickens, "Fifty Years of Emancipation," unpublished ms., January 12, 1913, Robert H. Terrell Papers. Library of Congress.,

66. Charles V. Roman, *American Civilization and the Negro*, p. 359.

67. DuBois, *Darkwater*, p. 183.

68. Grant, *Out of the Darkness*, especially p. 85.

69. Griggs, *Hindered Hand*, p. 198.

70. Houston *Informer*, November 1, 1919. See also the Helena (Arkansas) *Reporter*, February 1, 1900.

Black men were not alone in their efforts to maintain racial purity. Partially out of fear that white females could be attracted to black men, white racists like Page, Watson, and Dixon had charged that interracial sexual contact involving "their women" threatened racial integrity. On the other hand, they rarely mentioned sexual relations between white males and black females. Certain black activists were promoting the same kind of argument. Women had to be "loyal" to the men of their race in order to preserve racial integrity. Strangely, male "loyalty" was not as crucial to the purity of the black race.

Clearly, white Southern racists and black activists looked at women in similar terms. Both viewed the female as a second sex with distinctly limited privileges. But the parallel ran even closer. Since antebellum days, Southern planters had idolized the white woman as a jewel of the universe, adorning her in finery and speaking of her as a near goddess. At the celebration of Georgia's one-hundredth anniversary in the 1830's a toast brought twenty cheers: "Woman!!! The center and circumference, diameter and periphery, sine, tangent and secant of all our affections!" [71] Perpetuating the Cavalier literary tradition, Page referred to white women in the same exalted terms while Brownlow, Watterson, Watson, and Cable were only slightly more earthy in their descriptions. By the turn of the century, as articulate Negro activists busied themseves on the racial front, many thought in the same terms. Like whites of the "Brownlow tradition," they paid homage to the shrine of womanhood. But though they exalted and demanded protection for black women threatened by white assault and though the white male exalted a white woman who black males rarely endangered, men of both races considered "their" women in the same light. Both claimed guardianship over "their" women; both elevated the female above the state of mortals. Southern males, white and black, were therefore participating in the dehumanization of women. While they may have been manifesting an American or even a universal phenomenon, this did not mitigate the harsh effect of their conduct.

Thus, as certain activitists rebutted the white Southern charge that black males were predisposed to raping white females, they tried to augment the Negro's sense of worth and dignity; Caucasians, not blacks, lacked respect for the "purity of womanhood," for they assaulted the precious black female. But this black male counterattack introduced serious problems; it furthered a black male predisposition to idolize a black female to the point where she became a mere object. In male eyes, she lost her essential human qualities, and this may have precluded a viable man-woman relationship among many blacks. Throughout her autobiography, for example, Mary Church Terrell

71. Quoted in W. J. Cash, *The Mind of the South* (New York: Alfred A. Knopf, Inc., 1941), p. 89.

indicated that she had become bitterly disappointed over her marital relationship. She complained that her activist lawyer husband always seemed to treat her like fragile pottery, thwarting her activities in behalf of women's rights and racial justice for fear that she might be "tarnished." [72] The relationship between Booker T. Washington and his third wife, Margaret Murray Washington, resembled the relationship between the Terrells. Mrs. Washington wanted an active, functional life but her husband insisted that she had to be more "moderate" and "restrained." Frustrations ensued and marital life became almost pointless. Writing on the benefit of matrimony for Negro Americans, she could only maintain that it allowed a black man and woman to "unite their savings" and thereby enlarge their purchasing power. In "this order of helpmate may lie some of the reason for gain in the sacredness of the marriage tie," she concluded.[73] Marriage was practically reduced to a financial transaction. For Margaret Washington, its benefits were essentially monetary. If she had to be passive and "restrained"—to stand atop the pedestal of exalted womanhood—what else could be gained from living with Booker T. Washington?

The Terrell and Washington examples were probably not unique. Hence, the effort to fortify racial pride through exaltation of pure womanhood was likely as disastrous for the black race as for the white. The promotion of an untenable man-woman relationship through the dehumanization of women merely added to the many frustrations that plagued black Southerners.

VI

Clearly, Negro activists could hardly mitigate white racist pressures and the complex ramifications of those pressures. In most economic confrontations with white society, they were soundly defeated, while historical invention and exaltation of black womanhood were inadequate substitutes for economic power. The results were disheartening. Even before the turn of the century many activists were losing faith in the quest for black liberation. As the Brownlows, the Wattersons, the Pages, and the Watsons suppressed black resistance, they had justified their own barbaric conduct by alluding to the supremacy of white civilization and the necessity for black servility. Increasingly, many activists began to accept these justifications. As the white man had successfully turned back black efforts, many began to sense that

---

72. Mary Church Terrell, *A Colored Woman in a White World* (Washington, D. C.: Randell, Inc., 1940), pp. 102, 104, 106, 107, 115.

73. Mrs. Booker T. Washington, "The Gain in the Life of the Negro Women," *The Outlook*, LXXVI (January 30, 1904), 273.

the white race was supreme. White success did not cause Negro activists to let up on their fiery anti-white rhetoric. But in occasional moments of unguarded candor, several of them began to de-emphasize the struggle for racial dignity.

Notwithstanding the intensive campaign to exalt the black past, activists who spoke of black history in glorious terms occasionally began to acknowledge that Negroes had never led meaningful, inspiring lives. "The past of the Negro race has been one long story of pathos and sadness, of ignorance and ostracism," one observed. "Even the brief period of his freedom has been simply a mine of incidents rather than an epoch of that healthy, steady growth that has characterized the progress of other races." [74] Another activist noted that the black experience had been rooted in the very "depths of depravity . . . ." [75] Exploring the Negro imprint upon universal progress, many wrote and spoke in these same negative terms. [76] Many were starting to acknowledge what Watterson, Page, Watson, and other white racists had always said about the black cultural heritage: it was nonexistent.

To an extent, these acknowledgments underlined a growing preference by certain activists for white skin. Ray Stannard Baker, the perceptive Northern journalist, was impressed by the tendency toward racial repudiation as he toured the South in the first decade of the twentieth century: "Even among those Negroes who are most emphatic in defence [sic] of the race there is, deep down, the pathetic desire to be like the dominant white man." Beneath their glorifications of the black race, Negro activists were increasingly sensing that "whiteness stands for opportunity, power, progress." [77] Though Baker cited few examples to sustain his observation, examples were not difficult to uncover. In perhaps the most important black novel written before the Harlem Renaissance, *The Autobiography of an Ex-Coloured Man* (1912), James Weldon Johnson argued that a sensitive Negro was strongly attracted to the quality of life in white society. Aspirations for whiteness also explained the vast number of advertisements in black Southern newspapers by the turn of the century for skin lighteners and hair straighteners. [78] Watching white cadets drill in

74. Robert H. Terrell, "What of the Future," unpublished ms., May 19, 1898, Robert H. Terrell Papers, Library of Congress.

75. T. D. Tucker to Committee on Morals and Religion for the Hampton Negro Conference, 1901, Subject Files, Woodson Collection, Library of Congress.

76. See, e.g., Miller, *Voice of the Negro*, II (August, 1905), 540; Journal and Notebook, 1877–1881, entry for March 11, 1880, Charles W. Chesnutt Papers, Fisk University; Booker T. Washington, *Character Building* (New York: Doubleday, Page & Co., 1903), p. 119; William Archer, *Through Afro-America: An English Reading of the Race Problem* (London: Chapman & Hall, 1910), p. 32.

77. Ray Stannard Baker, *Following the Color Line: American Negro Citizenship in the Progressive Era* (New York: Harper Torchbooks, 1964), pp. 157–58.

78. See, e.g., the Raleigh *Gazette*, New Orleans *Observer*, Houston *Western Star*, Brandon (Mississippi) *Free State*, Waycross (Georgia) *Gazette and Land Bulletin*.

Sewanee, Tennessee, as a young boy, Ely Green recalled: "What a beautiful sight it was. I said to myself: 'It is really something to be a white man' . . . I decided I would never be a nigger or a Negro no matter what my grandfather had said. He was glad he was a nigger. The white men were so neatly dressed and my grandfather was so dirty and greasy and smelled like slop." [79] White was "beautiful" and "really something"; white cadets were a symbol of power. By contrast, a Negro was dirty, greasy, and smelly. He could not be a cadet; thus he could not have power. Though Green became increasingly scornful of local whites in subsequent years, he never shed this frame of reference. Rather, his abhorrence of blackness and powerlessness intensified.

Since white Southerners operated on the premise that "one drop of Negro blood makes a Negro," any lightly complected Negro whose ancestry was known or who seemed to have "Negro physical characteristics" had difficulty passing for white. For discouraged activitists who were sometimes prone to repudiate black culture but were known for their Negro ancestry or were simply too dark to cross the color line, there was one potential remedy. They could try to distinguish themselves from the black community-at-large. They could try to convince themselves and whites as well that there were two types of Negroes—the crude black folk and the genteel, respectable element. Thus, they readily admitted that the Negro masses were "ignorant," "backward," and "inferior" to the Caucasian.[80] This implied that white Southerners were right in discriminating against most Negroes. But *"most"* was not *"all."* Because they belonged to the "better" class of blacks, whites had to distinguish them from the masses. In a sense, this was the Negro activist's brand of differential segregation.

Thus, certain activists were gambling upon the possibility that class consciousness among wealthier whites would supersede the prejudice of racial caste—that the "better" class of whites would allow certain genteel members of the black bourgeoisie to join them in discriminating against the masses of both races. Charles Chesnutt articulated these ambitions in *The Marrow of Tradition* (1901). Members of the Negro social elite like the novel's honorable hero, Dr. Miller, should not be forced to associate with the black masses, Chesnutt pleaded. The black folk "were just as offensive to him [Dr. Miller] as to the [propertied] whites in the other end of the train." Indeed, the "better"

79. Green, *Ely*, p. 42.

80. See, e.g., Miller, *Voice of the Negro*, II (August, 1905), 538; Charles W. Chesnutt, "The Negro's Rights," typed ms., 1908, Chesnutt Papers, Fisk University; Sutton E. Griggs, *Overshadowed* (Nashville: Orion Publishing Company, 1901), p. 68; Griggs, *Pointing the Way Out*, as quoted in Robert A. Bone, *The Negro Novel in America* (New Haven: Yale University Press, 1958), p. 18; Jack Abramowitz, "Crossroads of Negro Thought: 1890–1895," *Social Education*, XVIII, No. 3 (March, 1954), 119.

elements of both races had to join together and isolate themselves from the scum, white and black.[81] In his novel, *Lillian Simmons* (1915), Otis M. Shackelford issued the same plea. Lillian "could understand why Jim Crow cars and all other forms of segregation in the South were necessary, but she could not feel that it was fair to treat all colored people alike, because all were not alike." Cultivated activists like Shackelford had to be allowed to mix with the "best" of the white race.[82] Testifying before the House Committee on Reform in the Civil Service, another Negro activist concurred. The "better" element of the black population represented no threat to propertied whites, he charged, for "those who rise will take sides with you people who are up." [83]

Thus, simultaneous with their crusade for black power and racial pride, activists explored alternative possibilities. William Hannibal Thomas represented an extreme example of this gradual reorientation in priorities. He was descended from a Northern family of racially mixed ancestry. For three generations at the very least, none of his ancestors had been bondsmen. Well-educated and enjoying moderate financial resources, he traveled South as a carpetbagger in 1871 fired with the hope of aiding the freedmen. Settling in Newberry County, South Carolina, Thomas practiced law and served as a trial justice. In 1876 he was elected to the state legislature, but later that same year South Carolina's Reconstruction government was overthrown and Thomas was forced to withdraw from active political life.[84]

In the years after 1876, Thomas campaigned assiduously throughout the South for Negro educational and church development. He warned blacks that the failure of the Reconstruction experiment in biracialism had proven that they could not depend upon white good will. Repudiating biracial cooperation, he urged blacks to develop their own institutions and to guard against villainous Caucasians. By 1888 he was calling for "aggressive resistance" to white racism: "The Negro must lay aside humility . . . and manfully protect himself, his family and his fireside from the lecherous assaults of white invaders." [85]

81. Charles W. Chesnutt, *The Marrow of Tradition* (Boston and New York: Houghton, Mifflin & Co., 1901), Chapter V, especially p. 60.

82. Otis M. Shackelford, *Lillian Simmons* (Kansas City: Burton Publishing Company, 1915), p. 139.

83. *Hearings on Segregation of Clerks and Employees in the Civil Service, House Civil Service Reform Committee*, 63rd Cong. (March 6, 1914), pp. 18–22. The activist was Archibald H. Grimké of the N.A.A.C.P.

84. William Hannibal Thomas, *The American Negro, What He Was, What He Is, and What He May Become* (New York: The Macmillan Company, 1901), pp. xi–xviii, provides a rather detailed factual account of the man's life through 1876.

85. William Hannibal Thomas, "Till Another King Arose, Which Knew Not Joseph," *A.M.E. Church Review*, V (October, 1888), 337.

As he called for vigorous black resistance against whites, Thomas began a lengthy and systematic study of Negro life. He soon became disturbed over the implications of his data. Always thoroughly middle-class in outlook and values, he concluded that the black masses were crude, pretentious, and backward. He was "moved to righteous indignation at the insensate follies of a race blind to every passing opportunity." He sensed that this "dense" race would never overcome white pressures.[86]

In *The American Negro, What He Was, What He Is, and What He May Become* (1901), Thomas summarized and analyzed all of his notes and observations. He openly acknowledged the validity of many racist stereotypes: the Negro was lazy, cowardly, stupid, and inferior.[87] De-emphasizing the "lecherous" Caucasian, he wrote of the Negro's imperious sexual impulse. Rigid color lines were required to contain the black man's "inordinate craving for carnal knowledge of white women." Segregation was imperative.[88] More than most other Negro activists, Thomas gave up on the black race. He constantly referred to Negroes as "they." Significantly, he also stressed that "the admitted degredation [*sic*] of the race is not characteristic of all persons of negroid ancestry [*sic*]." [89] Thus, he may have been hoping to dissociate himself from the black masses. But at the same time, he sensed that his lot was inextricably tied to theirs. In the eyes of the Caucasian, Thomas knew that he was no more than an "American Negro."

VII

There can be no doubt at this point that white Southerners totally misinterpreted the most outspoken representatives of the black community. For the men of the "Brownlow tradition" and for countless other whites, blacks had suddenly become "uppity," "dangerously cohesive," and secretive. The white man's desperate attempts to regulate Negro behavior did not seem to be working. However, analysis of Negro activists indicates that racist pressures were far more fruitful than Southern whites realized. After numerous unsuccessful attempts at rallying blacks and confronting whites, activitists grew sullen and dejected. Most continued to repeat anti-white rhetoric and to call for racial solidarity, but as time progressed the enthusiasm behind their words dissipated. Increasingly, many of them tried to dissociate themselves from the Negro masses. White racism left them bitter and directionless.

86. Thomas, *The American Negro*, p. xviii.
87. Thomas, *The American Negro*, pp. 117, 405.
88. Thomas, *The American Negro*, pp. 65, 176–77, 223.
89. Thomas, *The American Negro*, p. xxiii.

There were a number of reasons why whites so completely misread the intricacies of Negro life and the effects of white racism. The fact that they were particularly suspicious of Negro activists suggests that they perused activist writings searching for evidence to confirm their suspicions. Moreover, because such writings were not published in large quantities and were seldom promoted, most whites initially learned of the activist message through hearsay. Owing to the vague and inaccurate nature of hearsay evidence, the white racist mind could fantasize over preconceived notions of black insolence and misbehavior.

Even those whites who read activist prose and fiction attentively and somewhat objectively may have overlooked the author's disposition toward racial repudiation. The obvious themes in activist writing were the glories of blackness, the deficiencies of the white race, and the need for black solidarity. Very close reading was required to detect the rare phrase here and the sentence there indicating activist disillusionment. Then, too, some activists confined their more dispirited expressions to personal diaries and whites never learned of these.

If the white reader could not detect the activist's dejection in written materials, he could scarcely be expected to detect it from first-hand observation. With the rise of large, impersonal urban centers throughout the South, with the widespread acceptance of the myth that blacks were diseased, and with increasingly rigid enforcement of segregation barriers between the races, it was extremely difficult for whites to maintain close and continuous contact with Negro activists.

The general instabilities of American society during the late nineteenth and early twentieth centuries suggest another reason for the white Southerner's basic misinterpretation of black society. During these decades people were becoming increasingly sensitive to the shift of population and political power from the countryside to the city, immigration reached unprecedented levels, and large, bureaucratized monopolies tended more and more to replace small, independent businesses. Due to these seemingly vast and rapid changes, Americans sensed that they lived in "a society without a core." [90] Southerners did not experience this splintering process to the same extent as Northerners, yet the process still had a marked impact upon Southern life. The quality of daily existence below Mason-Dixon seemed "unnatural" and vastly "out of proportion." With the character of everyday life seeming to change in every respect, a white Southerner was bound to assume that Negro life was also destined to change. Choosing to believe that blacks had traditionally been docile, he was strongly disposed to assume that servile patterns of Negro behavior

90. This theme is thoroughly analyzed and documented in Robert H. Wiebe's outstanding study, *The Search for Order, 1877–1920* (New York: Hill and Wang, 1967).

were evaporating. Along with the family farm and the country store, the "old-time Negro" could easily pass from the scene. With this frame of mind, the white Southerner could only interpret the rhetoric of black racial pride as a challenge to the tradition of white supremacy.

Then, too, men like Watterson, Watson, and Cable had sought servile Negro behavior because it had afforded them relief from this confusing, unstable, and anxious quality of American life. But in order to "break loose" before a Negro through intimate personal confessions or through sadistic violence, the white man required a meek black population. The "uppity" Negro might strike back. This was why Negro assertiveness and separatism seemed so threatening. The slightest evidence of black aggressiveness and racial solidarity had to be regarded with neurotic alarm. For a Southern Caucasian who desperately needed Negro docility to relieve his anxieties, too much was at stake to allow any sign of black activism to go unnoticed.

Therefore, by the end of the first decade of the new century, racial anxieties among Southern whites were particularly acute. They needed a gallant knight on a white horse to come to their rescue, to explain the reasons for Negro "misconduct," and to restore Negro docility. Within a few years, Southerners thought that their knight had come and that his name was Woodrow Wilson.

Chapter Eight

A Nation of Savages

At the turn of the century, white Southerners were ideologically unprepared to cope with the problems of a seemingly new and unprecedented level of Negro insolence and secrecy. Judging from their dispirited commentaries, few were willing to insist upon rigid, across-the-board segregation of all Negroes from white society; most wanted desperately to communicate with docile blacks. But by this time urbanization, the widespread myth of Negro disease, and an increasingly inflexible Jim Crow system tended to preclude an effective program of differential segregation. This left whites with two unacceptable alternatives—complete integration or inflexible segregation.

Sometime between 1910 and the middle of 1912 the problem took a strange turn. The number of dispirited Southern commentaries decreased substantially and some whites began to manifest guarded optimism. This new hope was a response to efforts to place Woodrow Wilson of Virginia in the White House. If a Southerner could occupy the most powerful office in the land, some sensed that the troubled and anxious racial situation could be improved. With Wilson running Washington, a maximum of power and prestige could be deployed toward a solution of the "Negro problem."

As early as May of 1888, the vicious Negrophobe, Thomas Dixon, Jr., had suggested that Wilson was potential Presidential timber. Nominating the thirty-one-year-old professor of history for an honorary Doctor of Laws degree at Wake Forest College, Dixon boasted of him to the Board of Trustees: "He is the type of man we need as President of the United States, and on that platform I name him for the degree." [1] By 1906 Henry Watterson, a more astute political analyst than Dixon, predicted that Wilson could become President and was working for such an eventuality. Concerned with home rule above all else, Watterson reasoned that a Southern President could assure regional autonomy. Though Wilson was serving as President of Princeton, "Marse Henry" urged him to consider a move to the White

1. Thomas Dixon, Jr., "Southern Horizons: An Autobiography" (ms. unfinished), p. 289, as quoted in Raymond Allen Cook, *Fire from the Flint: The Amazing Careers of Thomas Dixon* (Winston-Salem: John F. Blair, Publisher, 1968), p. 73.

House, and a number of influential Democrats enthusiastically backed the suggestion.[2]

Owing to several personality conflicts and defections, a solid Wilson Presidential campaign organization was not established until the early months of 1912, during which time the candidate was Governor of New Jersey. When the Wilson campaign was finally organized, Southerners dominated it. William F. McCombs of Arkansas, Walter F. McCorkle of Virginia, and Walter Hines Page of North Carolina formed the Wilson high command. In time, they were assisted by William G. McAdoo of Georgia, Thomas Gore of Oklahoma, Thomas J. Pence of North Carolina, and Edward M. House of Texas.[3] Electoral efforts were most intensive below Mason-Dixon. Enthusiastic Wilson clubs crusaded in nearly every Southern county.[4] To elect the first Southern President since Andrew Johnson, overwhelming Southern support was considered imperative.

Outside of the South, Arizona was the only state where Wilson won over a majority of the voters.[5] In this sense, he was a regional candidate. Moreover, he was a white man's candidate; owing to widespread Negro disfranchisement below Mason-Dixon, a white Southern electorate sent him to the White House. Shortly before election day, North Carolina industrialist Daniel Augustus Tompkins remarked that the whites of his region sensed that victory was in the air and seemed more "confident of its [the South's] ability to handle both the race problem and politico-economic questions . . . ." [6] In the immediate aftermath of victory, Southern confidence rose to an unprecedented level. Controlling the nation's highest office, they would surely remedy regional ills. Thomas Nelson Page was exuberant. To him, something had occurred "which I had never expected to see, in which the South has come into her own with a broader horizon that carries her principles to the utmost bounds of our Country." [7] To Henry Watterson, Wil-

2. Eleanor Wilson McAdoo, *The Woodrow Wilsons* (New York: The Macmillan Company, 1937), p. 109; C. Vann Woodward, *The Origins of the New South, 1877–1913* (Baton Rouge: Louisiana State University Press, 1951), p. 470; Leonard Niel Plummer, "Political Leadership of Henry Watterson" (Ph.D. dissertation, University of Wisconsin, 1940), p. 211.

3. Arthur S. Link, "The South and the Democratic Campaign of 1912" (Ph.D. dissertation, University of North Carolina, 1945), pp. 67–68; Woodward, *Origins of New South*, p. 471.

4. Arthur S. Link, "The Democratic Pre-Convention Campaign of 1912 in Georgia," *Georgia Historical Quarterly*, XXIX, No. 3 (September, 1945), 149.

5. Edgar Eugene Robinson, *The Presidential Vote, 1896–1932* (Palo Alto, California: Stanford University Press, 1934), pp. 14, 51, 52.

6. Daniel Augustus Tompkins to Albert Bushnell Hart, September 18, 1912, as quoted in John B. Wiseman, "Racism in Democratic Politics, 1904–1912," *Mid-America*, LI, No. 1 (January, 1969), 58.

7. Thomas Nelson Page to John Sharp Williams, March 15, 1913, Page Papers, Duke University. See also Page to Charles E. Lyon, March 20, 1913, Page Papers.

son's "nomination and election look like destiny." [8] "The South is in the saddle," a white Texan proclaimed.[9] "Long ago I had despaired of ever seeing a man of Southern birth President," wrote a happy North Carolina judge. With victory in 1912 "we have the ascendancy of men of Southern birth and residence to the seats of power and responsibility such as has never been seen in our day." [10] The Southern mood was unmistakable. As Judson C. Welliver, an analyst of the Washington scene, pointed out, Dixie ran America and white Southerners knew it.[11]

Thus, in 1913 the South seemed assured of home rule and much more. With half the Wilson cabinet composed of Southerners, with more men of the region appointed as bureau chiefs, commissioners, and assistant secretaries than at any time since the Civil War, and with Southerners in control of nearly every vital Congressional position, the federal government had ceased to be an enemy.[12] Under these new conditions, white Southerners knew that the national government would not hamper their efforts to resolve local anxieties, particularly the all-important "Negro problem." With Wilson in the White House, the vast powers of the federal government would be deployed, for the first time in generations, to come to grips with regional difficulties. Only one worry remained. Should federal resources fail to solve the "Negro problem," a white Southerner could conclude that it had no solution at all.

II

It is not difficult to understand why many white Southerners looked to President Wilson as the manipulator of vast power and authority

8. Louisville *Courier-Journal*, November 9, 1912.

9. H. J. Fallon to Albert S. Burleson, September 2, 1913, Burleson Papers, Library of Congress.

10. Benjamin F. Long to Walter Hines Page, March 15, 1913, as quoted in Charles Grier Sellers, Jr., ed., *The Southerner as American* (Chapel Hill: University of North Carolina Press, 1960), p. 159.

11. Judson C. Welliver, "The Triumph of the South," *Munsey's Magazine*, XLIX, No. 5 (August, 1913), 738, 740. For similar analyses, see the New York *Times*, August 14, 1913, and James Weldon Johnson, *Along This Way* (New York: The Viking Press, 1933), pp. 300–301.

12. William G. McAdoo, Josephus Daniels, David F. Houston, Albert S. Burleson, and James C. McReynolds were the Southerners in Wilson's first cabinet. Woodward, *Origins of New South*, p. 480, notes high-level noncabinet appointments going to Southerners. The specifics of Southern control of Congress are provided in Woodward, *Origins of New South*, pp. 480–81; George Brown Tindall, *The Emergence of the New South, 1913–1945* (Baton Rouge: Louisiana State University Press, 1967), p. 3; Dewey W. Grantham, Jr., "Southern Congressional Leaders and the New Freedom, 1913–1917," *Journal of Southern History*, XIII, No. 4 (November, 1947), 441; Arthur S. Link, "The South and the 'New Freedom': An Interpretation," *American Scholar*, XX, No. 3 (Summer, 1951), 314.

who could solve the South's racial problems. Time and again, the man had proclaimed his utmost devotion to the region. "So I am obliged to say again and again," he charged, "that the only place in the country, the only place in the world, where nothing has to be explained to me is the South." [13] Most of Wilson's historical writings were glaringly pro-Southern.[14] The man openly acknowledged that his love for the South was unrivaled.[15] "There appear to be no limits to the possibilities of her [the South's] development," he boldly predicted.[16] Had he been of age at the outbreak of the Civil War, Wilson once told his daughter, he would have supported secession. Virginia and the South were more important than the nation.[17]

Like Watterson, Page, and Watson, Wilson's deep sectional loyalties were rooted in nostalgic yearnings for the restoration of antebellum Southern civilization. In his *History of the American People,* he persistently romanticized the Old South. Merely to think of that society helped to "connect me with my parents, and with all the old memories" and allowed him to "know again the region to which I naturally belong." [18] To this first Southern President since Reconstruction, the Old South was above all a stable and cohesive society. The region had been characterized by "homogeneity, a sense of community and a common understanding, the reservoir of emotions that lie at the head of all true patriotism." [19] More than any other factor, the "peculiar institution" was responsible for this cohesion and stability. "Great gangs of cheery Negroes" produced the necessities for the society and a responsible planter class looked after the Negroes.[20] Because they were familiar only with the chaos and the confusion of Northern society, critics of Southern life like Harriet Beecher Stowe and James Ford Rhodes could never appreciate the wonders of a culture based upon black bondage.[21] Drawing upon the unifying spirit of the Old

13. Woodrow Wilson, *Robert E. Lee* (Chapel Hill: University of North Carolina Press, 1924), p. v.

14. See, e.g., *Division and Reunion, 1829–1909* (New York: Longmans, Green, & Company, 1910); "The Southern Colonists" (unpublished ms.), April, 1907, Wilson Papers, Library of Congress; *George Washington* (New York: Harper & Brothers, 1897); "The Reconstruction of the Southern States," *Atlantic Monthly,* LXXXVII (January, 1901), 1–15.

15. Paul M. Gaston, "The New South Creed, 1865–1900" (Ph.D. dissertation, University of North Carolina, 1961), p. 85.

16. Woodrow Wilson to Charles A. Talcott, September 22, 1881, Ray Stannard Baker Papers, Library of Congress.

17. Ray Stannard Baker, "Memorandum of a Conversation with Mrs. Francis A. Sayre," unpublished ms., December 1, 1925, Baker Papers, Library of Congress.

18. Wilson, *Lee,* p. vi.

19. Atlanta *Georgian,* March 11, 1911.

20. Woodrow Wilson, *A History of the American People,* documentary ed. (New York and London: Harper & Brothers, 1901), VIII, 48, 52, 106; Wilson, *Division and Reunion,* p. 127.

21. Woodrow Wilson, "A Review of *History of the United States from the*

South, Wilson contended that contemporary Southerners could bring calm to a troubled, confused, postbellum industrial America. Seizing control of the "councils of the Nation," they would restore order to a troubled land.[22]

These remarks fail to explain Wilson's certainty that Negro slavery had eased tensions and anxieties in Southern society and his confidence that the spirit of a slave society could rescue postbellum America. But in other remarks he charged that slavery had disciplined Negroes to defer to the "superior" race and he described race relations in the same broad terms as the men of the "Brownlow tradition." Whites represented "civilization," "wisdom and moral feeling," "pride," and "responsibility."[23] Blacks stood for "wildness," "ignorance," and "barbaric aggression"; at base they were wild savages.[24] Because slavery had made blacks deferent, Wilson believed that it had checked their savage impulses. Through the "peculiar institution," whites had been able to associate with blacks with little fear. Civilized man had been able to do as he pleased with the savage race, knowing all the while that however he behaved, he was uplifting barbarism at no great physical risk. Because of the discipline of the slave system, the savage would not strike back.

The advantages that accrued to whites from such a biracial relationship may explain Wilson's constant and warm references to social intimacies between the races. They may also explain his penchant for telling "old-time Negro" dialect stories of antebellum racial life to his family and friends.[25] As a young boy, he had actually enjoyed the freedom that the antebellum white-black relationship had afforded. With tomahawk, bow, arrows, and Indian feathers, he had chased frightened Negro children and had enjoyed it immensely.[26] As a representative of white civilization, he had interacted with and therefore uplifted the black child-savages, refusing to recognize the crudity of his own conduct. This could explain why nostalgic yearnings for the white-black relationship of the old order never escaped him. Even

Compromise of 1850 by James Ford Rhodes," Atlantic Monthly, LXXII (August, 1893), 273; Wilson, Division and Reunion, p. 181; Wilson, History of American People, VIII, 16.

22. Atlanta Journal, April 17, 1912; Link, Georgia Historical Quarterly, XXIX, No. 3 (September, 1945), 145.

23. Wilson, Division and Reunion, p. 127, and History of American People, VIII. 154; Henry Blumenthal, "Woodrow Wilson and the Race Question," Journal of Negro History, XLVIII, No. 1 (January, 1963), 15.

24. See, e.g., Wilson, Atlantic Monthly, LXXXVII (January, 1901), 6; Wilson, Division and Reunion, pp. 125, 203.

25. Ray Stannard Baker, "Memorandum of a Conversation with Mrs. Francis B. Sayre," unpublished ms., December 1, 1925, Baker Papers, Library of Congress.

26. Jessie B. Brower to Ray Stannard Baker, May 9, 1926, Baker Papers, Library of Congress.

in 1912, amidst an otherwise cautious campaign for the Presidency, he told New Jersey Negroes that as a child of the Old South, he knew that white and black could be happy together.[27]

If Wilson yearned for antebellum Southern civilization, he thought of the Reconstruction experiment with anger and regret. Whereas the Old South had been a cohesive society, Reconstruction had introduced social disintegration and had created a tense, bitter, and divided America. During the postwar decade, the savage race had been exalted and white Southern civilization had been degraded. Blacks assumed the most prestigious positions in Southern society. Ultimately, the "instinct of self-preservation" forced the civilized race "to rid themselves, by fair means or foul, of the intolerable burden of governments sustained by the votes of ignorant negroes . . . ." [28] Whatever white civilization did to black savages was not only understandable but proper. But though Reconstruction was overthrown, Wilson remained troubled, for antebellum society was never restored. Rather, a horrid decade of "Negro rule" had "left upon us the burden of a race problem well-nigh insoluble . . . ." Since the Reconstruction period, Wilson charged, Southerners had never been able to experience true peace of mind. Like him, they could only dream of earlier days before blacks had learned to "lord over whites." [29]

It was painful for Wilson to observe contemporary racial events. He toyed with the notion that a black woman might one day be elected President of the United States.[30] Desperately, he tried to resist the "trend of the times." As President of Princeton in the first years of the new century, he discovered that blacks were trying to enroll as students. Such effrontery outraged him, for higher education for the servile race was "unprecedented" and "unwarranted." It was particularly hard for him to believe that Negroes would apply to a school with a heavy Southern enrollment and a Southern president. Though other Eastern universities were beginning to admit Negroes, he had letters distributed to all black applicants informing them that Princeton enjoyed a large Southern enrollment and that black students would feel out of place. All Negro applicants took the suggestion.[31] In addi-

27. Trenton *Evening Times,* July 31, 1912.

28. Wilson, *History of the American People,* IX, 58, and *Atlantic Monthly,* LXXXVII (January, 1901), 11.

29. Ray Stannard Baker and William E. Dodd, eds., *The Public Papers of Woodrow Wilson* (New York and London: Harper & Brothers, 1925–27), II, 18.

30. Henry Wilkinson Bragdon, *Woodrow Wilson: The Academic Years* (Cambridge: Belknap Press, 1967), p. 231.

31. Notes by Stockton Axson on Ray Stannard Baker's manuscript biography of Woodrow Wilson, October 31, 1928, Baker Papers, Library of Congress; Oswald G. Villard to Woodrow Wilson, August 28, 1912, Baker Papers. Wilson's action contrasted strangely with his statement to New Jersey Negroes in 1912 that whites and blacks could live together happily, unless happiness meant that Negroes were to play servile roles.

tion to his efforts at Princeton, Wilson was sure that Southern campaigns to disfranchise Negroes helped to "undo the mischief of reconstruction." [32] But the basic problem remained unsolved: Southern blacks had forgotten they were naturally and properly a servile race. Until they came to this realization, the wonders of antebellum Southern society would never return.

Wilson's strong nostalgic tie to the Old South and to the "peculiar institution" indicates that he lacked the sobriety and the sophistication to remedy the South's increasingly complex "Negro problem." A man who yearned nostalgically for the return of Negro slavery and a cohesive antebellum society would not use the vast powers of the Presidency subtly and realistically in racial matters. The Virginian was not capable of dispassionate analysis of the sources of black cohesion and secrecy, the origins and effects of the myth of Negro disease, and the tendency of urbanization to preclude flexible enforcement of segregation barriers. Southern whites needed a far less rigid racial mind than Wilson's in order to comprehend the enormously complex maze of difficulties they were meeting in their search for Negro docility. Though whites of the region looked to him as the one person with the power and prestige to resolve their racial nightmare, they had singled out a man remarkably ill-suited for the job. He might have displayed flexibility and subtlety on other matters, but when it came to race relations, Wilson had ready answers and could therefore ask no questions.

III

On inauguration day in March, 1913, the atmosphere in the nation's capital bore ominous signs for Negroes. Against a background of "Rebel Yells" and bands blaring "Dixie," Edward Douglass White, ex-Confederate, ex-Ku Klux Klansman, and Chief Justice of the United States Supreme Court, administered the oath of office to Woodrow Wilson.[33] Consonant with Southern tradition, an anonymous donor sent a possum to the new President.[34] An unidentified associate of the new Chief Executive warned that since the South ran the nation, Negroes should expect to be treated as a servile race.[35]

Not long after Wilson had moved into the White House, two fiery

32. Wilson, *History of the American People*, X, 186.,

33. Tindall, *Emergence of New South*, pp. 1–2.

34. James C. Walters to Oswald G. Villard, November 19, 1913, N.A.A.C.P. Papers, Library of Congress. According to Southern racist tradition, the possum represents the comic essence of the Negro.

35. E. H. Sutton to Oswald G. Villard, November, 1913, N.A.A.C.P. Papers, Library of Congress.

Negrophobes, James K. Vardaman of Mississippi and Benjamin R. Tillman of South Carolina, outlined their racial programs and urged the President to implement them. Predictably, they called for racial segregation among federal employees and a halt to Negro federal appointments.[36] But similar demands by white women employed in the federal departments at Washington, particularly the Treasury and the Post Office, drew far greater attention and concern from the President and his cabinet. These women (many from the South) insisted that Negroes in the federal employ had to be segregated. Separate Negro work rooms, wash rooms, and showers had to be installed to protect whites from "insolent" and "lazy" black employees. More crucial, the women argued that segregation would protect them from Negro diseases. With their own eyes, they had allegedly seen black women with vaginal infections. One veteran of the Office of the Recorder of Deeds, Maud B. Woodward, swore out an affidavit to that effect: "That the same toilet is used by both whites and blacks, and some of said blacks have been diseased, evidence thereof being very apparent; that one negro woman, Alexander, has been for years afflicted with a private disease, and for dread of using the toilet after her some of the white girls are compelled to suffer physically and mentally." Interestingly, Maud Woodward did not go on to explain how she discovered that black women had a "private disease." Nor did any of the other white women testify concerning the basis of their beliefs. Avoiding this embarrassing question, they charged that if blacks continued to use white wash rooms and showers, white employees could become seriously ill. Therefore, toilets, above all else, had to be segregated.[37]

Pressed and aroused by white female employees, Postmaster General Albert S. Burleson of Texas and Treasury Secretary William G. McAdoo of Georgia brought the matter to a head at an April cabinet meeting. Burleson explained that black and white could no longer work together in the railway mail service, for separate drinking and washing facilities were too difficult to provide. The safety of white employees was reason enough to keep white and black workers apart in all federal departments, the Postmaster added. McAdoo concurred and charged that he was going to establish a color line in the Treasury Department. Neither the President nor any other cabinet officials ob-

36. Vardaman is quoted in the New York *Evening Post*, August 4, 1913. Tillman outlined his program in a letter to Wilson dated June 12, 1913, Wilson Papers, Library of Congress.

37. *U.S. Civil Service Reform Comm., House. Segregation of Clerks and Employees in the Civil Service, Hearings* [H.R. 5968 and 13772], March 6, 1914, has information concerning the complaints these white women issued after Wilson assumed office. Maud B. Woodward is quoted on p. 6. See also Josephus Daniels to Franklin D. Roosevelt, June 10, 1933, Official File 237, Franklin D. Roosevelt Library.

jected. From the facts at hand, segregation seemed to be a common-sense policy for these white leaders.[38] Hence, largely owing to the notion that blacks were carriers of infectious diseases, Jim Crow made his debut in Wilson's Washington. He might have come anyway. Yet it is important to note that the Wilson Administration took its first step toward resolving the "Negro problem" by responding to the widespread fear that blacks were carriers of disease.

By early autumn of 1913, both the Treasury and the Post Office Departments in Washington had been quietly but thoroughly segregated. Secret letters and confidential conversations provided the necessary directives rather than executive orders or public proclamations. Publicity was avoided for fear of resulting controversy. Black employees were ushered into separate work rooms while special precautions were taken to keep them away from lunch tables and toilet facilities used by whites.[39]

These measures were soon implemented elsewhere in the capital city. The Bureau of Printing and Engraving set aside separate rest rooms, locker rooms, and work rooms for each race.[40] Public "safety and comfort" also dictated separate eating facilities at the Bureau. Hence, three hundred black female employees were assigned to a dining room designed to accommodate thirty-five or forty.[41] In their efforts to combat "Negro disease," none seemed to consider the possibility that grossly overcrowded dining facilities could produce serious health problems. In mid-July, the auditor of the Interior Department posted orders on department toilets designating the facilities that were to be used by whites and those for blacks. "Any violation of the rule will be promptly dealt with," the orders concluded.[42] Again, a sanitation craze was at the heart of the segregationist impulse.

38. E. David Cronon, ed., *The Cabinet Diaries of Josephus Daniels, 1913–1921* (Lincoln, Nebraska: University of Nebraska Press, 1963), pp. 32–33.

39. McGregor, "Segregation in the Departments," *Harper's Weekly Magazine* (December 26, 1914), p. 620; Constance M. Green. *Washington: Capital City, 1879–1950* (Princeton: Princeton University Press, 1963), p. 223; New York *Evening Post,* September 9, 1913; Oswald G. Villard, "Segregation in Baltimore and Washington," unpublished ms., October 20, 1913, Villard Papers, Harvard University; Kathleen L. Wolgemuth, "Woodrow Wilson and Federal Segregation," *Journal of Negro History,* XLIV, No. 2 (April, 1959), 160–61.

40. McGregor, *Harper's Weekly* (December 26, 1914), p. 620; Oswald Garrison Villard, "The President and the Segregation at Washington," *North American Review,* CXCVIII (December, 1913), 802; Wolgemuth, *Journal of Negro History,* XLIV, No. 2 (April, 1959), 160–61.

41. James C. Walters, Jr., to Oswald G. Villard, November 19, 1913, N.A.A.C.P. Papers, Library of Congress. See also Henry Lincoln Johnson, *The Negro under Wilson* (Washington, D.C.: Republican National Committee, 1916), p. 12.

42. R. W. Wooley to the Chiefs of Divisions and the Offices of the Office of the Auditor for the Interior Department, July 16, 1913, Villard Papers, Harvard University.

Similar precautions were taken in other departments. According to
W. E. B. DuBois, by the end of 1913 most black federal workers
faced at least some form of segregation.[43]

Of all high federal officials, only McAdoo and Wilson attempted to
justify the new segregation measures. Vague and ambiguous, their
statements were nonetheless revealing. Both hinted at the disease
problem. In addition, McAdoo articulated the traditional Southern
fear that black men would make sexual advances toward white women.
Before segregation had been implemented, he maintained, white
women had been "forced unnecessarily to sit at desks with colored
men" and this created "friction." "Elimination of such friction pro-
motes good feeling and friendship," he added.[44] Wilson, on the other
hand, cloaked his defense of federal segregation policy in paternalistic
language. The color line protected Negro employees from the antagonistic competition of Caucasians, the Virginian explained. Off by
themselves with only a white supervisor, blacks would not be forced
out of their jobs by energetic white employees. In a sense, the President was describing an antebellum plantation where a kindly master
directed "great gangs of cheery Negroes." [45]

By the end of 1913 and the early months of 1914, the segregationist
crusade in Wilson's Washington had diminished somewhat, though
it never subsided.[46] The House Civil Service Reform Committee continued to review bills proposed by Southern Congressmen for more
extensive and systematic federal segregation. Complaints of Negro disease appeared in the testimony that the Committee pondered.[47] In
August, 1916, the Superintendent of the State, War, and Navy Departments Building segregated all men's toilets after 9 a.m. Apparently Negro male diseases ceased before 9 a.m. and never invaded
women's rest rooms. Riddled with inconsistencies, the policy was soon
reversed, though the War Trade Commission continued to retain
separate toilets for blacks.[48] In other quarters the protection of white

43. W. E. B. DuBois, *Dusk of Dawn: An Essay Toward an Autobiography of a
Race Concept* (New York: Harcourt, Brace & World, Inc., 1940), p. 237.

44. William G. McAdoo to Oswald G. Villard, October 27, 1913, Villard Papers,
Harvard University. Also quoted in Villard, *North American Review*, CXCVIII
(December, 1913), 803.

45. Woodrow Wilson to Oswald G. Villard, July 23, 1913, Villard Papers, Har-
vard University; Wilson to H. A. Bridgeman, September 8, 1913, Wilson Papers,
Library of Congress; Wilson to Oswald G. Villard, August 29, 1913, Wilson Papers,
Library of Congress.

46. Moorfield Story, *et al.* to Woodrow Wilson, January 6, 1914, Wilson Papers,
Library of Congress; George C. Osborn, "The Problem of the Negro in Government, 1913," *The Historian: A Journal of History*, XXIII (May, 1961), 347; Wolgemuth, *Journal of Negro History*, XLIV, No. 2 (April, 1959), 171.

47. *U.S. Civil Service Reform Comm., House. Segregation of Clerks and Employees in the Civil Service, Hearings* [H.R. 5968 and 13772], March 6, 1914.

48. August Meier and Elliot Rudwick, "The Rise of Segregation in the Federal

women was a more central concern. In 1917, for example, Naval Secretary Josephus Daniels, a North Carolinian, toured the Naval Yard at Charleston. Black women had registered to work in a clothing factory in the Yard, and officials feared that white females who labored in the factory would be "endangered." Daniels took action. Reduced efficiency notwithstanding, factory production would take place in two buildings, one for each race. To the North Carolinian, the "health and safety" of the white female took precedence over low-cost production.[49] By 1918 the color line had extended into the Senate lunchroom and the Library of Congress restaurant.[50] Next to toilet facilities, dining rooms seemed to be the "worst" breeding grounds for both disease and Negro "insolence."

Clearly, the segregationist policy of the Wilson Administration was primarily inspired by the fear that blacks carried contagious diseases and secondarily moved by the feeling that blacks had become disrespectful to their white superiors. Among some Administration officials, these two apprehensions may have blurred into one—the insolent Negro was the diseased Negro. Yet even before "uppity niggers" were reprimanded, Administration officials felt that toilets and lunch rooms would have to be segregated. If they were to prevent a mass epidemic, no time could be lost.

When it came to federal appointment policy, these priorities were reversed. The white official who subscribed to the myth that blacks carried infectious disease must have felt that by cutting the number of black federal employees, he reduced health hazards. But the fact that Administration officials did not dismiss all or even a substantial number of black workers indicates that the disease theory was not foremost in their minds. Rather, the primary concern behind Administration appointment policy was to "officially" establish the Negro's place in American society as a servile laborer. As Postmaster Burleson predicted in December of 1912, a Negro might be a doorman or a messenger under the new administration, but nonmenial federal jobs were out of the question.[51]

Bureaucracy, 1900–1930," *Phylon*, XXVIII, No. 2 (Summer, 1967), 181; Rayford W. Logan, *The Betrayal of the Negro from Rutherford B. Hayes to Woodrow Wilson*, 2nd ed. (New York: Collier Books, 1965), p. 362.

49. Cronon, ed., *Cabinet Diaries*, p. 181.

50. Charles F. Kellogg, *NAACP: A History of the National Association for the Advancement of Colored People* (Baltimore: Johns Hopkins Press, 1967), I, 181; Meier and Rudwick, *Phylon*, XXVIII, No. 2 (Summer, 1967), 181.

51. Burleson's remark is noted in the New York *Age*, December 12, 1912. See also John P. Gavit to Oswald G. Villard, October 1, 1913, Villard Papers, Harvard University; August Meier, *Negro Thought in America, 1880–1915* (Ann Arbor: University of Michigan Press, 1963), p. 188; Kathleen L. Wolgemuth, "Woodrow Wilson's Appointment Policy and the Negro," *Journal of Southern History*, XXIV, No. 1 (February, 1958), 457–71.

The President acted accordingly. He dismissed fifteen of the seventeen Negroes that the prior administration had appointed; among his new appointments, only two went to blacks.[52] American ministers to Haiti and Santo Domingo had traditionally been Negro, but Wilson appointed Caucasians.[53] Owing to mild, half-hearted Southern opposition to a Negro nominee as Register of the Treasury, the Virginian once more broke precedent and withdrew the nomination.[54] Two other prestigious but traditionally Negro posts—the Auditor for the Navy and the Recorder of Deeds—were filled by whites.[55] Blacks ceased to be hired for the Washington, D. C., police and fire departments and very few were appointed to the War Trade Board.[56] Of all Administration personnel, Treasury Secretary McAdoo seemed most anxious to keep blacks out of authoritative positions. Dismissing a veteran black collector at the Port of Beaufort, McAdoo replaced him with a Caucasian. Learning that a Negro was Collector of Internal Revenue at Jacksonville, Florida, the Treasury Secretary begged Wilson to replace him with a white plantation owner.[57]

Influential figures in Wilson's Washington resorted to still other tactics to teach the Negro his "proper" station in life. Certain Congressmen were constantly drafting racist legislative proposals. Some of them sought to repeal the Fourteenth and Fifteenth Amendments and to expel Negro officers from the armed services.[58] McAdoo prodded the United States Railway Administration to prohibit Northerners from prepaying the transportation cost of Southern blacks who wished to travel to the "promised land." [59] When the United States entered the European conflict in April of 1917, the war effort was conducted with few Negro commissioned officers. Moreover, no blacks were trained for leadership roles at West Point or Annapolis.[60] Earlier, in 1914, the Army had prepared a memorandum to explain why blacks should not be officers: "While the negro makes an ideal

52. Wolgemuth, *Journal of Southern History*, XXIV, No. 1 (February, 1958), 467.
53. Villard, *North American Review*, CXCVIII (December, 1913), 802.
54. Villard, *North American Review*, CXCVIII (December, 1913), 801–2; "The President and the Negro," *The Nation*, XCVII (August 17, 1913), 114; Thomas P. Gore to William G. McAdoo, October 1, 1913, and William G. McAdoo to Thomas P. Gore, October 10, 1913, both in the McAdoo Papers, Library of Congress.
55. Meier, *Negro Thought*, p. 188.
56. Charles M. Thomas to Joseph P. Tumulty, August 5, 1918; Nevel H. Thomas to Woodrow Wilson, July 23, 1919; both in the Wilson Papers, Library of Congress.
57. McAdoo's efforts to dismiss the Negro Collector of the Port of Beaufort are reported in the New York *Times*, April 13, 1913. The Jacksonville collectorship issue is noted in William G. McAdoo to Woodrow Wilson, April 11, 1913, McAdoo Papers, Library of Congress.
58. Kellogg, *NAACP*, I, 175–76, 180–81.
59. Kellogg, *NAACP*, I, 221, note 49.
60. Nick Charles to Woodrow Wilson, August 19, 1918, Wilson Papers, Library of Congress.

follower, especially if led by a white man, history shows that he is not a success as a leader, and experience shows that the white officer inspires the negro soldier with a certain faith and confidence that it is impossible for a negro to inspire in a negro." [61] In a sense, this statement articulated the racial outlook of the federal government. Most Negroes were seen as health hazards and general irritants who could not associate with whites under any circumstances. Those who could would have to occupy distinctly subordinate roles and be happy with them.

Somewhere in the tangled web of color lines, discriminatory appointment policies, and other racist pressures in Wilson's Washington, one could vaguely detect the old "Brownlow tradition": contented, servile Negroes could associate with whites while the dangerous and the defiant had to be ostracized. Simultaneously, however, certain factors were undermining the "Brownlow tradition": the myth of the diseased Negro and growing urbanization. According to the 1910 census, Washington had become a major urban center of 331,069 inhabitants, 94,446 of whom were black.[62] Compared to most American cities, this represented an enormous concentration of Negroes. Hence, race relations were often impersonal and docile Negroes free of disease could not be singled out from the contagious and defiant black masses. Therefore, though Brownlow, Watterson, Page, and Watson had spent many years propounding differential segregation and though many in Wilson's Washington hoped and even sought to implement the concept, across-the-board segregation increasingly appeared to be the only possible course. Like Negro activists, Southern leaders in the Wilson Administration were experiencing conflicting ideological drives. Negro activitists had tried to glory in their blackness but some eventually began to entertain thoughts of passing for white. Many "Wilsonites" doubtless preferred differential segregation but found the idea increasingly unworkable and moved instead toward an opposite concept—the inflexible color line.

IV

The racial ideas that circulated through Wilson's Washington were not new. They came from the plantations, the crossroads, the hamlets, and the cities of the postbellum South. Reared in these areas, the men

61. "The Use of Colored Troops in Case of National Emergency and the Organization of a Colored Brigade," March 14, 1914. This memorandum was prepared for the Department of Agriculture. It is located in the Records of the Office of the Secretary of Agriculture (Record Group 16), National Archives.

62. Constance McLaughlin Green, *The Secret City: A History of Race Relations in the Nation's Capital* (Princeton: Princeton University Press, 1967), p. 200.

who ran the federal government—Wilson, McAdoo, Burleson, House, Daniels, Houston, McReynolds, Underwood, Martin, and others— merely carried regional culture to the nation's capital. Correspondence and visitations with "the folks back home" kept them constantly in touch with Southern values. In terms of the white-black relationship, the Southern way had become the federal way.

Moreover, as the Wilson Administration endorsed and promulgated Southern racial ideas, those ideas became even more entrenched on the local scene. Receiving prestigious federal commendation, they became even more tenaciously the Southern way. As a Negro activist from Nashville, Charles V. Roman, pointed out, "Segregation at the Capitol means degradation in the shrievalty. If a president condones discrimination the sheriff may practice unfairness." [63] After several months of intensified segregationist efforts in Washington, the editor of the influential *Progressive Farmer,* Clarence Poe, commenced his "South-Wide Campaign for Racial Segregation." Desirous of extending the color line to the farms and countryside of the South, Poe proposed forcing rural negroes into land reserves like those established in South Africa.[64] Late in 1913, the Arkansas superintendent of railroad mail service announced that white and black employees had to be separated.[65] In small communities about Jacksonville, Florida, postmasters constructed Jim Crow windows at the sides of their post offices and required blacks to wait outside by those windows. A Negro was not to be served until all whites within the building had been serviced.[66]

Appointment policies in several Southern localities also became increasingly discriminatory, resembling the federal model. High federal officials like McAdoo and Daniels frequently removed blacks from positions of authority in cities and ports throughout the South. On his own initiative, Atlanta's postmaster discharged thirty-five black employees.[67] Georgia's Collector of Internal Revenue announced that "there are no Government positions for Negroes in the South. A Negro's place is in the corn-field." [68]

63. Charles V. Roman, *American Civilization and the Negro* (Philadelphia: F. A. Davis Company, 1916), p. 47. For a similar analysis by Kelly Miller, see Nancy J. Weiss, "The Negro and the New Freedom: Fighting Wilsonian Segregation," *Political Science Quarterly,* LXXXIV, No. 1 (March, 1969), 69.

64. Jack Temple Kirby, "Clarence Poe's Vision of a Segregated 'Great Rural Civilization,'" *South Atlantic Quarterly,* LXVIII, No. 1 (Winter, 1969), 33–37; Oswald Garrison Villard to George Foster Peabody, January 23, 1914, Villard Papers, Harvard University; Kellogg, *NAACP,* I, 87.

65. Oswald G. Villard to A. Mitchell Palmer, November 20, 1913, Villard Papers, Harvard University.

66. James Weldon Johnson, *Along this Way,* p. 301.

67. Arthur S. Link, *Woodrow Wilson and the Progressive Era, 1910–1917* (New York: Harper Torchbooks, 1963), p. 65.

68. Atlanta *Georgian and News,* October 7, 1913.

V

Black reaction to the racial policies of the Wilson Administration was not uniform. The majority—the folk as well as most of the bourgeoisie—were silent and dejected. "I have never seen the colored people so discouraged and bitter as they are at the present time," Booker T. Washington observed.[69] Black activists were deeply pessimistic but far from silent. They were openly bitter and sarcastic toward Wilson and his aides. A Negro attorney from Washington asked the Virginian if the white South would ever realize "that the sentiment of the civil war is about dead?" [70] The business manager of Howard University warned Wilson: "If this segregation and discrimination is allowed to go on, there is but one future for the United States, and that is, a nation of *class* and *caste*." [71] After years of combat against the effects of white racism upon black people, Francis J. Grimké was among the most bitter and critical of the activitists. "As American citizens," he wrote, Negroes had a right to expect courage and integrity from an American President. A Chief Executive was duty bound "to stand between us and those who are bent on forcing us into a position of inferiority." But Wilson had been cowardly; he had been derelict in his responsibilities and black people suffered for it.[72]

The most dramatic confrontation between Negro activitists and the Wilson Administration came in November, 1914. Heading a black delegation, editor-journalist Monroe Trotter called upon the President to denounce federal racial policies, particularly federal segregation. Wilson told the delegation that "segregation is not humiliating but a benefit, and ought to be so regarded by you gentlemen." When Trotter fervently objected, the President replied emotionally that "if this organization is ever to have another hearing before me, it must have another spokesman. Your manner offends me." But Trotter did not back down; he refused to play the part of the inoffensive and "cheery" Negro that Wilson wanted. Rather, he insisted that if the Administration's racial policy was not altered, blacks could desert Wilson and the Democrats at the polls. Stunned by Trotter's boldness, Wilson retorted that he would not be influenced by this threat,

69. Booker T. Washington to Oswald Garrison Villard, August 10, 1913, Wilson Papers, Library of Congress; New York *Times*, August 18, 1913.

70. W. Calvin Chase to Woodrow Wilson, August 2, 1913, Wilson Papers, Library of Congress.

71. George W. Cook to Woodrow Wilson, September 11, 1913, Wilson Papers, Library of Congress. Emphasis added. A copy of this letter may be found in the N.A.A.C.P. Papers, Library of Congress.

72. Francis J. Grimké to Woodrow Wilson, n.d., N.A.A.C.P. Papers, Library of Congress.

that his racial policies would continue, and that the interview was terminated. The President seemed to be saying that because Trotter was an "uppity" and "insolent" Negro, he had to go away. Only the docile and the servile of the race could show their calling cards.[73]

From this encounter with Trotter and from the deluge of mail from other angry activists, Wilson was sure that he was encountering a great wave of black insolence. The day after the confrontation with the Trotter delegation, he confided in Josephus Daniels that he had never seen Negroes who had acted with such "disrespect" for the Caucasian and that it had infuriated him.[74] But even before the Trotter episode, the President had voiced discontent over the state of race relations. Reviewing Administration racial policy with Oswald Garrison Villard in August of 1913, he noted that something seemed to be going wrong: "I not only hope but pray that a better aspect may come upon it before many months." [75] A few months later, Wilson seemed even more depressed: "I say it with shame and humiliation, but I have thought about this thing for twenty years and I see no way out." [76] In the fall of 1914, he commented angrily on the mounting Negro criticism of Administration racial policy: "If the colored people made a mistake in voting for me, they ought to correct it." [77] By August, 1917, the racial situation seemed to an anxious and bewildered President to have become one large nightmare. Blacks were not the only people who appeared to be increasingly defiant. The civilized race was also conducting itself "improperly." Race relations had deteriorated so badly, Wilson charged, that he had learned of a cultivated white woman who had kissed and given money to a ragged black boy.[78] While the President longed for the happy, safe plantation darkie of antebellum days, Trotter and other disrespectful blacks had made him increasingly doubtful that servile Negro behavior could ever be restored. Very likely, this explains his growing doubts concerning interracial contact. He was coming to suspect that white civilization would do best to steer clear of black savagery. He was beginning to doubt the efficacy of the "Brownlow tradition."

By the end of 1913, Wilson was not the only white Southerner who was distressed and confused over white-black relationships. The

73. The details of the Trotter delegation interview with the President are supplied in Josephus Daniels to Franklin D. Roosevelt, June 10, 1933, Official File 237, Franklin D. Roosevelt Library; New York *Times,* November 13, 1914.

74. Josephus Daniels to Franklin D. Roosevelt, June 10, 1933, Official File 237, Franklin D. Roosevelt Library.

75. Woodrow Wilson to Oswald Garrison Villard, August 21, 1913, Villard Papers, Harvard University.

76. Quoted in Oswald Garrison Villard, *Fighting Years: Memoirs of a Liberal Editor* (New York: Harcourt, Brace & Company, 1939), p. 240.

77. New York *Times,* November 13, 1914.

78. Cronon, ed., *Cabinet Diaries,* p. 195.

honeymoon with his Administration was over. Southerners who had anticipated the restoration of the region to the nation's leadership and who had assumed that such an eventuality was bound to usher in a better racial day were also discouraged. To be sure, the President and his aides had intensified federal segregation, they had deprived Negroes of federal positions of authority, and they certainly had not interfered with home rule. With this record, white Southerners had few complaints. Yet somehow Administration policy did not seem to restore servile Negro behavior. To Southerners, blacks seemed as insolent and defiant as ever. Though Wilson did not appear to be doing anything wrong on the racial front, the first Southern President in many decades was not resolving the "Negro problem." Uncle Tom was nowhere in sight.

The fears and anxieties of white Southerners over their inability to control racial events were manifested in countless ways. Some whites continued to voice dismay at a seemingly vigorous and dynamic crusade for black solidarity behind a veil of secrecy. In 1914 Thomas Pearce Bailey complained that blacks were becoming "increasingly cautious and reticent with regard to racial secrets." [79] That same year, Mrs. L. H. Hammond, daughter of slaveholding parents and wife of the white president of Payne College for Negroes in Augusta, published an emotional volume—*In Black and White: An Interpretation of Southern Life*. She charged that blacks had ceased to love white Southerners. Rather, they viewed whites with "suspicion" and "mistrust" from behind a veil of racial cohesion.[80] According to Winfied H. Collins, historian and essayist from Reids Grove, Maryland, the brief Wilsonian period of hope had clearly passed. In the long run, it had counted for little: "It is hardly to be questioned that since the Civil War, the white man and the Negro have been drawing farther and father apart." [81]

Many whites saw black solidarity as merely another manifestation of the aggressive Negro behavior patterns that the Wilson Administration had not corrected. Thomas Dixon, Jr. was disturbed with the rhetoric of Negro activists. As he saw matters, this was proof that blacks had become so assertive as to eventually take up arms against whites.[82] Fretting over continued Negro "insolence," Benjamin R. Tillman feared that such conduct would eventually lead to massive sexual aggression against white women. From a racial perspective, the

79. Thomas Pearce Bailey, *Race Orthodoxy in the South and Other Aspects of the Negro Question* (New York: Neale Publishing Company, 1914), p. 192.

80. Mrs. L. H. Hammond, *In Black and White: An Interpretation of Southern Life* (New York, Chicago, Toronto: Fleming H. Revell Company, 1914), pp. 59-60.

81. Winfield H. Collins, *The Truth about Lynching and the Negro in the South* (New York: Neale Publishing Company, 1918), p. 101.

82. Thomas Dixon, Jr., to Rolfe Cobleigh, March 27, 1915, N.A.A.C.P. Papers, Library of Congress.

South was "on the edge of a volcano. . . ."[83] James K. Vardaman of Mississippi viewed racial affairs in these same terms.[84] A white woman from Shadydale, Georgia, had abandoned the quest for Negro docility: "There's no managing the neegahs now, they's got so biggety. . . ."[85]

In their frantic efforts to explain what had gone wrong, some Southern whites blamed the Wilson Administration. The unrealistic tone of their arguments showed how far they were from understanding the intricacies and complexities of the Southern racial dilemma. Once on very friendly terms with Wilson, both Henry Watterson and John Sharp Williams broke with the Administration over the proposed woman suffrage amendment. Watterson argued that because the amendment would allow black women to vote, it would promote "Negro domination" in the South. Only by defeating the amendment could racial ills be remedied. Williams took the argument to a more absurd level. Usually calm and level-headed, the Mississippian suggested that woman suffrage was at the core of the "Negro problem." If black women were enfranchised, this would somehow destroy "the purity and the integrity" of the "white race everywhere, but especially in my own native State."[86] For Tom Watson, the few Negro appointments that Wilson made were altogether too many; it was no wonder racial difficulties persisted.[87] To Hoke Smith, the powerful Georgia politician, Administration advocacy of a League of Nations correlated with the "Negro problem." Through its immigration jurisdiction, the League could somehow influence Southern race relations. Since it was a foreign institution, Smith concluded that its influence would be adverse.[88] Closely associated with the Wilson Administration as Ambassador to Italy, Thomas Nelson Page could not openly attack Wilson for failures on the racial scene. But in private correspondence during Wilson's second term, Page alluded to

83. Benjamin R. Tillman to Sophia Tillman Hughes, May 4, 1916, as quoted in Francis Butler Simkins, *Pitchfork Ben Tillman: South Carolinian* (Baton Rouge: Louisiana State University Press, 1944), p. 401.

84. *Congressional Record*, 65th Cong., 2nd Sess., 10778; "Our Subject Race Rebels," *Literary Digest*, LXII (1919), 25.

85. Quoted in Stephen Graham, *The Soul of John Brown* (New York: The Macmillan Company, 1920), p. 170.

86. The Fort Worth *Record*, February 24, 1918, quotes Watterson. For remarks by Williams, see the *Congressional Record*, 63rd Cong., 2nd Sess., 10770; and George C. Osborn, *John Sharp Williams: Planter-Statesman of the Deep South* (Baton Rouge: Louisiana State University Press, 1943), p. 326.

87. Thomas E. Watson, "Editorial Notes and Clippings," *Watson's Magazine*, XXIV, No. 2 (December, 1916), 117.

88. Dewey W. Grantham, Jr., *Hoke Smith and the Politics of the New South* (Baton Rouge: Louisiana State University Press, 1958), pp. 340–43. Unfortunately, Smith did not develop this argument. Thus, one cannot really assess its internal logic.

a continually deteriorating white-black relationship—a deterioration that those in power should somehow have arrested.[89]

None of these complaints revealed a genuine understanding of the factors that were undermining the search for Negro docility. Nowhere was there a systematic investigation of the myth of Negro disease or an analysis of the link between that myth and across-the-board segregation. None seriously considered the relationship between urbanization and the difficulty of distinguishing servile Negroes from the defiant. None pondered the fact that as segregation statutes accumulated on the books, differential enforcement became increasingly difficult. Most important, no white Southerner seriously and methodically examined the nature and causes of the new wave of black activism that diminished white hopes of attaining docile Negro behavior. Had a Watterson, a Wilson, or any other influential Southerner probed behind the fiery, anti-white rhetoric of the Negro activist, he might have enlightened other whites on the emotions behind activist statements. Then Southern whites might have learned that the blacks who caused them so much worry posed no great threat. Whites would have understood that as activists failed in repeated attempts to promote racial pride and black cohesion, they were losing their spirit and gradually de-emphasizing the struggle against white racism. Indeed, had whites only known of the effectiveness of their racism, they might have modified or discarded the long-standing image of the "uppity new Negro." The knowledge would not have restored white Southern faith in the increasingly unworkable notion of differential segregation, but it would have given whites some peace of mind. They would have sensed that they had some mastery over race relations.

VI

Rejecting critical, systematic analysis of racial affairs, white Southerners retreated into a world of myth and fantasy. In 1912 and the early part of 1913, they had looked to Woodrow Wilson as the man who would deploy the vast powers of the Presidency to resolve the "Negro problem." By 1915 they knew he had failed, and so did he.

Precisely at this time, Wilson's old friend from graduate student days at Johns Hopkins, Thomas Dixon, Jr., came to Washington to promote a film spectacular, "The Birth of a Nation." The movie was based upon his most strikingly racist novels, *The Leopard's Spots* (1903) and *The Clansman* (1905), and upon his 1905 play, "The Clans-

89. See, e.g., Thomas Nelson Page to Norval Richardson, November 18, 1919, and Thomas Nelson Page to Rosewell and Ruth Page, January 25, 1920, Page Papers, Duke University.

man." With these sources, with portions of Wilson's *A History of the American People,* and with the latest in technical innovations, David W. Griffith had fashioned a remarkable film production.[90] The movie focused upon a struggle in the Reconstruction South, with white Congressional Radicals and Negroes pitting themselves against white Southerners. Though the white Radicals were depicted as scheming, unprincipled men, their black allies were characterized far more grossly. A happy and contented labor force under the "peculiar institution," the race became vicious and wild with emancipation. Freedmen in the film were usually coarse, dirty, and ill-behaved, thereby threatening the welfare of white society. In marked contrast, white Southerners were characterized as a cultivated, heroic, well-mannered people—the height of civilization. Through force and violence, they heroically battled the blacks and overthrew "Negro rule." In the end, their leader proclaimed that "civilization has been saved, and the South redeemed from shame." With civilization restored, Radicals fled from the South and blacks returned to their traditional role of servility.

"The Birth of a Nation" illustrated the contradictory ideas and aspirations of early twentieth-century white Southern racial thought. It reflected the desires of the men of the "Brownlow tradition" for docile Negro behavior. The old-time darkie of antebellum days emerged as an ideal for which whites struggled. The movie also reflected the dichotomy in white Southern thought between black savages and white civilization. White skin entitled Caucasians to behave barbarically toward blacks as they overthrew "Negro rule." Yet because whiteness represented civilization, the conduct of the whites was not characterized as actual barbarism. Only blacks could behave like savages.

Whereas "The Birth of a Nation" solidly embraced the essence of the "Brownlow tradition," it also embraced forces that were undermining that tradition. Most blacks in the film were clad in filthy rags that covered dirty bodies, and some suffered from visible skin blemishes. Clean, cultivated whites would not allow these blacks into their homes. Such a portrayal reinforced the myth of the diseased Negro— a myth that suggested the futility of differential segregation and emphasized the need for rigid color lines. Moreover, the film was set in an urban locale—a moderate-sized Southern town where whites knew many but not most local blacks. Since an unfamiliar Negro represented a potential threat, the difficulty of applying differential segregation and the need for across-the-board segregation were obvi-

90. John Hammond Moore, "South Carolina's Reaction to the Photoplay *The Birth of a Nation," Proceedings of the South Carolina Historical Association* (1963), p. 36. I am indebted to Bert Wayne of Los Angeles, a veteran Hollywood lighting expert, for sharing his memories on the technical production of "The Birth of a Nation."

ous. Finally, as the film concluded, white civilization "let loose" with forceful and violent assaults upon black savages. But the savages were not the servile "blind Tom" or "Hannah, the faithful" that white Southerners had traditionally depended upon for emotional release. Instead, the savages had become defiant Negroes, indicating that the search for Negro servility had once more been aborted.

Coming to grips with the social significance of the movie, these subtleties must not be overemphasized, for Griffith had designed a film to make people feel but not to think. In the darkness of the movie house, white Southerners simply viewed bold, courageous men of their region heroically forcing the "uppity nigger" into his place. This represented all that they had hoped for; the "Negro problem" was finally being resolved. A movie producer from the 1930's, Paul Bern, used to say that a good "film man" asked himself what people sensed that they lacked in their everyday lives and gave it to them on the screen.[91] Under Dixon's wise council, Griffith had done just that. In a world of fantasy—the movie house—he had given white Southerners the sense that they had the power and the insight to cope with a horrendous difficulty. Even President Wilson could not match that achievement.

Intent on promoting "The Birth of a Nation" on a national basis, Dixon came to Washington early in 1915 and visited his old friend, the President. He asked Wilson to assemble his cabinet and preview the movie. Recalling that Dixon had nominated him for an honorary degree at Wake Forest twenty-seven years earlier when he had been an unknown, Wilson consented: "I want you to know, Tom, that I am pleased to be able to do this little thing for you, because a long time ago you took a day out of your busy life to do something for me. . . . I've always cherished the memory of it." [92] The film was screened in the East Room of the White House for the President and his cabinet. The next night it was shown to the Supreme Court and members of Congress with the consent of Chief Justice Edward White, a former Klansman.[93] Wilson was deeply impressed by the film: "It is like writing history with lightning, and my only regret is that it is all so terribly true." [94] White was glad that "the true story of that

91. "The Illusion of Good News," *The Nation*, CCIX, No. 5 (August 25, 1969), 130.

92 Thomas Dixon, Jr., "Southern Horizons: An Autobiography" (ms. unfinished), p. 426, as quoted in Cook, *Fire from the Flint*, p. 170.

93. Thomas R. Cripps, "The Reaction of the Negro to the Motion Picture *Birth of a Nation*" in Dwight W. Hoover, ed., *Understanding Negro History* (Chicago: Quadrangle Books, Inc., 1968), p. 227; Moore, *Proceedings of the South Carolina Historical Association* (1963), p. 36.

94. Quoted in David M. Chalmers, *Hooded Americanism: The First Century of the Ku Klux Klan, 1865–1965* (Garden City, New York: Doubleday & Company, Inc., 1965), pp. 26–27.

uprising of outraged manhood" would finally be revealed to the nation.[95] The anguish of the white Southern racial dilemma was at last being publicized.

The film was scheduled for its first public screening in New York's Liberty Theater in early March of 1915. Opponents of the movie appealed to the city magistrate to close down the theater and the magistrate complied. In desperation, a defense attorney announced that the film had been shown at the White House. Hastily, the magistrate reversed his decision. Wilson's power and prestige were enough to sanction the Dixon-Griffith production.[96] Dixon and his lawyers proceeded to launch a national advertising campaign with the theme that the film was a "federally endorsed" production—that the President and the Chief Justice had recommended it.[97] Despite an unprecedented two-dollar admission fee, enormous audiences attended throughout the country. After only six months, Dixon reported to Wilson that two million people had seen the movie and predicted that fifty million more would see it within two years. It was "transforming the entire population of the North and West into Sympathetic Southern voters." It was teaching the entire nation the wisdom of the Wilson Administration's racial policies.[98] Dixon was saying, in effect, that Wilson's Washington had been responding to the "Negro problem" like heroic Southern whites had done in the screen spectacular and that Americans were coming to understand the propriety of this policy.

It is impossible to conclusively confirm or refute Dixon's interpretation of audience reaction. One can only conjecture whether Northerners grasped the essence of the Southern racial dilemma as they watched the "Presidentially endorsed" film, for available evidence is necessarily vague and imprecise. Most spectators were touched deeply and emotionally. The day after the movie's first showing at Liberty Theater, New York newspapers described audience reaction. According to the *Evening Telegram,* it "went wild" with excitement. The film "swept a sophisticated audience like a prairie fire in high wind," the *Evening Mail* confirmed. It "had a profoundly moving effect on those who saw it," the *Press* concluded.[99] Audience reaction in Los Angeles was similar. At one showing of the film, ballots were distributed to evaluate audience opinion. Twenty-five hundred wrote decidedly favorable comments and only twenty-three found the movie

95. Chalmers, *Hooded Americanism,* p. 27.

96. Cook, *Fire from the Flint,* p. 173.

97. Arthur S. Link, *Wilson: The New Freedom* (Princeton: Princeton University Press, 1956), p. 253; Cripps in Hoover, ed., *Understanding Negro History,* p. 233.

98. Thomas Dixon, Jr., to Woodrow Wilson, September 4, 1915, Wilson Papers, Library of Congress.

99. New York *Evening Telegram,* March 4, 1915; New York *Evening Mail,* March 4, 1915; New York *Press,* March 4, 1915.

objectionable.[100] The reaction by South Carolinians was strikingly similar—emotional and overwhelmingly favorable.[101]

"The Birth of a Nation" captivated an entire nation. The Southerner's "Negro problem" became a vital national concern. On the screen, the "problem" was solved—the white South overthrew "Negro rule" and restored blacks to their traditionally servile roles. But when the lights went on in theaters throughout the country, the reality of a horrendous racial dilemma had to be faced. Claiming that the film "triggered race riots in many parts of the nation," Professor Rayford W. Logan may have been guilty of some oversimplification.[102] Nonetheless, the film was surely one of several causes of the riots. Millions of white Americans sat at the edge of their seats and cheered as violent, barbaric white conduct toward blacks became heroism in defense of civilization. Identifying, as spectators incline to do, with the heroic, many doubtless left the theater in the heat of passion, hurried off to "niggertown" and "let loose" before the savage race. In Knoxville and in Chicago, in Washington, D.C., and in Omaha, in Elaine, Arkansas, and in East St. Louis, Illinois, whites rioted against blacks. The fantasies of the theater had become the realities of American racial existence. White savagery reigned supreme.

100. Cook, *Fire from the Flint,* pp. 179–80.
101. Moore, *Proceedings of the South Carolina Historical Association* (1963), especially pp. 38–39.
102. Logan, *Betrayal of the Negro,* p. 351.

Bibliographical Note

The White Savage is based on hundreds of sources, and most of them have been cited in the footnotes. Nonetheless, a few brief comments on the nature and scope of the most important sources may be helpful.

The student of postbellum Southern race relations should begin with C. Vann Woodward's publications, particularly *Origins of the New South, 1877–1913* (Baton Rouge, 1951) and *The Strange Career of Jim Crow* (New York, 1955). Whether one accepts, modifies, or rejects Woodward's conceptual framework, it is well worth pondering. Two other general studies should also be reviewed at an early date: Claude H. Nolen, *The Negro's Image in the South: The Anatomy of White Supremacy* (Lexington, 1967) and Guion Griffis Johnson, "The Ideology of White Supremacy, 1876–1910," in Fletcher M. Green ed., *Essays in Southern History* (Chapel Hill, 1949), pp. 124–56. Though there are numerous state studies of race relations in the postbellum decades, three are particularly valuable: George B. Tindall, *South Carolina Negroes, 1877–1900* (Columbia, South Carolina, 1952); Vernon Lane Wharton, *The Negro in Mississippi, 1865–1890* (Chapel Hill, 1947); and Joel Williamson, *After Slavery: The Negro in South Carolina during Reconstruction, 1861–1877* (Chapel Hill, 1965). In addition to historical studies, the writings of sensitive contemporary observers merit attention and concern. Thomas Pearce Bailey, *Race Orthodoxy in the South and Other Aspects of the Negro Question* (New York, 1914); Ray Stannard Baker, *Following the Color Line* (New York, 1908); Maurice S. Evans, *Black and White in the Southern States* (London, 1915); and Stephen Graham, *The Soul of John Brown* (New York, 1920) are filled with rich insights. W. E. B. Du-Bois, *The Souls of Black Folk: Essays and Sketches* (New York, 1903) and Kelly Miller, *Race Adjustment* (New York, 1908) view the Southern racial scene from unique and sensitive black perspectives.

Unfortunately, few historians have bothered to systematically analyze white Southern racial thought during the Civil War. Nonetheless, important and useful data can be gathered from a number of historical publications. Harvey Wish's "Slave Disloyalty under the Confederacy," *Journal of Negro History,* XXIII, No. 3 (October, 1938), 435–50 and Bell I. Wiley's *Southern Negroes, 1861–1865* (New Haven, 1938) are very good, though one should also consult H. J. Eckenrode, "Negroes in Richmond in 1864," *Virginia Magazine of History and Biography,* XLVI, No. 3 (July, 1938), 195–200; Thomas R. Hay, "The South and the Arming of the Slaves," *Mississippi Valley Historical Review,* VI, No. 1 (June, 1919), 34–73; and Charles H. Wesley, "The Employment of Negroes as Soldiers in the Confederate Army," *Journal of Negro History,* IV, No. 3 (July, 1919), 239–53. Southern newspapers are invaluable in comprehending white racial attitudes during the war years, particularly the Charleston *Daily Courier,* the Columbus (Georgia) *Daily Enquirer,* the Macon *Daily Telegraph,* and the Meridian (Mississippi) *Daily Clarion.* A number of informative Southern Civil War diaries have been published. Ben Ames Williams, ed., *A Diary from Dixie by Mary Boykin Chesnut* (Boston, 1949) and Kate Mason Rowland and Mrs. Morris L. Croxall, eds., *The Journal of Julia Le Grand: New Orleans, 1862–1863* (Richmond, 1911) are by far the most lucrative, though one can profit from John Q. Anderson, ed., *Brokenburn: The Journal of Kate Stone, 1861–1868* (Baton Rouge, 1955) and Spencer Bidwell King, Jr., ed., *The War-Time Journal of a Georgia Girl, 1864–1865, by Eliza Francis Andrews* (Macon, 1960). Finally, no phase of Civil War history can be comprehended without one hundred and thirty very basic volumes —R. N. Scott, *et. al.,* eds., *War of the Rebellion: A Compilation of the Official Records of the Union and Confederate Armies* (Washington, D.C., 1880–91).

Though William G. Brownlow may have been the major white Southern racial theorist of the Reconstruction decade, historians have slighted his intellectual qualities. E. Merton Coulter presents the essential facts of the parson's life in *William G. Brownlow: Fighting Parson of the Southern Highlands* (Chapel Hill, 1937). Much has been written about Brownlow's political and journalistic activities in Tennessee, but one can profit most from James W. Patton, *Unionism and Reconstruction in Tennessee, 1860–1869* (Chapel Hill, 1934) and Thomas B. Alexander, *Political Reconstruction in Tennessee* (Nashville, 1950). Professor Coulter lists all of Brownlow's published writings, and these are required reading for all who wish to understand the parson's mind. Brownlow was an editor for many decades, and his editorials in the Tennessee *Whig* (Elizabethtown), 1839–1840, the Jonesboro (Tennessee) *Whig and Independent Journal,* 1840–1849, the Knoxville *Whig,* 1849–1869, and the Knoxville *Whig and Chronicle,* 1875–1877, are both exciting and revealing. Unfortunately, the parson's private correspondence is hard to uncover. The Brownlow Papers at the Library of Congress are no more than a small stack of letters. Some important Brownlow letters are also included in the Andrew Johnson Papers at the Library of Congress and the Thomas A. R. Nelson Papers at Knoxville's Lawson McGhee Library.

"Wattersonia"—the road certain white Southerners selected to ease Northern animosities and restore home rule—is becoming increasingly significant to historians. Nonetheless, Paul H. Buck's *The Road to Reunion, 1865–1900* (New York, 1937) remains the most sensitive analysis of the topic. One can also profit from Rayford W. Logan, *The Betrayal of the Negro from Rutherford B. Hayes to Woodrow Wilson* (New York, 1965) and Paul M. Gaston, "The New South Creed, 1865–1900" (unpublished Ph.D. dissertation, University of North Carolina, 1961). Leslie H. Fishel, Jr.'s outstanding Ph.D. dissertation, "The North and the Negro, 1865–1900: A Study in Race Discrimination" (Harvard University, 1953), outlines a number of Yankee assumptions that "Wattersonians" appealed to. Though Henry Watterson was perhaps the shrewdest proponent of Southern home rule, his biographers have not understood his manipulative, deceptive qualities. Though Joseph Frazier Wall's *Henry Watterson: Reconstructed Rebel* (New York, 1956) and Isaac J. Marcosson's *"Marse Henry"* (New York, 1951) are scholarly and competent studies, they de-emphasize both Watterson the tactician and Watterson the racial theorist. *"Marse Henry": An Autobiography* (New York, 1919) is more helpful in grasping the essence of the man, while Watterson's editorials in the Louisville *Courier-Journal* from 1868 to 1921 are indispensable. But the sly scheming core of the man's personality revealed itself best in private correspondence. The Library of Congress has the most extensive collection of Watterson Papers though the collection at the Technical Journalism Division of Colorado State University must also be consulted. Other interesting Watterson letters can be found in the Horace Greeley Papers (New York Public Library) and the Samuel J. Tilden Papers (New York Public Library).

Little has been written about Thomas Nelson Page and his new Cavalier literary tradition. In *Thomas Nelson Page: A Memoir of a Virginia Gentleman* (New York, 1923), his brother, Rosewell Page, revealed certain significant details about the man's personal life. Harriet R. Holman's Ph.D. dissertation, "The Literary Career of Thomas Nelson Page, 1844–1910" (Duke University, 1947) and Theodore L. Gross' *Thomas Nelson Page* (New York, 1967) are detailed scholarly reviews of the man's literary production but do not really appraise Page's ideology or personality. Thus, the serious Page student must read and reflect upon his many novels, short stories, and prose essays, all of which are listed in Gross' study. In addition, one should review the extensive Thomas Nelson Page Papers at Duke University.

Though historical investigations of Tom Watson and Southern

Populism abound, none is as thoroughly researched and carefully written as C. Vann Woodward's *Tom Watson: Agrarian Rebel* (New York, 1938). Nonetheless, critical review of the primary sources does not sustain Woodward's interpretation of the "rebel's" racial ideology. Watson's papers in the Southern Historical Collection at the University of North Carolina and his pronouncements in the *People's Party Paper* (Atlanta, 1891–1898) were instrumental in provoking my disagreement with Woodward, though analysis of many of Watson's published writings was surely contributory.

There are a number of biographies of the "heretical" Mr. Cable. Philip Butcher's *George W. Cable: The Northampton Years* (New York, 1959) and Kjell Exström's *George Washington Cable* (Cambridge, Massachusetts, 1950) are competent and scholarly, but Arlin Turner's *George W. Cable: A Biography* (Durham, North Carolina, 1956) represents literary biography at its best. Though I disagree with Turner's interpretation of the "heretic's" racial ideology, I have only respect for his exhaustive research and his closely reasoned analysis. Turner's bibliography lists Cable's many published writings, and the serious student must consult all of them. Three New Orleans newspapers are also useful—the *Picayune*, the *Times-Democrat*, and the *Semi-Weekly Louisianian*. Cable's private papers at Tulane University are voluminous and invaluable, though smaller Cable collections at Columbia University, Duke University, and Harvard's Houghton Library should also be consulted. In addition, the Charles W. Chesnutt Papers at Fisk University include a number of revealing letters from Cable to Chesnutt on the "Negro question."

There are innumerable sources to consult on black activist reaction to the white Southern quest for docility. The Booker T. Washington Papers at the Library of Congress are the most valuable, for they shed light on many activists besides the head of the "Tuskegee machine." Four other collections at the Library of Congress also reveal a great deal about the "black mood"—the N.A.A.C.P. Papers, the Mary Church Terrell Papers, the Robert H. Terrell Papers, and the Carter G. Woodson Collection. The Negro newspaper microfilm project of the American Council of Learned Societies and the Library of Congress provides another marvelous source, for it gives one access to many black Southern newspapers published in the late nineteenth and early twentieth centuries which have been discontinued. Historians have generally overlooked the Negro novels of the period, but those of writers like J. W. Grant, Sutton E. Griggs, and Thomas H. B. Walker reveal a great deal about changing black activist ideological patterns. Finally, all students of the black experience in postbellum America are indebted to August Meier for his study, *Negro Thought in America, 1880–1915: Racial Ideologies in the Age of Booker T. Washington* (Ann Arbor, 1963). Though Meier may have interpreted black activist rhetoric too literally, his research is impeccable and his contribution to human knowledge is substantial.

The researcher has little difficulty gathering material on the reaction of Wilson's Washington to apparent changes in the black community. A number of exciting and well-researched articles must be consulted, particularly Henry Blumenthal, "Woodrow Wilson and the Race Question," *Journal of Negro History*, XLVIII, No. 1 (January, 1963), 1–21; Arthur S. Link, "The Negro as a Factor in the Campaign of 1912," *Journal of Negro History*, XXXII, No. 1 (January, 1947), 81–99; George C. Osborn, "The Problem of the Negro in Government, 1913," *The Historian*, XXIII (May, 1961), 330–47; Nancy J. Weiss, "The Negro and the New Freedom: Fighting Wilsonian Segregation," *Political Science Quarterly*, LXXXIV, No. 1 (March, 1969), 61–79; and two fine articles by Kathleen L. Wolgemuth: "Woodrow Wilson's Appointment Policy and the Negro" *Journal of Southern History*, XXIV, No. 1 (February, 1958), 457–71, and "Woodrow Wilson and Federal Segregation," *Journal of Negro History*, XLIV, No. 2 (April, 1959), 158–73. In addition to secondary materials, a number of manuscript collections should be exploited. The Woodrow Wilson Papers at the Library of Congress and the Oswald Garrison Villard Papers at Harvard's Houghton Library are the most informative, though one should also review several other Library of Congress collections: the Ray Stannard Baker Papers, the Albert Sidney Burleson Papers, the William G. McAdoo Papers, and the N.A.A.C.P. Papers. The *Congressional Record* and the New York *Times* are also mandatory reading for the years of the Wilson Presidency.

Finally, two books must be noted that deal neither with the post-bellum South nor with white attitudes toward blacks—Kai T. Erikson's *Wayward Puritans: A Study in the Sociology of Deviance* (New York, 1966) and Roy Harvey Pearce's *The Savages of America: A Study of the Indian and the Idea of Civilization* (Baltimore, 1953). Analyzing New England Puritans, Erikson pointed to a human predisposition toward negative self-identification. Charging that certain people are social deviants and calling them "devils" or "barbarians," an insecure person can sense that he is "orthodox" and "civilized." Focusing upon the attitudes of early American whites toward Indians, Pearce detected this same human quality. Together, *Wayward Puritans* and *The Savages of America* helped to form the conceptual framework for *The White Savage* and to enlarge my sensitivity to the human condition.

Index

ST. MARY'S COLLEGE OF MARYLAND
ST. MARY'S CITY, MARYLAND